India's Rising: 2030

INDIA'S RISING: 2030

Dr. Ajay Parmar

PRASHANT PUBLISHING HOUSE
DELHI-110094

Published by :
Prashant Publishing House
C-34, 28 Foota Road, Gali-3,
West Karwal Nagar, Delhi-110094
Phone : 011-22963970, Mob. : 9810396373
e-mail.: prashantpublishinghouse@gmail.com

India's Rising: 2030

First Published 2017

ISBN 978-81-934253-29

PRINTED IN INDIA
Published by Mr. R.K. Jha M/s Prashant Publishing House and Published at H.S. Offset House Press, Delhi.

Contents

Preface

US intelligence has predicted that in 2030, India could be the rising economic powerhouse of the world as China is seen today and that it will continue to consolidate its power advantage over Pakistan. "In 2030 India could be the rising economic powerhouse that China is seen to be today. China's current economic growth rate - 8 to 10 per cent - will probably be a distant memory by 2030," said the fifth installment of the 'Global Trends 2030: Alternative Worlds', of National Intelligence Council (NIC), released on Monday.

As the world's largest economic power, China is expected to remain ahead of India, but the gap could begin to close by 2030. "India's rate of economic growth is likely to rise while China's slows," said the report which is aimed at providing a framework for thinking about the future. According to the report, the total size of the Chinese working-age population will peak in 2016 and decline from 994 million to about 961 million in 2030.

India is one of the world's largest importers of weapons and manufacturing is still at a nascent stage, but there are strides being made in the defence sector as the country finally starts to try to break away from its dependence on imports. Indian Prime Minister Mr. Modi is pushing for India to become a global manufacturing centre under his "Make in India" campaign, and the defence and aerospace industry is a key part of this. Two years ago, India opened up the defence sector to 49 per cent foreign direct investment (FDI) from a previous limit of 26 per cent. In June this year, the government liberalised the rules even further, permitting FDI of 100 per cent in the sector.

India has been one of the biggest importers of advanced conventional weapons in the last thirty years, but this sustained rearmament has not altered India's strategic position. The armed forces push for modernization, but do not have the authority to mount the national campaign necessary for transforming the security condition of the country. Budget increases delivered by a rapidly expanding economy and access to western technology previously denied to India have led to optimism about Indian military power, but the dysfunction in India's civil-military relations reduces the impact of rearmament. Arming without aiming has some purpose in persuading other great powers of India's benign rise, but it cannot be the basis of military planning.

As the book addresses this crucial issue quite deftly, it is hoped that it would prove to be a source of great information for the reader.

—Editor

1

India's Rising Superpower

India has long been an important nation on the international stage; its massive population and rapidly growing economy have the potential to propel it forward even further. While there have been ebbs and flows–the recent recession strongly impacted the sub-continent–things may be looking up. There's a new Prime Minister and India is on the rise yet again. Read on to learn about India's growth, the relationships it has with other nations, and the challenges that the country will face in coming years.

A LOOK INTO THE PAST

Like China and Mesopotamia, India is often considered one of the birthplaces of civilization. The first civilization in India was founded over five thousand years ago. Since then, India saw the rise and fall of countless empires, invading forces, and ideas. Buddhism and Hinduism were also founded in India; and Islam, when it reached the area in the eighth century, came to exert a powerful influence, as well.

The story of modern India however, picks up at the beginning of the eighteenth century, when the declining Mughal Empire was conquered piecemeal by the British East India Company. The British outcompeted their French rivals and bit by bit took over the sub-continent. Yet British rule was not to last either, with a large-scale mutiny in the middle of the nineteenth century hinting at the rise of Indian nationalism.

This came to fruition after years of protest that featured leaders such as Mahatma Gandhi when India finally achieved independence in 1947. This independence, however, did not come about smoothly. The same year India became independent, it also broke into twoseparate nations, Hindu India and Muslim Pakistan. As many as 12.5 million people migrated to one country or the other depending on their religion. Up to one million people died in the ensuing chaos.

INDIA: THE EMERGING ASIAN SUPER POWER

Singapore's defence minister Ng Eng Hen stated last month that his country wanted India to play a bigger role in the South China Sea. The leaders of Vietnam and the Philippines have also made similar statements in recent years. This "invitation" extended to India by the leaders of Southeast Asia to participate in that region's security affairs is tantamount to India's emergence as a great power in Southeast Asia, and by extension, in Asia itself.

Southeast Asia connects the Indian and the Pacific Oceans, and includes some of the most important maritime chokepoints, is likely to be the site of order-making in Asia in the context of the rise of China.

Thomas Donilon, who was the American National Security Advisor when the US said its "pivot/rebalancing" has explained that the pivot is not just about "rebalancing towards Asia" but also includes rebalancing "within Asia" as America has begun to focus "in a renewed way on Southeast Asia and Asean." Furthermore, the Asian-institutional architecture is Asean-centric and Asean-led.

Therefore, India's emerging profile in Southeast Asia is significant and marks its arrival as a great power.

Solid grounds

There are two main reasons that explain the benign perception of India's rise in Southeast Asia. First, there are no territorial disputes between India and its immediate neighbours in Southeast Asia. India has a land border with only one

Southeast Asian state, Myanmar, which was fixed by their British colonial rulers in 1937.

India has maritime borders with three Southeast Asian states: Myanmar, Thailand, and Indonesia. India's maritime boundaries with Thailand and Indonesia were fixed through a trilateral agreement in 1978, while India's maritime boundary with Myanmar was finalized in 1987.

Second, India is not pursuing any unilateral or hegemonic policies towards Southeast Asia. In 2012, former Prime Minister, Manmohan Singh, explicitly noted that New Delhi believes that "Asean centrality is essential in the evolving regional architecture," endorsing Asean's leading role in regional diplomacy.

Similarly, at the military/maritime level, India not only prefers to be invited into the region , but former defence minister, Pranab Mukherjee, noted in 2006 that India was willing to assist the regional states in "any capacity" for security in the Strait of Malacca subject "to the desire of the littoral states."

In other words, despite India's more advanced military capabilities, New Delhi is not claiming the mantle of leadership there but prefers to work in accordance with the local norms and mores.

Therefore, it is not surprising that Lee Kuan Yew, Singapore's recently deceased statesman, welcomed India's presence in Southeast Asia in 2007 by noting that there was "no fear" that India had "aggressive intentions."

India has now transcended its home region of South Asia due to its growing power in Southeast Asia, thus becoming a key component of the Asian security architecture along with the region's other great powers: the United States, Japan, and China. Notably, all three Asian great powers also seem to be willing to work with India in Southeast Asia.

Strategic edge

US President Obama has urged India to "act East" on a number of occasions. Furthermore, the US and India released a joint vision statement earlier this year in which they specifically called for "safeguarding maritime security and ensuring freedom of navigation and over flight throughout the region, especially in the South China Sea." On his part, Japanese Prime Minister Shinzo Abe sees the India-Japan relationship as a "confluence" of the Indian and Pacific Oceans.

Notably, Southeast Asia is geographically — and geopolitically — located at this confluence. The Japan-India statement on their strategic and global partnership that was released last year especially noted the launch of their "bilateral dialogue on Asean affairs." Finally, China also seems to be willing to work with India, even if begrudgingly, in the region's economic and institutional affairs.

Through their 2008 shared vision document, China and India agreed to "explore ... a new architecture for closer regional cooperation in Asia, and to make joint efforts for regional integration of Asia." This statement, which explicitly identified the Asean-led East Asia Summit as an avenue where China and India can work together is significant simply because China was hitherto unwilling to recognize India as a major power in Asia beyond South Asia.

In other words, the regional states of Southeast Asia, as well as the great powers active in Southeast Asia, now seem willing to grant India the status of a great power in that region.

This has two noteworthy implications. First, these acts 'legitimise' India's status as a great power in Asia as well as its role in the security affairs of a region outside of India's home region in South Asia. As such, India is not seen as an interloper. Second, this empirically demonstrates that the rise of a new great power need not disrupt the extant order as is normally assumed. In fact, the rise of a new great power — in this case, India — can be seen as contributing to the maintenance of the regional order.

Security angles

India has three main security-related interests in Southeast Asia. First, as noted by Mukherjee in 2005, India's "Look East" strategy is based on the principle of "the maintenance of an equitable strategic balance."

India does not want Southeast Asia to be dominated by any single great power. Consequently, India is upgrading its naval and air assets in the Andaman and Nicobar Islands. Located at the mouth of the Strait of Malacca, India's maritime and air capabilities in the Andamans help India meet its second security interest in the region: the security of the Strait itself. Finally, India's growing maritime and air capabilities — cantered on diverse platforms such as the P-8I aircraft, the C-130Js, the C-17 Globemasters, Sukhoi-30 MKIs, aircraft carrier(s), nuclear submarine(s), and landing dock(s) — allow India to project military power into the South China Sea from the Andamans.

After all, India's third security interest in Southeast Asia is to ensure the freedom of navigation in the South China Sea. In fact, India's regional partnerships — including docking rights at Vietnam's Nha Trang port — may further augment India's capabilities.

At the same time, India has been providing a range of security-related public goods in Southeast Asia such as the provision of humanitarian and disaster relief assistance as well as military capacity-building in regional states.

Despite these modest but significant efforts, Southeast Asian states want India to "do more" pro-actively. The crucial question now is whether India's political leaders will grasp the geopolitical opportunity to ensconce India in the emerging Asian order or if a lack of vision and the exigencies of domestic politics will effectively force New Delhi to squander the chance to shape Asia. At the very least, India needs to expedite its economic engagement with Southeast Asia while enhancing physical connectivity – land and maritime – in order to demonstrate its seriousness.

WILL INDIA EVER BE A TRUE GLOBAL SUPERPOWER?

This is possible, but not at all easy. For the sake of long-term analysis, let's neglect some of India's current weaknesses which may get resolved in 10-20 years, but focus on fundamentals and their manifestations.

India's economy is projected to reach the #3 spot by 2020 (by at least some analysts and metrics; it's already there by PPP), surpassing Japan, and trailing only China (#1) and the US (#2). In view of China's recent economic troubles and suspicious accounting, China's ascent is in doubt, but India's upward path seems more certain (say, by 2030), as its excesses have been smaller so far.

Of course, India's economy must become more robust and structurally sound, while the legal system must strengthen as well, and corruption must be addressed. Going forward, India has huge potential due to its large population, a long-standing tradition of democracy and stable government system with non-violent transitions, convenient location for trade, proximity to major oil exporters, decent standing in the world, a large English-speaking population, massive engineering education that is gradually improving in quality, and a system of R&D institutions.

India's current weakness is limited global reach. In particular, the BRICS group is looking less and less promising due to significant divergence between its members (some are in deep recession, some need oil to be expensive, while others prefer cheap oil, etc). However, G20 has been increasingly relevant. Should India and China reach the status of developed economies (perhaps in 20 years), they may be added to the G7 forum. In general, faster development of the world economy should help developing countries to catch up, but in a slower world economy the developed countries will preserve their lead.

India's military is ranked #4 in 2015 by Global Firepower after the US, Russia, and China, and followed by the UK. While this is unlikely to change by 2020, I expect Russia to drop out from the top three in 10-20 years, due to the effects of protracted financial crisis, economic stagnation, and deteriorating demographics. In contrast, both India and the UK are primed to significantly increase their military strength by 2025. With two new super-carriers, the UK will have a stronger Navy (currently, UK's Navy is considered slightly weaker than India's). The recently-announced massive new purchase program for strike aircraft can make the UK Air Force stronger as well (it is currently considered weaker than India's, and is a lot smaller).

India's initial bet on Russian fifth-gen fighters (PAK FA) has gone sour. The supersonic cruise missile Brahmos jointly developed by India and Russia hasn't been deployed by Russia for some reason (despite its availability) and does not have direct analogues in NATO countries, while NATO can technically develop one. This raises doubts about the operational effectiveness of this primarily anti-ship missile.

Even today, India cannot project power away from its borders nearly as efficiently as the UK can (due to UK's bases and close defense relations with NATO). And India has no military alliences like NATO and the Five Eyes. India is likely to remain the #4 military power through 2030, but if Russia is replaced by the UK in the top three, this can increase India's significance because the UK is a part of the already-strong NATO. It's really hard to guess the military developments by 2050, but the NATO militaries will clearly become increasingly unmanned, negating population handicaps and leveraging new technology, while other countries are likely to lag behind. The extent of this trend will be determined by specific technology developments and economic health of the countries involved.

India's diplomatic standing and international reach. India hasn't been involved in many international conflicts and also has relatively little political influence on other countries (despite being the third largest contributor to UN Peacekeeping Forces worldwide). This may start changing as India's economy and international trade grow.

The big diplomatic prize would be an enhanced status in the UN. India is arguing for a permanent seat in the UN Security Council, but any UN SC reform looks impossible in the next five years. Some changes may become realistic by 2025, especially after major political upheavals that some experts predict for this timeframe. A UN reform is looking more likely by 2050, especially if 20 years pass without major conflicts. Here, the key for India is to wisely navigate between other world powers, make good bets, and avoid major pitfalls, while contributing to the world peace in essential and unique ways. The current conflict with Pakistan is a serious shackle, as it confines India to the status of a regional power and limits India's support among Muslim nations (India's collaboration with Israel on defense matters is another issue for Muslim nations). The rule of three. I'd like to postulate that there can be at most three global superpowers on this planet (with more comparable powers, each will hold too little sway to count as a superpower).

There is little doubt that the US will remain a superpower, even if China's economy becomes larger. As of 2025, the EU will likely become the second global superpower, and some may argue that it already is (the EU economy is currently larger than the US economy, the EU definitely has global political, diplomatic, and economy-related reach, while enjoying two seats on the UN Security Council, etc).

It is not clear if there will be a third superpower, especially because the US and the EU are so tightly allied in most regards. But the main candidates are China and India (Russia's economy is way too small, and its global reach has significantly shrunk in 2014-2015 due to political adventurism and bad bets, while the overall trajectory remains negative). Both China and India have limited global reach today, and both are trying to reach the status of developed economies. Both need to provide better education to their citizens, improve their legal/enforcement systems and cut down corruption.

Both have questionable human-rights records, although India seems in a better shape. Both have thorny relations with some of their neighbors that are unlikely to get resolved. China has a head start on economy size, while India has a head start on the political system. In the short-term, economy is more tangible, but in the longer term the political system is at least as important (as this is critical to fixing the legal system, setting up effective law enforcement, and rooting out corruption).

INDIA: A CENTURY OF STRUGGLE AND THE RISE OF A SUPERPOWER

The monograph "A History of India: The Twentieth Century" is an outstanding work embracing the eventful period of Indian history, from political processes in colonial India to India's path of development today. In this major work, the authors present a thorough, in-depth analysis of the crucial socio-political and economic processes taking place in contemporary India.

The monograph offers readers a definitive, multifaceted study. The first part of the work reviews key political processes in colonial India and the history of the country's struggle for independence, in which Mahatma Gandhi played a major role. The second part analyses the formation and implementation of socio-political and economic policy in India since independence. The third part explores the fundamental priorities of the foreign policy in independent India, as well as its military doctrine and the build-up of its armed forces.

The work investigates the activities of India's key political parties, above all the Indian National Congress and the Bharatiya Janata Party, as well as achievements and failures of left-wing and regional parties. A study of the role of religions and religious castes constitutes an integral part of the study of India's domestic political processes.

Some chapters address specific aspects of the formation and implementation of economic strategy in modern India that can be traced to the time when the governments of both Jawaharlal Nehru and Indira Gandhi, and parties opposing the Congress Party were in power. The review of India's economic reforms of the 1990s emphasises that, despite its focus on economic liberalisation, India did not renounce its previous achievements, specifically national economic planning. The market economy can and must be used as a measure of the exigencies and requirements of the people.

The work stresses the positive role of the Indian diaspora, numbering over 25 million people. Remittances from emigres make a significant contribution to the country's balance of payments. By the same token, Indians living abroad are proactively and successfully lobbying for India's interests in relation to the commerce, economies and political lines of their countries of residence. Furthermore, they even helped India secure the right to use the know-how they had accumulated to develop and upgrade its own economy.

India's social development experience since independence has demonstrated that its progress resulted from a national focus in the social, economic, and political development model. India's search for development options has been based largely on its own historical traditions. In its political practices, as well as in building its political and social systems, India has been relying on methods rooted in the specifics of Indian society. This, however, has not implied creation or pursuit of any autarchic model. Indians have localised the best achievements of other nations (for instance, the democratic system of governance) and cautiously, without ever forcing them on society, built them into their system of values, lending them a national hue.

Meanwhile, India's spiritual and political elite has never given up the further search for solutions to outstanding problems and new challenges. The key criterion in this search has been the capacity of a particular model to solve problems rather than a commitment to a certain ideology.

The section of the book that provides an overview of the foreign policy of independent India, including its contribution to the Non-Aligned Movement and the nature of its relations with its major international partners: the Soviet Union (succeeded by Russia), the United States of America and China, deserves separate mention. It deals largely with a study of India's policies in South Asia and the Asia-Pacific region, armed conflicts and wars with China and Pakistan.

The monograph emphasises that at all stages of India's independent development and its foreign policy have served as a major tool for securing its national interests based on equality, justice, and democratisation of both economic and political international relations. Simultaneously, India has always sought to respond flexibly to global changes by making tactical adjustments, yet remaining adamantly committed to consistently observing the fundamentals of its foreign policy that go back to the first years of its independence.

India's evolution into a nuclear superpower is discussed in this work separately. The monograph highlights the role of India's confrontation with Pakistan, specifically the Indo-Pakistani war of 1965, and the armed conflict with China in 1962, in India's emergence on the nuclear arena.

Still, India's way of securing an independent nuclear position cannot be called easy or, still less, rash. The book discusses why India, which had repeatedly promoted moves to create a nuclear-free world, nevertheless refused to sign the Nuclear Non-Proliferation Treaty (1970). In 1974, the country tested a nuclear device as a warning to its rivals on the international arena and demonstrating India's scientific and technological potential. And finally, 24 years later, in May 1998, it test-fired a nuclear weapon. After the breakup of the USSR and the end of the bipolar world, India was faced with reinforcing its national security in the new environment, including through use of nuclear weapons.

The monograph is a fundamental work, building its conclusions on a broad reference base. This book's clear advantage is that, alongside official documents, works by Russian and foreign India-scholars and researchers engaged in broader studies, as well as press publications from all over the world, it features personal observations and assessments by its authors formed resulting from many years spent working in India.

The wealth of information and the unconventional assessments and conclusions this book features make it an interesting reading not only for specialists in Oriental studies, but also a wider readership.

RISE OF MODERN INDIA

After the end of colonial rule, India initially adopted a planned economic approach. The idea was to increase consumer savings, which would then lead to greater investment in the economy and growth. The plan was to create a prosperous India that was financed by its own economy and not beholden to outside forces.

While the plan had some success, however, growth remained limited in India at an average of four percent annually in the 1950s, 60s, and 70s. The plan was also plagued by unbridled population growth and inequality. The proverbial corner was turned beginning in the late 80s and early 90s when the economy was finally opened up. Growth shot up to over 6.5 percent annually, while the service sector in particular began to take off.

Move to a Market Economy

The key to the turn-around for India economically was when it moved from a series of five-year plans, as part of a planned economy adopted from its then-ally, the Soviet Union, to a market economy, which is similar to those of Western nations. Originally India adopted a socialist model as the means to improve its economy. This meant most industry, licensing, and investment infrastructure was controlled by the government. The whole idea behind this logic was to build strong home-grown industries in India, and in the process prevent the inequality notorious in capitalist societies from spreading there.

The planned economy proved ineffective. This was mainly due to low growth rates and the failure to generate high savings rates. In fact the state, far from succeeding in building up savings, actually began running up higher and higher deficits as its programs proved ineffective. Thus, spurred by this ineffectiveness and a rise of the price of oil as a result of the first gulf war which nearly caused the country to default, India made a change. The government did a complete 180, reducing state control and planning, liberalizing trade and investment, and reducing the deficit.

Following the success from the 1990s and with continued reforms, the Indian economy continued to hum along in the first decade of the 2000s, averaging greater than six percent growth annually. Rapid growth stalled, however, as it did in much of the rest of the world, following the Great Recession.

The reason that India was hit so hard was because of a failure to further liberalize policy concerning labor, energy, land reform, and infrastructure improvement. Namely the issue was in many ways the same that had been affecting India during its planned economy, despite the reforms the country had enacted in the past two decades. First labor laws were still very restrictive so it made it hard for people to move around in search of jobs. Secondly, the infrastructure was not adequately developed in India so that its manufacturers could easily export their products. Third, the country was still plagued by shortages in essential goods, such as energy. This was all compounded by the government's vain effort to prop up the country's currency, the Rupee. Not only has this led to a higher deficit, but also inflation, which eats away at people's savings and makes them poorer. This led to growth rates closer to four or five percent during the recession.

After the Recession

Nevertheless, India's economy has rebounded in the last two years and in 2014 outpacedChina for the first time. This was due to several improvements. First, both the manufacturing and financial sectors improved dramatically. In addition, new Prime Minister Modi and other political leaders have worked diligently to reduce debt. Lastly, the drop in the price of oil has dramatically helped India, as most of its import deficits were due to the importation of oil to fuel its growing need.

While India has seemingly regained its status as a rapidly growing emerging market, this also comes with caveats. First, the growth figures that show it outpacing China had to be recalculated due to some errors, so many economists are treating them with skepticism. Secondly, according to a *New York Times* study from 2011-2012, 30 percent of Indians still live in extreme poverty, which translates approximately to 363 million people. That is more people than live in the United States. Thus, although India may recoup its status as a major, up-and-coming economy, there is still room for improvement. The following video gives an outlook on the impact reforms could have on India's economy.

INDIA'S FRIENDS AND ENEMIES

Pakistan

When discussing international concerns for India, the discussion always starts with Pakistan. The two nations were founded at the same time when British rule in India ended; however, the division of the two countries was plagued by extreme violence and a persistently strong feeling of animosity. The situation has in no way improved by the three wars and ongoing proxy war being waged over Kashmir. The conflict in Kashmir stems back to the separation of India and Pakistan.

At the time of independence, there were 562 princely kingdoms that were independent from either country and could choose which one they wanted to join. Both countries therefore were eager to recruit these principalities–Kashmir was one of the most coveted. Pakistan seemed to have the upper hand, as 70 percent of the population was Muslim; however, at the time, the ruler was Hindu so India claimed the area on that argument and still occupies it to this day. Aside from the direct conflicts there, Pakistan has also waged a guerrilla campaign to free the territory from India and incorporate it into the Muslim state of Pakistan.

On top of all that, both countries possess nuclear weapons and flaunt their capabilities, an example of which was the corresponding nuclear tests during the 90s. The video below provides a summary of the two nations' conflict.

Nonetheless, hopes for thawed relations came when Prime Minister Modi was elected last year–one of his campaign promises was to improve relations between the two countries; however, lately Modi's speeches have been full of aggressive rhetoric and the Pakistani military continues to support anti-

India terror groups so change has yet to come. An example of this is when he suggested Pakistan was, "waging a proxy war" in Kashmir. He has also canceled several meetings with Pakistani officials, including one potential rendezvous at the United Nations.

China

India's other major neighbor in Asia is China. Like Pakistan, India also fought a brief warwith China in 1962 and has since maintained a relatively tense border with the country in the Himalayas. Tthe relationship with China has steadily improved in other areas as the countries have signed a number of trade agreements. The relationship was tested in 2013 with a Chinese incursion into Indian territory; however, no apparent serious harm came of it. The lack of consternation may be rooted in how the countries view each other. In India, China is seen as a chief rival and also a source of emulation economically. For China, which is stronger militarily and economically, India is not regarded as much of a rival.

United States

Like its relationship with both Pakistan and China, India's relationship with the U.S. is complicated. The countries originally shared strong ties, with the U.S. aiding India during the conflict with China. Relations were strained following America's decision to side with Pakistan in its 1971 war with India. Things were further exacerbated by an arms treaty signed between India and the USSR and India's testing of nuclear weapons in the 70s.

Relations seemed to be improving in the 1990s as India opened up its economy and moved to a free market approach. But once again ties between the nations weakened in 1998 when India again tested nuclear weapons, which drew condemnation and sanctions from the U.S. The sanctions were quickly repealed though and the two nations became close once more over a commitment to combat terrorism. The two sides have continued to grow closer since then, signing everything from trade to weapons agreements. In 2013 an Indian delegate was arrested for committing visa fraud, causing major waves. The two sides have seemed to yet again overcome this hiccup though, following the president's recent trip to India where he reaffirmed the U.S. commitment to friendship.

The relationship with the U.S. also seems likely to continue to improve, despite numerous setbacks, many of which were over nuclear policy that now seem settled. While the U.S. may want to utilize India against a rising China, the two sides also value each other as trade partners. The relationship is further enhanced by the U.S.'s further distancing itself from Pakistan.

DOMESTIC CONCERNS FOR INDIA

While India navigates the dangerous game of international politics, it has internal issues to consider, as well. First and foremost is the status of women. While seemingly no country in the world can boast of total equality between men and woman, the situation is especially bad in India. While some women may enjoy access to lucrative lifestyles, there is a virtually systemic oppression of women in education, marriage, and the economy. A grisly example was the gang-rape of a woman by six men in Delhi in 2013 that resulted in the woman's death. While four of the men were eventually sentenced to death, their crime highlighted a culture where women are often blamed for rape and where the courts are slow to act.

Women, of course, are not the only group to be institutionally marginalized in India. Thecaste system has existed for a long time. In this system people are born into and can expect to rise no further than a particular caste or class, which is often associated with some type of profession. While some efforts have succeeded at down-playing caste origins in jobs, castes still play a large role in social interactions and romantic relationships.

The persistence of discrimination, both against women and people of lower classes, speaks to the issue of inequality in the country. According to a report from the United Nations – Economic and Social Commission for Asia and Pacific (UNESCAP), incomeinequality actually increased in India from the 1990s to late 2000s. India's population is the second largest in the world at more than 1.2 billion people. With birth rates still outpacing death rates, that number is only going to continue to increase until it is expected to plateau in 2050. The population of India is also expected to surpass that of China for the world's largest along the way, in 2025. All these extra people mean more food, housing, and jobs for a country that is already hard pressed to generate them at current levels. The accompanying video highlights the issues with poverty in India.

Domestically, though changes have been made incrementally, the sweeping changes necessary to fix many of India's societal ills seem unlikely. As the infamous Delhi rape trial showed, while courts can be forced into action when thrust into the spotlight, they have been very slow to protect women. This also speaks to a problem of institutionalized marginalization for a large chunk of society, which has lasted for many years and thus is unlikely to simply go away now. Couple these issues with continued population explosion and the poverty that haunts India is likely to continue. Particularly with inequality rising and wealth being consolidated into the hands of the elites, much as it is in western nations.

CONCLUSION

After initially struggling following independence, India has enjoyed strong recent growth. While that growth was threatened by the great recession, India was able to pull through and even outpace China, if the numbers are to be believed. Going forward, Asia's other potential superpower has many issues to deal with. Internationally, serious issues still exist concerning the relationship between India and Pakistan. India's relationship with Asia's affirmed rising super power is also in question as India moves closer to fellow democracy in the United States, while China seemingly drifts closer to fellow autocrat Russia.

Domestically it is more of the same, with concern over the economy dominating. Yet other issues also exist, namely an entrenched class system and the low status of women. Thus, while India has come very far, there is still a long way to go.

Therefore while it is still possible for India to act on its superpower potential and one day rival China as Asia's premier power, reforms and improvements are likely required along the way.

A SUPERPOWER IN THE MAKING?

The rise of this growing nation will change the balance of power in Asia—and potentially the world. With nearly 1.1 billion inhabitants, India is the second largest country on earth in population, and seventh largest in geographical area, over 1.1 million square miles. This is almost 1,000 people for every square mile of area nationwide—much denser than even China.

Since achieving independence from British rule in 1947, it has seen its share of conflict, struggle and setbacks. Although India still faces many challenges, it is now poised to reach a higher position on the world scene than at any previous time.

The Indian economy has grown an average of around 6% annually over the past decade and 8% per year over the past three years—among the fastest rates in the world. It boasts an emerging middle class and increasing gross domestic product, exports, employment and foreign investment. This is complemented by a roaring stock market (index value up by a third in 2005 and by 200% since 2001), low external debt and large foreign exchange reserves.

Recent visits from leaders and officials from the United States, France, Germany and Russia have spotlighted India's rise. These wealthier nations see India as a trading partner with enormous potential.

Although it has not yet matched the financial performance of China—currently the fastest-growing economy in the world—according to some analysts, India shows even more long-term potential for rapid growth.

Leaders from both nations have discussed the creation of a Chinese-Indian common market based on the European Union model. Although only an idea at present, if realized, it would be the largest economic system in the world, home for about

2.5 billion consumers—almost 40% of the human race (or 3 of every 8 people on earth)!

India's growth becomes more impressive in light of the fact that it is driven by a fraction of its population. Much of the nation remains a picture of rural poverty. Nearly all foreign investment in India goes to its six most urban states, with 22 other less developed states virtually ignored. This gap between city and country is keenly felt in places such as Gurgaon, a suburb of the Indian capital New Delhi: "In a land still plagued by deep poverty and backwardness, Gurgaon has become a renowned home of international call centers, business-processing operations, and information-technology firms. There are gleaming, glass-paned high-tech towers, condominium blocks, multiplexes, and shopping malls, where Indians dine at Ruby Tuesday, browse for Samsung electronics, or kick the tires at a Toyota, Ford, or Chevy dealer. If one overlooks the dusty pockets of poverty nearby, a few water buffaloes picking at garbage near shantytowns, the look is more Southern California office park than the India of yore" (*U.S. News and World Report*).

Despite the problems seen in India's underdeveloped countryside—for example, massive unmet infrastructure needs; more illiterate citizens than any other single nation—there are several areas in which the nation excels. These particular specialized talents have allowed a tiny percentage of the populace—perhaps less than 1%—to spearhead its move toward a higher standing in the world order.

Intellectual Capital

India's economy is divided between agriculture (which accounts for a quarter of the gross national product), manufacturing (constituting another quarter) and the high-tech service sector, which now makes up fully half of the gross national product. Striving to become a "knowledge superpower," it hopes to skip the intermediate step of industrial development that has preceded other nations' march into the Information Age.

Scientific and information technology companies from around the world are opening research and development labs in India—more than 100 in the past five years.

One mainstay of the new economy is software development, with ever more global firms outsourcing to India the time-intensive work of programming. Businesses worldwide also rely on the country for customer service—phone calls from around the world are directed to call centers in Indian cities such as Bangalore.

Other developing markets include pharmaceutical and biotechnology research. Currently, the majority of top American companies send some of their IT work to India, and there is little evidence of a slowdown in this trend.

The business world is also looking in India's direction. Graduates of the nation's business programs are in high demand among multinational corporations, with each graduating class commanding a higher average salary than the one before. Those who complete MBA degrees at schools such as the Indian Institute of Management can now expect starting salaries ranging from $75,000 (USD) at Indian firms to over $200,000 outside the country. This is comparable to graduates of top American business schools such as Harvard, Stanford and Dartmouth—testimony to the market value of Indian talent in this area of study.

Military Buildup

As its clout has grown, India has placed a high priority on improving its military capabilities as well. New Delhi has not joined 187 other nations in signing the Nuclear Non-proliferation Treaty (NPT), and appeared on the world's radar screen as a nuclear-armed nation in May 1998, with the detonation of five warheads in the desert near the border of Pakistan.

This disturbed many governments around the globe, naturally including that of Pakistan, which responded with nuclear tests of its own.

This stand-off was the turning point that began India's pursuit of a full-fledged nuclear weapons program. According to *The Bulletin of the Atomic Scientists*, additional nuclear missile tests occurred in the summer of 2004; since then, the Indian Defense Ministry has earmarked $2 billion annually to build 300 to 400 weapons over the next 5 to 7 years.

India maintains a "no first strike" nuclear policy, and asserts that it only seeks enough nuclear weaponry to effectively deter aggressors. U.S. President George W. Bush, during a March 2006 visit with Indian Prime Minister Manmohan Singh, announced cooperation between the two countries on civilian nuclear programs, and had previously called India a "responsible" nuclear nation (*Der Spiegel*). These measures drew an American diplomatic line between India and other nations that have nixed participation in the NPT, such as North Korea and Iran.

Whatever its nuclear aspirations, the country has a long military shopping list. Last year, it announced plans to build the first aircraft carrier ever put to sea by a developing nation, and to lease two nuclear submarines from Russia. America has openly discussed the sale of naval vessels, combat aircraft, patrol aircraft and helicopters to India. One former U.S. ambassador to India opined, "Of course we should sell advanced weaponry to India. The million-man Indian army actually fights, unlike the post-modern militaries of many of our European allies" (*The Economist*).

A Turning Point in Relations With China?

Many have compared India's pattern of growth to its neighbor, China. The countries have much in common—physical borders, immense populations, similar challenges, ancient civilizations, and quickly-rising economies. India also measures itself against China, coveting its economic power and international standing, including its permanent seat on the United Nations Security Council.

Though a degree of tension does remain between the two nations, with lingering memories of the brief 1962 war in which China soundly defeated India, the relationship between these two Asian giants is warming up. Trade between them is now increasing at a vigorous pace, and diplomatic relations are at a post-1962 highpoint. Chinese Prime Minister Wen Jiabao, during a recent visit to New Delhi, hailed cooperation between the two nations as the driving force of a new "Asian Century." Indian Prime Minister Singh spoke of the potential for India and China to rearrange the world order by working together.

Many have pointed out that their economic strengths seem to be tailor-made for a partnership. India seeks to be a major player in the computer software world in the same way that China is in the area of hardware. Cooperation between Beijing and New Delhi could prove a dominant force in the information technology market.

Both nations have a voracious appetite for natural resources, and a recent energy deal neatly symbolized the new Sino-Indian dynamic: India acquired a 20% share in the development of the largest onshore oil field in Iran. The venture happens to be operated, and 50% owned, by Sinopec—China's state-run oil company.

However, India could seek to undercut China's manufacturing prices (as China did with many Southeast Asian countries in the 1990s). But it is more likely to pursue a different segment of the world market by producing higher-quality goods, as well as entirely different products.

Time will tell exactly how the relationship will mix competition and cooperation. These two nations both aspire to "first-world" status—and economic gains could be the incentive for a more tightly allied Asia.

Between East and West

With its newfound power, India faces a dilemma: Should it ultimately pursue closer ties with Western nations, or with other Asian countries?

After India gained independence, its first prime minister spoke of an Asian renaissance, envisioning a tightly bound continent changing the post-World War II landscape. Though premature at the time, the idea is now more feasible than any time since the Cold War era. Along with the improving relations with China, India is also friendly with Russia and Japan. And, as of 2004, the valuc of India's trade with other Asian nations surpassed that of exchange with the United States and Western Europe put together (*International Herald Tribune*).

But the United States—after courting India's arch-rival Pakistan as an ally in the war on terror after the September 11 attacks—is now distancing itself somewhat from the current Islamabad regime led by Pakistani President Pervez Musharraf, focusing on India instead. India's common ground with the U.S. includes liberal democratic government, capitalism and, among the more educated urban residents, the English language.

However, America's courting of India is viewed by some as a way to limit and contain Chinese influence in Asia. Some Indians resent this perception of their nation as a pawn of the U.S. Though they appreciate the American lifestyle and culture, much of the Indian population still sees this lone superpower as a bully.

While it may be able to dance with both partners alternately for a while, India will eventually be forced to choose. Which way will this nation turn?

"Kings of the East"

We need not merely guess where world events will ultimately lead. While many of the details remain to be seen, the overall framework of the future has been recorded in advance in one book—the Holy Bible.

In nations such as India, the size of population alone pulls them toward superpower status. Bible prophecy describes global power blocs—superpowers, or groups of superpowers—that will be prominent at the end of the age, shortly before Jesus Christ returns.

These powers will be based in the north (Europe), the south (the Arab world), and the "kings of the East"—a group of Asian nations that will band together, eventually fielding a standing army of*two hundred million* (Rev. 16:12; 9:16; Dan. 11)!

The nations of the West, including the United States, are headed for hard times as a result of their national and personal sins against the God that inspired the Bible. He reveals that they will be forsaken by their allies, called "lovers" in Scripture:

"And when you are spoiled, what will you do? Though you clothe yourself with crimson, though you deck yourself with ornaments of gold, though you rend your face with painting, in vain shall you make yourself fair; your *lovers* will despise you, they will seek your life...All your *lovers* have forgotten you; they seek you not; for I have wounded you with the wound of an enemy, with the chastisement of a cruel one, for the multitude of your iniquity; because your sins were increased" (Jer. 4:30; 30:14).

India is today one of these "lovers," but one that will soon prove to be something very different. So will other nations that Western countries now consider to be allies.

Keep watching India's growth toward superpower status—just one part of the inevitable rise of Asia!

FUTURE SUPERPOWERS - THE WORLD TO 2100

Most projections of future trends in national power fail to appreciate the importance of three crucial factors: (1) the declining EROEI of energy resources (including, but not limited to, "peak oil"); (2) the importance of human capital to economic growth, especially in developing countries' attempts to "catch up" to the advanced world; and (3) the impacts of climate change, which are projected to be more and more catastrophic with every passing year. Disregarding these trends produces predictions such as George Friedman's (STRATFOR) argument that Mexico – a low human capital country experiencing plummeting oil production and growing water stress – will become a superpower by 2100. Using my current estimates of Comprehensive National Power as a base (an index of power that attempts to express a nation's economic, military, and cultural power in a single number), I will *specially stress* the above factors in my analysis of future global power trends.

Some results will look plausible and familiar (e.g. China overtaking the US as a superpower by the 2020's); others will appear utterly bizarre (e.g. Canada becoming a major Great Power in by the end of the century, while India and Brazil plummet back into obscurity). But they are nonetheless all plausible and even likely outcomes, derived from bringing together worlds that all too often are considered independently of each other: the economy; human capital; geopolitics; energetics; and climate change.

There may of course be unexpected discontinuities – popularized as Black Swans by Nassim Taleb – that unravel these projections (the probability of their happening increasing exponentially over time). This will be covered in greater depth below. In the meantime, bear this caveat in mind as you read the rest of the post.

The End of Pax Americana (1980-2025)

The US is the current superpower, but China is rapidly making up ground. Its real GDP is now at $10 trillion, though according to some estimates it has already overtaken the $14.5 trillion American economy.

Some critics claim that nominal GDP is a better measure of power, even using these figures to claim that even at 10% growth it will be decades before China surpasses the US. This is a product of economic illiteracy, because it doesn't take into account the convergence of Chinese price levels to those of developed countries (its nominal GDP has been expanding *at more than 20%* in the last 5 years).

There are a number of other factors that are often quoted to predict the doom of China's rise, such as: (1) Growing regional disparities; (2) Income inequality; (3) Environmental degradation; (4) Bad loans and financial collapse, aka Japan; (5) Aging population; (6) Excessive export dependency; (7) Social unrest; (8) Authoritarian nature of its Marxist-Leninist political model.

Suffice to say that they are either common to most industrializing countries (1-3, 7); will only seriously affect it by the time its already developed (4-5); are overestimated (4, 6); or it is unclear why they should derail its economic ascent for long even if they lead to a democratizing revolution (7-8). I address all these points in detail here.

In any case, most of these are factors have yet to be realized, whereas many of the same trends undermining US power are already in evidence. You can point out the accumulating weight of China's bad loans, but it is the Western financial system that had to be bailed out in 2008 at social expense; you can argue that the aging of China's population will bankrupt its (minimal) social net, but it is the US that is facing a budget deficit of >10% of GDP and a national debt soaring into the stratosphere.

China is already the world's largest manufacturing power. On current trends, it is due to overtake the US economy by the mid-2010's (followed in nominal terms sometime in the 2020's, as restrictions on the yuan are lifted and it appreciates). Since China produces its own military hardware, real GDP is what matters; consequently, it will take *less relative effort* for the PLA to match and overtake the US (especially in the crucial East Asian region and the Indian Ocean). As Paul Kennedy noted in *The Rise and Fall of the Great Powers* (of which, incidentally, the Chinese are great fans) military and political power follows naturally in the wake of economic power, whereas trying to achieve results from the opposite directions leads to the "imperial overstretch" that contributed to Soviet collapse and is now undermining American power.

Which brings us to the last point. China's population is four times bigger than America's, and human capital among the youngest generations is now as good as the US average. This makes its per capita convergence – and consequently, its ascent to economic primacy – almost inevitable.

But rather than assessing the situation dispassionately and preparing for a strategic retreat, the US is digging in all fronts: foreign wars, deficit spending, oil dependence, political gridlock, etc. This increases the probability that US decline will take the form of a sudden collapse, as of Argentina's in 1999-2002, instead of fading away like the British Empire after 1945.

The Return of the Middle Kingdom (2020-2075)

The cultural decline will be slower. It took Latin more than a millennium after the collapse of the Roman Empire to lose its status as a *lingua franca*. Needless to say, the US will still retain a great deal of power by virtue of its large population and developed economy, it will remain in second place, almost no matter what, well into the 21st century. Furthermore, it will retain its deep ties – economic, cultural, etc. – with the Anglo-Saxon world (the UK, Canada, Australia, New Zealand) and, to a lesser extent, Europe. Hollywood, Silicon Valley, and the Ivy League will remain staples of global culture and technology.

However, there's only so much power you can exercise through the English language, Google, or even Chuck Norris. For everything else there's China – after a two hundred year break (a mere blip in its millennial history), the Middle Kingdom will have returned to its rightful place at the center of the world.

China is now roughly where South Korea was in 1990. A similar growth profile will by 2030 leave its economic power *equal to 25 of today's Koreas*. Imagine that!

It's unclear what political system China will have by then. Democratization on the Taiwanese model is not inevitable. The Chinese Communist Party (CCP) has studied the Soviet collapse in rigorous detail and is determined not to repeat its liberalizing mistakes. What I consider at least equally likely is an emergence of a "consultative Leninism", in which the current NEPist model is opened up to democratic elements (e.g. competitive local elections; policy-making based on opinion polling) but under the continuing hegemony of the CCP. This could be China's own, sovereign road to democracy.

Other possibilities are also possible, e.g. a Singaporean authoritarianism, or "managed democracy" in the style of Putin's Russia. But short of a reversion to Maoism – which is exceedingly unlikely, given that China now has a commercial class that would strongly oppose it – it's unclear how the widespread mantra that political change must be accompanied by a cessation of economic growth can be justified. China's rise will be accompanied by the flock of BRIC's trailing in its wake: Brazil, Russia, and India. The first two will enjoy a massive resource windfall from selling their plentiful energy, mineral, and water (in the form of food) reserves to a world made increasingly ravenous by depletion elsewhere and the effects of an increasingly destructive and chaotic climate. Russia will remain a first-class Great Power, and India will join its ranks; Brazil will be the most prominent of the second-class powers, which will also include France, Canada, Germany, Japan, the UK, Turkey, and Korea.

As with China, there are many reasons cited to explain for why Russia will fail to achieve its promise, such as (1) demographic decline; (2) corruption; (3) resource-based economy; (4) crumbling infrastructure; (5) authoritarianism. All these factors are either exaggerated (1-5), typical of most middle-income countries (2, 4), or it is unclear why they are necessarily negatives at all (3, 5). But it also has great strengths. Russia combines the BRIC's fiscal sturdiness and economic dynamism (both lacking in the West) with a GDP per capita that is almost twice that of the next richest BRIC, Brazil. Its human capital is on a par with the developed world's, allowing for an easy convergence. Crucially, Russia is perfectly positioned for the coming age of "scarcity industrialism", in which food, energy, and energy prices soar and global warming opens up vast regions of the country, including the Arctic, to shipping, energy production, agriculture, and habitation. Even at current growth rates of 4% per year, Russia should converge to European income levels by 2020-25 and spend the next few decades comfortably, its energy riches shielded by its nuclear umbrella.

Obviously Russia lacks the population mass, at least at this stage, to become a true superpower (even if it absorbs the other post-Soviet nations into a Eurasian union). This is not the case for India, which will overtake China to become the world's most populous nation by 2025. But within that fast-growing population illiteracy is still rife and 47% of children remain malnourished. Though it suffers from many the usual ailments of low-income countries – creaky infrastructure, caste-based inequalities, sluggish courts and bureaucracy, etc. – it's India's low level of human capital that is the primary cause of its falling so far behind China (manufacturing output is an order of magnitude lower, and the poorest Chinese provinces are equal to the Indian average). Nonetheless, India has the coal to power itself, and temperatures will remain within acceptable bounds for producing stagnant grain harvests for at least the next few decades. And quantity counts. That is why India will become a first-rank Great Power, equaling Russia and approaching the US.

With its ample lands and resources (e.g. iron, oil), not to mention its successes with sugar cane-derived ethanol, Brazil is set to enjoy – much like Russia – a comfortable existence as a regional hegemon in a world of high prices for food, energy and minerals. Its military strength is paltry, but irrelevant given its distance from other Great Powers. It is also the least corrupt of the BRIC's. However, its prospects for true superpowerdom are constrained by relatively low human capital; as its economy wasn't distorted by a legacy of socialist mismanagement (as with China or Russia), its GDP per capita is already, more or less, "where it should be." In the background, Canada will be getting very rich off supplying fuels and water to an increasingly parched and energy-starved US. However, for the time being its profile will remain modest.

The European Union is conspicuous by its absence. Europe is no longer united by the memory of war and the Soviet threat, and each country concerned above all for its own national interests. This is not a stable foundation for a union, and as such it will likely retreat into something like a glorified free trade area by the 2020's. Real power will be concentrated among the big European Powers, which will carve out spheres of influence and compete with each other for neo-colonial influence: e.g. France (Maghreb); Germany (East-Central Europe); Turkey (Balkans, Azerbaijan, Arab world); the Scandinavian bloc; the Visegrad bloc. Arguably there is already evidence of this in the Anglo-French effort to oust

Qaddafi. No European Power will have the mass to become a first-rank Great Power, though it may be (marginally) possible for France and definitely possible for coalitions of European Powers. By themselves, all the European nations will be lingering near the bottom of the CNP scale.

There is no point discussing any other country or alliance. NATO is becoming more irrelevant with each passing year. Japan is technologically advanced, but reliant on the US for its security and dependent on the same oceanic supply routes as China; as soon as the latter becomes the new regional hegemon, Japan's effective sovereignty is history. Indonesia is similar India, but five times smaller. South Africa, Mexico, Australia, Nigeria, Iran, and Saudi Arabia are all some combination of (1) too underpopulated, (2) too underdeveloped, and (3) too vulnerable to climate change.

Towards a Russian Century? (2075-?)

Beyond 2050 we are getting into very foggy territory. Just think of an educated European observing the world one century ago, in 1911 – could he have predicted Germany's utter collapse and occupation, and the rise of Russia (now known as the USSR) as a superpower along with the (vastly stronger) US superpower? And could that observer in 1951 have predicted that a China only recently consolidated under Communist control, after a century of stagnation, invasions and warlordism, would just fifty years later have overtaken a Russia that had become a basketcase?

Any number of black swans may have intervened by 2050, steering any projections wildly of course. Here are a few examples:

- *China and the US cooperate to build a massive global geoengineering project in the 2040's that succeeds at checking global warming.* This removes the conditions for Russia's rise to a dominant position.
- *Facing desiccation in the West and flooding in the South, the US annexes Canada.* As a result, it becomes the greatest Power in the world.

- *There is a total war between nuclear Powers, perhaps triggered by a Chinese land grab for the Russian Far East.* Whoever "wins" (if that's the right term), well, wins.
- *The development of nuclear fusion, space-based solar power, or some other technology, that reverses the secular trend towards declining EROEI.* This massively undercuts the power of major resource exporters, such as Russia, Canada, and Brazil.
- *A transition to sustainable development.* With global CO2 emissions setting a new record in 2010 (just one year after the deepest global recession in the past half-century), and setting the 2C warming target practically out of reach, there is little hope of that without geoengineering (after 2C the process is expected to display a runaway dynamic due to positive feedback loops). But miracles happen, sometimes.
- *A technological singularity.* Perhaps this catapults the nation where it first appears into a dominant leadership position, much like Britain during the industrial revolution; or maybe it is so transnational and transformative in its scope that it makes the very idea of nations and national power obsolete. By definition, a technological singularity is beyond the "event horizon" of our limited imaginations, so there's little more I can say on this.

For the purposes of completing the scenario to 2100, I will assume that the above don't occur. Instead, the dominant forces in previous decades – economic convergence; declining EROEI and minerals accessibility; accelerating climate change – remain constants.

By the second half the century, climate change will start to dominate over everything else. The latest projections tend to lean towards the high end of the IPCC's 1-6C warming range for the next century (the scariest of them show that by 2300 most of the world outside the Arctic may become downright lethal during summer). Warming of 4C is the point at which agriculture starts to not only experience difficulties but outright collapse throughout most of the equator and mid-latitudes.

[*Map of global drought under aggregated runs of IPCC's models. Most of the US, southern Europe, the Middle East, Africa, and Latin America will be in an unprecedented mega-drought. Read more here.*]

All the problems currently experienced by China and India with stagnant grain harvests will increase further, requiring very costly counter-measures. Now this is not to say that there will necessarily be mass famine and "dieoff", as doomers like to predict. It is certainly a possibility, especially under the most severe warming scenarios, but growing food production in Russia, Canada, and even East Africa may make up the difference. In particular, China should be relatively safe, because by then it should be a developed country.

On the other hand, the Chinese state will have its hands full mitigating disaster after climate disaster. The spate of rebuilding after the flooding of New Orleans, which actually boosted US GDP, was one thing; when commercial metropolises like Shanghai are getting flooded and coastal property prices devaluing to nothing, it is economic and financial apocalypse.

What's possible, then, is the following scenario. By the 2070's, the Chinese state becomes so preoccupied with maintaining food stability, and the energy and mineral flows that enable industrial society in general, that the surplus resources and administrative capacity to do anything else diminish. This is not a new development in its history. For much of the 19th century, Qing China was the world's biggest economy by GDP, even though Britain was becoming far more industrialized. This was because China was at its Malthusian limits; the population level was stable, but it was always on the edge of famine, and presided over by a government made weak by lack of taxable surpluses and unable to check the corruption and independence of its own public officials. The state was unable to defend itself, to modernize the country, or to guarantee its independence.

India is in a worse bind, and not just because it will likely remain less developed than China to that time. The Chinese, at least, have the reserve option of migrating some of their surplus population to Tibet (or East Africa, if they conquer it). India doesn't have that, and faces the unwelcome prospect of a further flood of excess population – this time from a collapsing Pakistan (the Indus to run dry by late century, as Himalayan glaciers melt) and inundating Bangladesh.

A consequence is that states with far smaller populations and economies, but greater surplus resources – will emerge as new Great Powers. Primarily, this means Russia, but Canada would also be in this category, as will Scandinavia, Alaska, and (in one or two more centuries) whoever settles or controls Greenland. By virtue of their control over most of the world's *remaining* critical resources – water (not only for food, but electricity); gas; coal; metals; whatever's left of oil – they will wield unprecedented strategic power over the countries to the south.

Perhaps a colonial relationship will develop, in which the Arctic nations send resources and allow southern workers to farm their lands in exchange for selling off their industrial assets and eventually ceding political sovereignty. In the very long term, this will logically lead to the development of caste-based societies in Russia and Canada, as the sheer magnitude of climate refugees would mean that in any integration policy, it would be the indigenous inhabitants who would have to do most of the integrating (and hence politically impracticable).

2

India's Rising Military Power

China has taken serious note of India's growing military power over the last decade. India, which has traditionally talked of the power of argument began to talk of the argument of power. In fact, the 1998 nuclear tests themselves were indicative of the fact that India had begun to realize the role of hard power in securing its national interests and also in making her voice heard in international politics.

India's growing military profile is especially evident in the maritime domain. The Indian navy has emerged as the net security provider in the Indian Ocean over the last decade. In 2004, it unveiled its first-ever naval doctrine that defined India's legitimate areas of interest stretching from the Persian Gulf to the Malacca Straits.

It released its updated version in 2009, incorporating the rapid changes in the geo-strategic environment involving India. India's defense ties with the US have developed at a frenetic pace, which has played the central role in India's military modernization. For example, recent defense contracts signed with the US include US$ 1.1 billion for C-130J Super Hercules transport planes and US$2.4 billion for 10 Globemasters airlifters. In January 2009, the Indian Navy signed an agreement with the U. S. to buy eight P-8I planes worth nearly US$2.1 billion, so as to replace the aging long range aerial reconnaissance fleet of eight Russian-made Tu-142s and five IL-38 planes.

The tests of its China-centric Agni series missile systems and the development of a Ballistic Missile Defense system. India's future military plans are even more ambitious, which further complicates China's strategic calculations. For example, the Indian Ministry of Defense in late 2011 announced its biggest expansion package to date, a US$13 billion military modernization plan. Under this plan within next five years, the Indian army is set to deploy 90,000 more soldiers and raise four new divisions along India's border with China, the largest such mobilization since the Sino-Indian border clashes of 1962.

INDIA'S POLY/MULTI-ALIGNED DIPLOMACY

The India that China defeated in 1962 was guided by a foreign policy doctrine called *non-alignment* vis-à-vis the superpower rivalry, and it remained the cornerstone of India's international diplomacy for more than four decades. However, this foreign policy paradigm underwent a U-turn when it metamorphosed into *poly/multi-alignment* under the new leadership in New Delhi in 1998. The new foreign policy outlook broadly had two components, namely, *improving relations with the US* and its *Look East Policy-II*.

The turnaround in India-US relations from being "estranged democracies" during the Cold War to "engaged democracies" in the 2000s has played a central role in bringing out a shift in China's India posture over the last decade. The anti-China element in the dramatically improving Indo-US relations was not very difficult to discern. Chinese scholar Jing-Dong Yuan notes that the warming of US-Indian relations took place at a time when China-US relations were undergoing serious setbacks in the late 1990s. In 1999, NATO bombed the Chinese embassy in the former Yugoslavia (the only embassy that it targeted); in May of that year, the Cox Report charged Chinese nationals with nuclear espionage and accused China of proliferation activities. hostile attitude toward the PRC further exacerbated tensions in early 2001. Also, the revised Nuclear Posture Review (NPR) included China as a nuclear target.

Meanwhile, in a diametrically opposite turn of events, India-US relations suddenly displayed signs of dramatic improvement. US President Bill Clinton visited India in March 2000 (the first presidential visit since Carter's visit in 1978). The US' National Security Strategy Report of 2002 released by the White House redefined India-US relations, stating that because of "India's potential to become one of the great democratic powers of the twenty-first century," the United States would "invest time and resources [for] building strong bilateral relations with India," and "work hard to transform our relationship accordingly." Consequently, the years 2002-03 witnessed a series of high-level meetings and substantial cooperation between the two democracies. Yet another contrast was the U.S.'s approval of Israel's sale of the Phalcon airborne warning and control systems to India in 2003 after the blockage of a similar sale to China in 2000.

Another Chinese security analyst Du Youkang argues that the US strategy of maintaining the balance of power in South Asia during the Cold War has gone beyond the balance of power and has tilted toward India. He cites the Clinton administration's pro-India attitude during the Kargil conflict, and his subsequent official tour to South Asia, where he spent six days in India compared to five hours in Pakistan. The growing strategic ties between the two countries provides a dangerous historical precedent for Beijing. During the Cold War, China perceived India-USSR relations in terms of an anti-China alliance in South Asia. So the strategic partnership between India and the US in the 2000s is, from China's perspective, the revival of the same anti-China alliance – the only difference being that the US has replaced the Soviet Union. Zhang Guihong compared the US-India Western Pacific.

The other pedestal of India's multi-aligned diplomacy included its *Look East Policy-II*. India's Look East Policy-I was officially initiated in 1992. Like most of the previous Indian policies it was reactionary and an outcome of ad hoc-ism. The main driver behind this policy was the economic doldrums of early 1990s, and India saw Southeast Asia as a springboard to join unfolding globalization. However, India displayed an uncharacteristic proactiveness in projecting the Look East policy in its second incarnation in the first-ever India ASEAN summit in Phnom Penh, Cambodia in 2002. India added a politico-security dimension to this policy. It developed security ties with the ASEAN group. From ASEAN's perspective, developing such ties with India (apart from the US presence in the region) provided them a sense of strategic reassurance given their territorial disputes in the South China Sea with a rapidly growing, authoritarian China.

An important highlight of India's Look East Policy-II, from China's viewpoint, has been a transformational improvement in India-Japan relations. Although the ice between their relations was broken with the visit of Prime Minister Mori Yoshiro to India in August 2000, their relations broadened and deepened in the second phase. The April 2005 joint statement issued during Koizumi Junichiro's visit to India introduced a "strategic" dimension to the partnership. The establishment of the Strategic and Global Partnership between India and Japan in December 2006 elevated relations to a new level. In 2006 Japan became only the second country with which India had a bilateral annual summit apart from Russia. When then Prime Minister Shinzo Abe visited India in August 2007, the joint statement sought to provide a roadmap for new dimensions to the strategic and global partnership. The October 2008 joint statement during Prime Minister Manmohan Singh's visit to Japan mentioned the advancement of the strategic and global partnership, making Japan the only country

Partnership Agreement (CEPA) which came into force in August of the same year. In late December 2011 India's External Affairs minister visited Japan in October 2011 for the Fifth round of the India-Japan Strategic Dialogue. Japanese PM Yoshihiko Noda visited India for the sixth annual meeting of the leaders of India and Japan. It was the success of India's Look East Policy-II (and not Look East Policy I) that made China remark that India's Look East Policy is "look to encircle China."

India Emerging as an Economic Giant

India and China had similar per capita income by 1974. However, China surged well ahead of India thanks to its deep economic engagement with the US after the Policy of Reform and Open Up (*gaige kaifang*) by Deng Xiaoping in 1978. While China's Open Door policy was a well-thought-out initiative, India, following its legacy of taking radical initiatives only while in crisis, embarked upon its own version of Open Door policy in 1991. The much-needed reforms removed obstacles to economic freedom, and India began to play catch-up, steadily re-integrating into the global economy. A Goldman Sachs report from 2007 found another watermark in India's economic history since 1991 when it pointed out that since 2003 India has been one of the fastest growing major economies, leading to rapid increases in per capita income, demand, and integration with the global economy.

The story of India's economic success has captivated Chinese attention over the last decade. Among Chinese scholars a new discourse has begun over India's economic success story, especially in the IT and consensus that China is a great success in exports, inside China, focusing on China's lag in information technology, Chinese researchers ask why India has become so competitive in the international software market when India has many unattractive features."

Chinese scholars now debate an "Indian Model" as an alternative to the "Chinese model" for developing countries. The Indian model, as understood by Chinese scholars, is characterized by avoiding its weaknesses and exploiting its strengths. For example, India leapfrogged from the primary sector (agriculture) to the tertiary sector (services) by exploiting its inherent advantages in the IT sector which includes a vast, young English-speaking population, the entrepreneurial genius of its private sector, computer literacy, a sound banking sector, and a culture that respects the rule of law.

Chinese analysts have especially taken notice of what they call "India New Economy" which is acting like an engine to the

Indian Model. Ma Jiali argues that although India is a baby elephant in the manufacturing industry, it is a "doughty tiger" in the information sector. Another set of scholars attributed India's success in this sector to its diaspora. It opined, "India's IT success is also attributed to the large cohort of educated overseas Indians who have good connections and invested heavily in their home country in recent years as a result of favourable government policies. The dynamism brought by the overseas Indians was comparable to the boost brought by the overseas Chinese since the 1978 economic reform in China."

RISE OF MILITARY POWER PROJECTION IN INDIA

The range of foreign policy tools employed by independent India, military power projection may not come readily to mind. Indeed, the conventional wisdom is that India's traditional foreign policy orientation all but precludes projection of military power beyond its territory. Such a belief not only fails to appreciate India's past and likely future use of military power abroad, it also ignores the fungibility of military tools for projecting both "hard" and "soft" power.

In the past five years, all three branches of the Indian armed forces have articulated the need to be able to operate beyond India's borders. The navy's 2007 maritime strategy speaks repeatedly about the need to "project power" as a means of supporting foreign policy objectives and achieving national aims.

In particular, the Indian Navy is keen to boost .its ability to decisively influence military operations on land. For his part, when Air Chief Marshal S. P. Tyagi was chief of the Air Staff, he argued that India needed "a strategic reach to safeguard our national interests," while official statements note that the Indian Air Force "is increasingly used for power projection beyond South Asia."

Similarly, a local defense analyst reports, "[T]he Indian Air Force's revised war doctrine envisages its transformation into an aerospace power capable of conducting full-spectrum operations and extending its strategic reach from the Persian Gulf to the Strait of Malacca." Even the traditionally inward-looking army is reportedly focusing on expeditionary warfare, with discussions at a recent infantry commanders' conference focused on transforming the infantry into an "expeditionary force" for use in an "out of area contingency." Unsurprisingly, a number of analysts both inside and outside of India look at recent military acquisitions and perceive that

India has begun inducting power-projection platforms, such as aircraft carriers, nuclear-powered submarines, long-range combat aircraft with mid-air refueling capability and landing platform dock ships for expeditionary warfare and humanitarian missions and is also developing an intercontinental ballistic missile with a strike range in excess of 5,000 km—all with the collective aim of influencing events far from home.

Similarly, external observers such as Ashley Tellis contend that "India is slowly maturing into a conventional great power," while the *New York Times* has run headlines proclaiming the "Land of Gandhi Asserts Itself as Global Military Power."

Such language and actions certainly run counter to the traditional view of India's early leaders, who profoundly believed that "power, especially military power, was the cause of evil," as well as contemporary civil and military leaders who believe that India has little need to develop the capacity to project military force far beyond its borders. As one former joint secretary in the Ministry of Defence bluntly remarked to the author, "India does not believe in power projection." Similarly, a former cabinet minister discounted the notion that India would ever militarily intervene in another nation's internal affairs, with the remark that "India would never do a Grenada." Even some retired flag officers believe that India will never undertake out of area power projection, claiming the concept is "not in the Indian psyche."

Instead, it is often suggested that India seeks only to project "soft power"—the attractive qualities of its culture and society—abroad to gain influence without resorting to military force. The idea of projecting India's culture, religions, art, and political morality abroad has traction within the Indian government, and some officials go so far as to suggest that India will seek to become a "soft power superpower." In that vein, several recent academic studies of Indian "power projection" have tended to focus largely, or even exclusively, on the non-military aspects of India's efforts to influence neighboring regions.

Is India poised to become a "global military power" with the ability to forcibly "influen[ce] events far from home," or will it retain its well-documented allergy toward military power projection? As with many things in life, the truth lies somewhere between these two extremes. This article argues that, in the medium term, the limitations of political will and military capacity will prevent India from achieving some of the more ambitious power projection goals discussed by defense analysts and members of the strategic community.

On the other hand, this article demonstrates that the idea that India has rejected and will continue to reject military power projection is untenable. This latter view appears to be based on an incorrect understanding of both the concept of military power projection and the fungibility of military tools for the projection of both hard and soft power, as well as India's needs in a changing geopolitical environment. Moreover, the notion that power projection is alien to India's strategic thinking overlooks the fact that India has not hesitated to "sort out" its neighbours when New Delhi felt that its interests were threatened. In comparison to a superpower such as the U.S., India's power projection needs are limited, but they are nonetheless real.

This article seeks to bring analytical clarity to the concept of military power projection in the Indian context and to explore the potential range of power projection capabilities India may possess in the coming years. To accomplish this goal, the article proceeds in three parts. First, the concept of military power projection is defined, and nine types of power projection missions are identified. Second, India's past use of power projection and future needs are briefly discussed in the light of contemporary strategic priorities. The final section discusses the utility of each of the three components of conventional military power (sea, air, and land) to fulfil the nine missions and examines India's potential power projection capability in these three areas. Given the previously noted focus by other scholars on Indian soft power projection, this article focuses solely on the use of military tools to shape political events abroad.

EXAMINING MILITARY POWER PROJECTION

To some, the phrase "power projection" suggests imposing regime change on a state far away from home for strategic gain. In this view, a prototypical example might be Operation Iraqi Freedom, the 2003 U.S.-led invasion of Iraq. While such a conceptualization captures some key elements of power projection, it is far too narrow. The U.S. Department of Defense (DoD) defines power projection much more broadly as being "[t]he ability of a nation to apply all or some of its elements of national power—political, economic, informational, or military—to rapidly and effectively deploy and sustain forces in and from multiple dispersed locations to respond to crises, to contribute to deterrence, and to enhance regional stability."

Focusing specifically on the final element of national power in the DoD's definition—the use of military tools—it is possible to disaggregate military power projection into nine different aspects based on the political goals being sought and the level of force employed. Four of these relate to the employment of "soft" military power (securing sea lanes of communication, non-combatant evacuation operations, humanitarian relief, and peacekeeping), and five are primarily concerned with "hard" military power (showing the flag, compellence/deterrence, punishment, armed intervention, and conquest).

Soft Military Power Projection

Securing Sea Lanes of Communication. The protection of shipping lanes from attack by hostile states or irregular threats. As the Indian Navy's maritime doctrine notes, trade is increasingly critical to the Indian economy, which makes the protection of the sea lanes transiting the Indian Ocean a significant priority. Following the attacks of September 11, 2001, the Indian Navy played a high-profile role in escorting U.S. shipping through the Straits of Malacca.

More recently, Indian naval vessels have been deployed to the Gulf of Aden, where they have thwarted several attempted hijackings by pirates.

Non-combatant Evacuation Operations. The evacuation of Indian or friendly third country civilians from a foreign country when they are endangered by war or civil unrest. For example, during Operation Sukoon (Urdu: Relief) the navy evacuated 2,280 Indian, Sri Lankan, and Nepalese civilians from Lebanon ahead of the 2006 Israeli-Hizbollah War. Several orders of magnitude larger was the airlift of over 100,000 Indians from Iraq and Kuwait ahead of the 1991 Gulf War.

Humanitarian Relief. The use of military forces abroad to assist in the aftermath of a natural disaster. Following the 2004 Asian tsunami, the Indian Navy mobilized 32 ships and over 20,000 naval personnel to evacuate casualties, as well as provide emergency sources of power and water to the peoples of Sri Lanka, the Maldives, Indonesia, Thailand, and Malaysia.

Peacekeeping. Military operations designed to support diplomatic efforts to reach a long-term political settlement to an ongoing dispute. India has been one of the most significant contributors to U.N. peacekeeping missions. As of 2009, the Indian Army had roughly 8,000 personnel deployed in the Democratic Republic of Congo, Lebanon, East Timor, the Ivory Coast, and the Golan Heights.

Hard Military Power Projection

Showing the Flag. The symbolic deployment of military forces to a region to demonstrate political interest, resolve, or willingness to take more forceful military action. For example, in June 1987 the Indian Air Force violated Sri Lankan airspace when it undertook Operation Poomalai (Tamil: Garland), the forced airdrop of relief supplies to ethnic Tamils during the siege of Jaffna. This action sent a clear message to the government in Colombo about New Delhi's desire to see a negotiated end to the conflict and helped lead to the signing of the Indo-Sri Lankan accord. More recently, the Indian Navy has undertaken several high-profile deployments to the South China Sea and the Persian Gulf, which have been interpreted as important signals of Indian interest in these regions.

*Compellence and Deterrence.*The use or the threat of military force against another state to induce it into or dissuade it from pursuing a given policy. In this form, power projection acts as a diplomatic tool, attempting to influence the decision-making process and calculus of foreign actors. For example, the governor of East Pakistan's decision to surrender to India in 1971 has been attributed to the compellence effect of well-timed air strikes on his residence in Dhaka at the very moment he was conducting a crisis response meeting. In the same conflict, the destruction of East Pakistani airfields after the air force in the territory had been attritted was an exercise in deterrence by denial that sought to preclude intervention by an outside power.

Punishment. The punitive use of force against another state in response to its pursuit of a given policy. Aside from limited punitive strikes on Pakistani posts across the Line of Control in Kashmir in response to militant activity (not an expeditionary use of force), punishment has not been widely employed by the Indian military.

Armed Intervention. The forcible movement of military units into another nation's territory to influence the internal affairs of the target country, short of outright conquest. Historical examples in India's immediate neighborhood range in size from the 1988 deployment of a parachute battalion to the Maldives (Operation Cactus) to put down a coup to the 1971 intervention in East Pakistan by three corps of the Indian Army to assist guerillas fighting for independence.

Conquest. The offensive use of military assets to forcibly occupy non-contiguous territory controlled or claimed by another state. This has not been an aspect of power projection pursued by independent India, although at the time some observers believed that the use of military forces in Hyderabad (Operation

Polo), Goa (Operation Vijay), and elsewhere as part of the post-Independence consolidation of the Indian Union was "an act of military aggression and conquest."

Given this disaggregation, it is clear that power projection is a much broader concept than mere invasion seeking regime change. Military assets, depending on how they are employed, can advance a state's foreign policy goals by facilitating the projection of either hard or soft forms of military power. Moreover, since Independence, India has employed at least seven, and perhaps eight, of the nine aspects of military power projection.

INDIA'S CONVENTIONAL MILITARY AND POWER PROJECTION

The three varieties of conventional military power—sea power, air power, and land power—all contribute to power projection in different ways. As Table 1 indicates, sea power has a high degree of fungibility across various power projection missions and will likely form the foundation of India's global reach in coming years. This is particularly true in India's "extended neighborhood," since the region stretching "across [Asia's] sub-regions—be it East Asia, West Asia, Central Asia, South Asia or Southeast Asia" is largely a maritime domain. In contrast, air and land power play more limited, but nonetheless important, roles in India's power projection capabilities.

Sea Power

In light of the fact that roughly 90% of India's external trade by volume and 77% by value is seaborne, Indian maritime power has a role to play in sustaining domestic economic development. Indeed, a host of observers dating back to the pre-Independence period has argued that India's economy is "at the mercy of the power which controls the sea." In the northern Indian Ocean, securing sea lanes of communication will be facilitated by the Indian Navy's ability to exercise "sea denial" (negating an enemy's ability to use the sea but at the same time making no attempt to control the sea itself) in a region stretching from the Arabian Sea in the west to the Straits of Malacca in the east. Moreover, as India looks farther away for energy resources, its political and military leaders are explicitly linking this effort with the need for the Indian military, particularly the navy, to be able to "protect the country's economic and energy interests" in key parts of the Indian Ocean.

Aircraft carriers, surface ships and submarines equipped with land-attack cruise missiles, and amphibious landing ships—the latter of which are discussed with land power below—are the key maritime power projection platforms that can influence events on land from the sea. While submarines can rely on stealth to approach an enemy coastline, task forces of cruisemissile-armed surface platforms, amphibious assault ships, and aircraft carriers require the assistance of attack submarines, maritime patrol aircraft, and modern destroyers to protect them from hostile submarines, aircraft, and anti-ship cruise missiles. Tankers and supply ships sustain maritime forces with food, fuel, and ammunition when operating a significant distance from friendly ports.

In 2008, then-Chief of Naval Staff Admiral Sureesh Mehta foresaw that the navy of 2020 would be "capable of influencing the outcome of land battles and performing a constabulary role in the Indian Ocean region." Achieving this will require a significant upgrade in capabilities. Naval planners envision a three-carrier fleet as the cornerstone of India's future blue-water navy: the 44,500-ton, Russian-built INS *Vikramaditya* (Sanskrit: Brave as the Sun) which is expected to join the fleet after 2012, and two domestically built aircraft carriers of the Vikrant class weighing in at 40,000 tons (INS *Vikrant*) (Sanskrit: Powerful) and 64,000 tons (INS *Vishal*) (Sanskrit: Great), scheduled to enter service in 2015 and 2018, respectively. At the same time, the introduction of the fourth-generation supersonic MiG-29K Fulcrum provides India with the most powerful naval strike aircraft in the region and increases its force projection capacity by an order of magnitude.

However, these optimistic projections mask a dark reality: at present India's existing 28,000-ton aircraft carrier, launched in 1953, is on its last legs. Should the induction of the *Vikramaditya* or the *Vikrant* be delayed beyond the middle of the decade, as some informed observers speculate, the navy could find itself without a carrier for several years. At the same time, only 11 of the 30 Mk. 51 Sea Harrier fighters that were in service in the 1980s remain, and at the time of this writing, there is yet to be a test flight of the naval version of Hindustan Aeronautics Limited's domestically designed Tejas lightweight fighter, which is supposed to replace the Harriers in providing air defense to the carriers.

Furthermore, the *Vikramaditya* and the *Vikrant* will carry only 16 fighters each. Assuming that the bigger *Vishal* will accommodate a larger complement of aircraft (50–60), analysts say it would have to operate in tandem with one of the 40,000-ton carriers to produce "as much striking power as a single U.S. Nimitz-class carrier. Even armed with precision-guided munitions, a contingent of this size could sustain only a modest land bombardment, and only for a modest time." Moreover, a three-carrier fleet will only ensure that the navy has at least one carrier at sea at all times, given the repair, training, and deployment cycles for modern naval vessels. To be able to implement Admiral Mehta's constabulary role in the Indian Ocean, the navy would need to have the ability to maintain two carriers at sea at all times, which would suggest a need for twice as many flattops. With an estimated unit cost of $1.5 billion, against an annual naval procurement budget of $2.3 billion, building each additional carrier over six or seven years could easily tie up 9% to 11% of the acquisition budget per platform, making a rapid expansion of the fleet unlikely.

The Indian Navy's surface-strike capability centers on the 290-kilometerrange supersonic BraMos cruise missile. A joint venture between Russia and India, the BraMos can achieve Mach 2.5 speed, which is three times faster than the U.S. Tomahawk cruise missile. While highly effective in an anti-shipping role, the BraMos is less useful as a land-attack weapon because it possesses only one-tenth the range of the U.S. Tomahawk. This latter characteristic is also true of the land-attack variants of the Russian-designed 3M-54 Klub cruise missile (275 kilometer range) also in service with the Indian Navy. The relatively short range of these missiles would render surface-launched cruise missile strikes against a state with even modest anti-access capability (attack submarines, anti-ship missiles, or supporting surveillance systems) a risky proposition. According to published reports, the Defence Research and Development Organization is currently developing a subsonic cruise missile with a reported range of 1,000 kilometres. Code named *Nirbhay* (Sanskrit: Fearless), it could fill an important gap in the navy's land-attack capability. However, test flights of the missile have been repeatedly delayed.

Finally, the Indian Navy's ability to project maritime power in the Indian Ocean and beyond is constrained by the fact that it is currently decommissioning surface ships faster than it is adding them. At present, large portions of India's fleet of 57 surface combatants, including five of its eight destroyers and seven of its 11 frigates, are approaching the end of their service life. The navy requires these types of platforms, equipped with advanced anti-aircraft and anti-submarine systems, to operate in hostile littorals. Moreover, to achieve a real power projection capability, the navy will require several additional fleet replenishment tankers and modern replacements for its cadre of Soviet-era minesweepers.

Air Power

Air power projection comes mainly in two forms: strikes against ground-based targets and the transport of ground troops. Since the latter role is primarily a supporting one, it is taken up in the discussion of land power below. As a tool for power projection, the use or threat of air power is primarily used for compellence/deterrence or to punish another state, should the initial efforts fail to bring about a desired policy change. Affecting targets at a range beyond a few hundred miles requires advanced strike aircraft (typically operating in conjunction with refueling tanker aircraft) capable of penetrating enemy air defenses, longer-range cruise missiles, or ballistic missiles.

The chief of the Air Staff, Air Chief Marshal F. H. Major, has argued that Indian air power needs "a strategic reach to safeguard our national interests," which requires a "long-range presence, persistence and 'forward-basing arrangements'." In this vein, the IAF's revised war doctrine is reportedly structured around "both pre-emptive action and swift retaliation" across a region stretching from the Persian Gulf to the Straits of Malacca. However, the air force has long suffered from the piecemeal acquisition of aircraft, and much of its fleet is facing obsolescence—raising questions about future combat power.

Nonetheless, the IAF has pushed for an independent strategic role in future conflict, arguing that air power can influence the battle space through deep-strike missions. The air force "aims to achieve this objective by operating advanced, long-range platforms with air-to-air refueling capability" and "must be equipped for long-reach, persistence, all-weather, precision, air dominance, networked, and space-enabled force capabilities." Most notable in this regard are efforts to induct long-range strike aircraft—particularly 272 fourth-generation Sukhoi Su-30s. The combination of SU-30s with precision-guided munitions, such as the AS-14 air-to-surface missile, would produce a significant ability to strike targets across the immediate neighborhood. Even though long-range strike Sukhoi aircraft are quite capable, their ability to operate at a significant distance depends on the IAF's in-flight refueling capability. Although the IAF does have six IL-78MKI Midas tanker aircraft (which doubles the Sukhoi's range to 6,000 kilometres), this only amounts to, in the words of one retired air marshal, "baby steps towards acquiring the capability of projecting combat power in the region.

At this point in time, the capability is limited to a token force and cannot be described as significant." In this regard, the IAF's hope to acquire an additional six new Airbus Military A330 Multi-Role Tanker Transports is a positive step. However, to support an expeditionary strike package of 60 aircraft, which would provide a modest ground-attack capability against multiple targets, at least 15 IL-78/A330 tankers would be required, notwithstanding the need for reserves or simultaneous capability in other areas. If the entire fleet of Sukhois were to be so supported, the IAF would require nearly 60 tanker aircraft. Beyond existing procurement plans, achieving the capability to support 60 Sukhois with tankers would require an additional $1.13 billion, while equipping the entire fleet would cost $11.7 billion, against an annual IAF procurement budget of $4.19 billion.

Strike aircraft are not the only way that offensive air power can contribute to compellence/deterrence or punishment type power projection missions. Given the simultaneously increasing lethality of air defense systems and the cost of combat aircraft, India may instead increasingly rely on surface-tosurface missiles for "deep strike against heavily defended targets in depth, such as airfields." This could presage an increased role for India's ballistic missile forces, which just saw the 3,000-kilometer range Agni III approved for induction into the army. The follow-on 6,000-kilometer range Agni V intercontinental ballistic missile is expected to be tested in 2011. While these missiles are commonly associated with India's strategic nuclear program, they could be employed in a conventional role if necessary, thus having potentially coercive effects on neighboring powers.

Land Power

The employment of expeditionary land power requires the facilitation of airlift or sealift capabilities, as well as specially trained forces (such as airborne troops or marines), long-range command and control capabilities, and a significant logistical ability to support and sustain troops once an initial landing has been made.

The chief of Army Staff, General Deepak Kapoor, had argued that "in keeping with our growing regional aspirations," the army needed to develop the capability to deploy ground forces for an out of area operation. In that vein, at a 2009 infantry commanders' conference, the army's senior leadership explored the idea of transforming into an "expeditionary force" capable of responding to an overseas contingency on short notice.

Although such capability may be required to fulfil U.N. peacekeeping obligations, there is some evidence that senior army leaders have been pressing for an increased overseas presence, "even outside the U.N. banner." "Given its emerging regional power status," one former Indian flag officer contends, "India may be called upon to project power in the region, which may involve airlift of large military forces to areas of interest . . . outside of our borders and [the capability] to provide sustained logistic support."

This would, in turn, require a substantial expansion of the country's strategic airlift capability, which some argue is virtually nonexistent. Lacking sufficient assets to suppress air defenses, some analysts believe that India's transports lack the ability to operate in hostile air environments. However, other observers contend that India has sufficient civilian airlift capacity to move and sustain up to a brigade of troops in a permissive environment—provided there is access to secure airfields.

The strategic reach provided by heavy airlift also has utility in noncombatant evacuation operations and humanitarian relief missions. In 1991 the IAF, along with civil air assets, played a key role in evacuating 100,000 Indian nationals from the Persian Gulf ahead of the Gulf War. More recently, India's airlift capabilities have reached across the extended neighborhood to ferry supplies and humanitarian aid during crises in venues from Lebanon to China.

For future power projection, Brigadier Gurmeet Kanwal (Retd.), the head of the Indian Army's principal think tank, the Centre for Land Warfare Studies, argues that India requires a dedicated air assault brigade by early 2012. The Agra-based 50th (Independent) Parachute Brigade might form the core of an air assault capability. But such a unit would require extensive organic fire support in the form of Lancer and Hind attack helicopters, to compensate for the lack of artillery possessed by such highly mobile troops. Moreover, the ability to move such a force in a rapid reaction scenario would require a significant increase of airlift capability. The IAF is rumored to be interested in buying 10 Boeing C-17s for heavy lift. However, moving a single battalion 2,000 kilometres in one day to respond to a crisis in the immediate neighborhood, as was done during the 1988 coup in the Maldives, would necessitate a lift capacity of 19 C-17 equivalents.

Furthermore, the ability to do so with an entire brigade would require 55 C-17 equivalents. Although the former is notionally within the capacity of present airlift assets, questions persist about the condition of these aircraft, raising doubts about the military's capacity in an emergency. Achieving the latter target by 2012 appears unrealistic because acquiring the equivalent of 55 C-17s would cost an estimated $9.1 billion, not including spare parts and maintenance. Against an IAF procurement budget of $4.19 billion, even if these aircraft were phased in over the next decade, it would still tie up 20% of the IAF's annual budget for new transport aircraft for the period.

In terms of amphibious lift, the navy's present ability to move 3,000 troops plus vehicles and equipment is centered on the INS *Jalashva* (Sanskrit: Sea Horse), a 16,900-ton, American-built Landing Platform Dock (LPD) that can transport nearly 1,000 soldiers and six medium helicopters. Acquired in 2007, the *Jalashva* addresses India's lack of heavy sea-lift and mass-landing capability, while also providing a potential command-and control platform for fleet operations in an amphibious landing or emergency response scenario. There is great interest in acquiring more LPDs through a combination of foreign acquisition and indigenous development. The present complement of Magar-class Landing Ship Tanks—which can transport 500 men or 15 armored vehicles—will be supplemented by four new amphibious assault ships.

In line with these developments, a joint doctrine for amphibious warfare was developed by the tri-service Integrated Defence Staff and tested in exercises in 2005 and 2007. Earlier this year, the army formally stood up a dedicated amphibious brigade, the 3,000-man 91 Infantry Brigade based at

Thiruvananthapuram, which is expected to form the core of a larger amphibious force in the future. The navy has expressed a desire to double the size of its own Marine Commando Force, which focuses on maritime counterterrorism operations and offshore raids, from its present strength of 2,000. Yet, such efforts will likely be hindered by budgetary constraints.

The *Jalashva*, operating together with one of the new carriers and a pair of Landing Ship Tanks, provides roughly the same size amphibious force as a typical U.S. Marine Expeditionary Unit in terms of deployable troops, armored vehicles, fighter aircraft, and helicopters.

With proper logistical support and training, this force could provide India with an expeditionary intervention force that could respond to contingencies or crises of limited scope or duration in its "extended neighborhood."

As with the carrier battle groups, the ability to operate close to hostile shores requires assistance from surface vessels with advanced anti-submarine and anti-aircraft capabilities. Should the Indian military reach its target amphibious lift capacity of 10,000 personnel, which would require both new amphibious platforms and more amphibious-ready troops, New Delhi would notionally be able to mount an operation like the 1983 U.S. intervention in Grenada. Similarly, it could respond to a major humanitarian crisis or non-combatant evacuation mission. This would go a long way toward Admiral Mehta's stated goal of playing a constabulary role in the Indian Ocean littoral region.

The army's ability to conduct expeditionary operations is no doubt enhanced by its long history of involvement in U.N. peacekeeping missions, which provides practical experience in small-unit operations as well as support functions: intelligence, medical, logistics, transportation, and engineering. However, one should not take the parallel too far because traditional peacekeeping operations are conducted in more-benign environments— which makes deployment, logistical support, and intelligence gathering significantly easier.

WILL INDIA PROJECT MILITARY POWER IN THE FUTURE?

There is good reason to believe that India will have at least as great a need for military power projection in the future as it has in the past. New Delhi's primary strategic priority over the next decade—deepening internal consolidation— requires sustained economic development and enhanced internal security. This, in turn, is at least partially dependent on developments in the country's immediate neighborhood. As current National Security Advisor Shivshankar Menon has argued, "[U]nless we have a peaceful and prosperous periphery, we will not be able to focus on our primary tasks of socioeconomic development." Furthermore, the achievement of regional peace and stability in South Asia will be a necessary precondition for India to claim great-power status.

Unfortunately, many of the countries on India's periphery are weak or fragile states. For example, *Foreign Policy* magazine's 2010 index of failed states included five of India's neighbours (Afghanistan, Pakistan, Bangladesh, Burma, and Sri Lanka) in the top 25. Although many of the challenges plaguing India's immediate neighborhood are political and economic in nature, and therefore not necessarily directly amenable to solutions based on the application of conventional military power, New Delhi may periodically require the ability to shape events in these countries that military power projection provides.

Further afield, successive political leaders in India have identified the arc from the Persian Gulf to the Straits of Malacca as "a legitimate area of interest . . . for the first quarter of the 21st century." As a result, the Indian Navy's maritime strategy states that "whatever happens in the [Indian Ocean littoral region] can affect our national security and is of interest to us." India's interests in this region are largely economic in nature, with energy access and growing regional economic engagement meshing with concerns about the safety of ships transiting the entire Indian Ocean littoral. In recent years, official statements have been increasingly blunt about the importance India attaches to energy security, which is deemed "vital for an assured high rate of [economic] growth." At present India imports over half of its natural gas and 70% of its oil, the vast majority of which comes from the Persian Gulf. Over the next 20 years, India's oil consumption is expected to grow at an annual rate of 5% to 7%—more than three times the global average rate of increase—which will more than double present day consumption by 2025. To sustain its high rates of economic growth, India must secure access to new sources of hydrocarbon energy.

The ability to influence events in this broader region may take on increasing importance as India's comprehensive national power grows. Scholars of international relations argue that as a state's wealth and material power increase, it "will select a larger bundle of security and welfare goals than a less wealthy and less powerful state." In terms of foreign policy preferences, scholars also argue that rising powers have generally sought to expand their spheres of influence— as state power increases, so do political interests abroad. This expanded material capacity and broadening of political interests are expected to translate into an increased interest in favourably shaping the state's strategic environment. Therefore, it is reasonable to assume that India will have at least the same level of need for power projection missions going forward as it has in the past. It will, in fact, most likely make increased use of such tools in the future.

The New Delhi has already employed its power projection assets to provide regional public goods (e.g., humanitarian relief, non-combatant evacuation operations, and securing sea lanes of communication) in parts of the Indian Ocean littoral in a manner befitting a regional hegemon. One key difference between great powers and other states is that great powers create external security for their region beyond merely protecting their own borders. Any country can have regional interests, but great powers also have regional responsibilities. As the dominant regional power in South Asia and an aspirant to a seat on the

U.N. Security Council, India is likely to be called on in the future to take an increased role in ensuring international peace and security, either under U.N. auspices or as a part of various multilateral coalitions.

While some in New Delhi may hope India can free-ride to great-power status, including ducking hard decisions and avoiding shouldering a burden, this status is unlikely to be achieved without bearing more responsibility. It is not possible to precisely identify in advance the specific contingencies that could compel India to project hard military power abroad, but, beyond the historical instances already noted, India may find several additional reasons to send its armed forces beyond its borders.

Future Military Roles

Support Forces Deployed on Peacekeeping Missions. It is hardly inconceivable that Indian peacekeepers (or those of friendly nations) could be targeted by belligerent parties during the course of their duties, thus potentially requiring a forcible extraction or rescue operations along the lines of Operation Khukri in Sierra Leone, where Indian forces rescued 230 U.N. peacekeepers who had been held hostage for over 75 days by the rebels of the Revolutionary United Front. Because India's local U.N. partners in the region were too weak to respond effectively, the success of this operation depended in large part on the rapid introduction of a battalion of Indian grenadiers and para-commandos airlifted directly from the Kashmir Valley, as well as a flight of Indian Air Force (IAF) attack helicopters.

Protecting Indians Abroad. Several recent events highlight the increasing salience of this issue. Following the 2000 coup in Fiji that ousted Prime Minister Mahendra Chaudhry, an ethnic Indian, there was significant pressure on the Indian government to take steps to protect Fiji's large Indian community. However, the lack of naval capacity rendered such an operation impossible. Of even more concern are the five million Indians employed in the Persian Gulf. A contingency in this region is hardly unthinkable, given the 1991 and 2006 emergencies that required major evacuations of Indian nationals from conflict zones.

Prevent Open Hostility from Immediate Neighbours. Aside from the domestic pressure brought by ethnic Tamils within India, the geopolitical imperative behind India's 1987 intervention in Sri Lanka was to preempt intervention in the conflict by an extra-regional power. Although the Sri Lankan conflict has ended, the imperative remains. If, for example, a neighboring country such as Burma were poised to emerge as a full-fledged satellite of China, New Delhi might feel compelled to act to protect its own interests.

Recognizing that India will likely have an increased need and desire for power projection in the future is not the same as arguing it will employ these capabilities indiscriminately around the globe. Such operations will still have to be in response to a threat to a vital national interest and have significant support from the population, if not, ideally, the international community. Nonetheless, these instances are likely to increase as India gains in international stature.

3

India's Rising Global Power

After disappointing itself for decades, India is now on the verge of becoming a great power. The world started to take notice of India's rise when New Delhi signed a nuclear pact with President George W. Bush in July 2005, but that breakthrough is only one dimension of the dramatic transformation of Indian foreign policy that has taken place since the end of the Cold War. After more than a half century of false starts and unrealized potential, India is now emerging as the swing state in the global balance of power. In the coming years, it will have an opportunity to shape outcomes on the most critical issues of the twenty-first century: the construction of Asian stability, the political modernization of the greater Middle East, and the management of globalization.

Although India's economic growth, its new foreign policy has been less noted. Unlike their U.S. counterparts, Indian leaders do not announce new foreign policy doctrines. Nonetheless, in recent years, they have worked relentlessly to elevate India's regional and international standing and to increase its power. New Delhi has made concerted efforts to reshape its immediate neighborhood, find a modus vivendi with China and Pakistan (its two regional rivals), and reclaim its standing in the "near abroad": parts of Africa, the Persian Gulf, Central and Southeast Asia, and the Indian Ocean region. At the same time, it has expanded relations with the existing great powers — especially the United States.

India is arriving on the world stage as the first large, economically powerful, culturally vibrant, multiethnic, multireligious democracy outside of the geographic West. As it rises, India has the potential to become a leading member of the "political West" and to play a key role in the great political struggles of the next decades. Whether it will, and how soon, depends above all on the readiness of the Western powers to engage India on its own terms.

THREE STRATEGIC CIRCLES

India's grand strategy divides the world into three concentric circles. In the first, which encompasses the immediate neighborhood, India has sought primacy and a veto over the actions of outside powers. In the second, which encompasses the so-called extended neighborhood stretching across Asia and the Indian Ocean littoral, India has sought to balance the influence of other powers and prevent them from undercutting its interests. In the third, which includes the entire global stage, India has tried to take its place as one of the great powers, a key player in international peace and security.

Three things have historically prevented India from realizing these grand strategic goals. First, the partition of the South Asian subcontinent along religious lines (first into India and Pakistan, in 1947, then into India, Pakistan, and Bangladesh, in 1971) left India with a persistent conflict with Pakistan and an internal Hindu-Muslim divide. It also physically separated India from historically linked states such as Afghanistan, Iran, and the nations of Southeast Asia. The creation of an avowedly Islamic state in Pakistan caused especially profound problems for India's engagement with the Middle East. Such tensions intertwined with regional and global great-power rivalries to severely constrict India's room for maneuver in all three concentric circles.

The second obstacle was the Indian socialist system, which caused a steady relative economic decline and a consequent loss of influence in the years after independence. The state-socialist model led India to shun commercial engagement with the outside world. As a result, India was disconnected from its natural markets and culturally akin areas in the extended neighborhood.

Finally, the Cold War, the onset of which quickly followed India's independence, pushed India into the arms of the Soviet Union in response to Washington's support for Pakistan and China — and thus put the country on the losing side of the great political contest of the second half of the twentieth century. Despite being the largest democracy in the world, India ended up siding with the opposite camp on most global issues.

The last decade of the twentieth century liberated India from at least two of these constraints; state socialism gave way to economic liberalization and openness to globalization, and the Cold War ended. Suddenly, New Delhi was free to reinvent its foreign policy — positioning itself to face the rise of China, shifting its strategic approach to its other neighbours, and beginning to work closely with the world's existing great powers.

VARIETIES OF INFLUENCE

India's recent embrace of openness and globalization has had an especially dramatic effect on the country's role in the region. As the nations of the subcontinent jettison their old socialist agendas, India is well positioned to promote economic integration. Although the pace has been relatively slow, the process has begun to gain traction. The planned implementation of the South Asian Free Trade Agreement this summer signals the coming reintegration of the subcontinent's markets, which constituted a single economic space until 1947.

At the same time, optimism on the economic front must be tempered by an awareness of the problematic political developments in India's smaller neighbours. The struggle for democracy and social justice in Nepal, interminable political violence and the rise of Islamic extremism in Bangladesh, and the simmering civil war in Sri Lanka underscore the potential dangers of failing states on the subcontinent. There are also the uncertain futures of Pakistan and Afghanistan: defeating religious extremism and creating modern and moderate states in both countries is of paramount importance to India. A successful Indian strategy for promoting peace and prosperity within the region would require preventing internal conflicts from undermining regional security, as well as resolving India's own conflicts with its neighbours.

In the past, great-power rivalries, as well as India's own tensions with Pakistan and China, have complicated New Delhi's effort to maintain order in the region. Today, all of the great powers, including the United States and China, support the Indian objective of promoting regional economic integration. The Bush administration has also started to defer to Indian leadership on regional security issues. Given the new convergence of U.S. and Indian interests in promoting democracy and countering extremism and terrorism, New Delhi no longer suspects Washington of trying to undercut its influence in the region. As a result, it is more prepared than ever to work with the United States and other Western powers to pursue regional goals.

Meanwhile, the external environment has never been as conducive as it is today to the resolution of the Indo-Pakistani conflict over Kashmir. The conflict has become less and less relevant to India's relations with the great powers, which has meant a corresponding willingness on New Delhi's part to work toward a solution. Of particular importance has been the steady evolution of the U.S. position on Kashmir since the late 1990s.

The support extended by President Bill Clinton to India in its limited war with Pakistan in 1999 removed the perception that Washington would inevitably align with Islamabad in regional conflicts. But India remained distrustful of the Clinton administration's hyperactive, prescriptive approach to Kashmir. It has been more comfortable with the low-key methods of the Bush administration, which has avoided injecting itself directly into the conflict. The Bush administration has also publicly held Pakistan responsible for cross-border terrorism and has extracted the first-ever assurances from Pakistan to put an end to the attacks. New Delhi does not entirely believe these promises, but it has nonetheless come to trust Washington as a source of positive of influence on Islamabad.

These developments have opened the way for a peace process between the two governments. With the growing awareness that the normalization of relations with Pakistan would end a debilitating conflict and help India's regional and global standing, New Delhi has begun to negotiate seriously for the first time in decades.

Although the pace of talks has not satisfied Pakistan, the two sides have agreed on a range of confidence-building measures. Indian Prime Minister Manmohan Singh has rejected the idea of giving up territory, but he has often called for innovative solutions that would improve living conditions and for common institutions that would connect Kashmiris across the Line of Control. Singh has made clear that the Indian leadership is ready to risk political capital on finding a diplomatic solution to Kashmir.

India's recent effort to resolve its long-standing border dispute with China has been just as bold. New Delhi decided in 2003 to seek a settlement with Beijing on a political basis, rather than on the basis of legal or historical claims. As a result, during Chinese Premier Wen Jiabao's visit to New Delhi in April 2005, India and China agreed on a set of principles to guide the final settlement. The two governments are now exploring the contours of mutually satisfactory territorial compromises.

India's search for practical solutions to the disputes over Kashmir and its border with China suggests that the country has finally begun to overcome the obsession with territoriality that has consumed it since its formation. Ironically, the nuclearization of India and Pakistan in 1998 may have helped in this regard: although nuclearization initially sharpened New Delhi's conflicts with both Islamabad and Beijing, it also allowed India to approach its territorial problems with greater self-assurance and pragmatism.

INDIA AND THE GLOBAL POWER SHIFT

The international security environment is witnessing a power shift from the developed Western states to Asia led by the rise of China and India. This power shift will have a significant impact on global geopolitics. Although a unipolar global order has been in place for a decade and a half, a non-polar world (as against a multipolar world) is in the making. Political, economic and demographic trends have made it inevitable.

As Richard Haass has noted, "In contrast to multipolarity — which involves several distinct poles or concentrations of power — a nonpolar international system is characterized by numerous centers with meaningful power. " He adds that while "the United States is and will long remain the largest single aggregation of power... power and influence are less and less linked in an era of nonpolarity. " According to Haass, "today's nonpolar world is not simply a result of the rise of other states and organizations or of the failures and follies of U. S. policy. It is also an inevitable consequence of globalization. "

Analysts assess that despite its pre-eminence in military, scientific and economic fields, the US remains a country in relative decline. Even if that decline is unlikely to make a difference in the near future, the certainty of new powers rising to be global players augurs for a new global power balance. Explosive rates of population and economic growth in Asian states are indicators of a new world order in which power will be more dispersed. The critical question is, if this multipolar world will have a benign or malign form. There are two likely possibilities on this. The world could fragment into competing blocs that attempt to resolve their differences through power politics as nation states did in the 19th and 20th centuries. Robert Kagan has talked of an 'axis of democracy', including the US, EU, India and Japan, counterbalancing a 'club of autocrats', including Russia, China and Iran. 2 The other possibility is of existing and rising powers choosing to manage their relations through mutual interdependence, as has been attempted successfully in Europe over the second half of the last century. Global shifts happen rarely and are even less often peaceful. The transfer of power from west to east will dramatically change the context of dealing with international challenges. In the early 20th century the imperial order and the aspiring states of Germany and Japan failed to adjust to each other. That led to wars which devastated the better part of the world. The coming shift in power will have a greater impact globally and will require assimilation of diverse political and cultural systems. Today's rising powers seek redress of past grievances, are proudly nationalistic and want to claim their rightful place in the comity of nations. Asian rise in economic terms will translate into greater political and military power, thus increasing the potential damage from conflicts. Former British Prime Minister Tony Blair has noted that "In the next two decades China and India will undergo industrialisation four times the size of the United States and at five times the speed... For the first time in many centuries, power is moving East. " Blair added that

"In this new world, we must clear a path to partnership, not stand off against each other competing for power. The world...cannot afford a return to the 20th century struggles for hegemony. "

It is also clear that military power, however strong, is in itself insufficient to obtain the political objectives of a war. The capacity of weaker opponents to impose high costs through asymmetric or 4th Generation War fighting is enough to make even the strongest military power think carefully before embarking on a military option.

The costs of managing Iraq after an easy military victory offer a clear indication of a fundamental shift in military affairs. As Fareed Zakaria has written, "On every dimension other than military power — industrial, financial, social, cultural — the distribution of power is shifting, moving away from U. S. dominance. That does not mean we are entering an anti-American world. But we are moving into a post-American world, one defined and directed from many places and by many people.

Recent studies on managing the consequences of the waning US hegemony have in turn led to the need to choose between two policy approaches. One reflects a desire to use US military capacity in 'full spectrum dominance' and its global reach to contain rising powers.

The other looks at the evolving global power shift as an opportunity to build a new basis for global order, which would be predicated on cooperation and equity. According to Kishore Mahbubani, "The application of the three western principles of democracy, rule of law and social justice will go a long way towards creating a more stable world order.

But the West will not be able to apply them on its own... Hitherto the most successful partnerships have been West-West, for example the Trans-Atlantic Alliance. Equally strong East-West partnerships must be created. But in working with partners from other cultures and civilizations the West will have to curtail its ideological impulses and learn to be more pragmatic."

Bill Emmott has noted that "both the US and the EU should, as a matter of urgency, scrap or reform all the top organizations of global governance in which China, India and Japan are not properly and fully represented." This would include the G8 and the UNSC. He also recommends that "the US should support the EAS (East Asia Summit) as Asia's principal political and economic forum and state that it sees Asian integration and intra-regional cooperation as desirable.

"Recent US policies in the wake of 9/11, clearly demonstrated the former approach. Its consequences in Iraq and the anti-American mood in the Islamic world have raised doubts on the viability of such a policy. What strategy initiatives will emerge from the principal determinant of the global order, i.e. the US, remains to be seen.

US Seeks to Maintain Primacy

The US has sought to maintain its position as the pre-eminent power by following a policy of defence transformation, which leverages its technological superiority. As the US National

Security Strategy states, “Innovation within the armed forces will rest on experimentation with new approaches to warfare, strengthening joint operations, exploiting US intelligence advantages, and taking full advantage of science and technology. ”7 Transformation is designed to help address not only the traditional threats but also the emerging asymmetric threats from both state and non-state actors.

According to the US Quadrennial Defence Review, “although the U. S. military maintains considerable advantages in traditional forms of warfare, this realm is not the only, or even the most likely, one in which adversaries will challenge the United States during the period immediately ahead. Enemies are more likely to pose asymmetric threats, including irregular, catastrophic and disruptive challenges. ” The National Security Strategy notes that the US is “pursuing a future force that will provide tailored deterrence of both state and non-state threats,..while assuring allies and dissuading potential competitors. ”

Thus the US simultaneously has to prepare against threats from state as well as non-state actors, which have acquired greater significance post 9/11. With respect to non-state actors, the primary threat comes from Al Qaeda and associated groups against whom the US is in the midst of fighting the so-called Global War against Terror, which it admits is going to be a ‘Long War’.

The Global War against Terror includes overseas fronts like Iraq and Afghanistan and also homeland defence against future terrorist attacks on US soil.

The US recognizes the asymmetric nature of the threat from China, which is unable to match US military capabilities and is hence seeking to negate US superiority by targeting its technological dependence.

The Chinese anti-satellite test in January 2007 is an example of the new kind of asymmetric threat posed by China. Since the US depends heavily on space-based assets, this has led to fears of a new arms race in space. According to the US National

Space Policy of 2006, "The United States considers space capabilities — including the ground and space segments and supporting links — vital to its national interests. Consistent with this policy, the United States will: preserve its rights, capabilities, and freedom of action in space; dissuade or deter others from either impeding those rights or developing capabilities intended to do so; take those actions necessary to protect its space capabilities; respond to interference; and deny, if necessary, adversaries the use of space capabilities hostile to U. S. national interests."

With respect to state actors, the Quadrennial Defence Review suggests that the primary threat comes from China. As it notes, "Of the major and emerging powers, China has the greatest potential to compete militarily with the United States and field disruptive military technologies that could over time off set traditional U. S. military advantages absent U. S. counter strategies."

The US is strengthening its alliances in the Asia-Pacific with Japan, South Korea and Australia as well as building bridges with emerging powers like India. This quest for building up its alliances and partnerships is primarily designed to hedge against the possibility that the rise of China may place it on a collision course with the US. Although an outright war is unlikely, the possibility that tensions in the Taiwan Straits could escalate into military action, drawing in the US cannot be ruled out.

China's Emergence as a Peer Competitor

Pentagon's 2005 report to Congress on China's military power acknowledges that its goal of modernizing national defence is proceeding well: "China does not now face a direct threat from another nation. Yet, it continues to invest heavily in its military, particularly in programs designed to improve power projection.

The pace and scope of China's military build-up are, already, such as to put regional military balances at risk. Current trends in China's military modernization could provide China with a force capable of prosecuting a range of military operations in Asia – well beyond Taiwan – potentially posing a credible threat to modern militaries operating in the region. "

China has gone to great lengths to assure its neighbours that its path to development will be peaceful. A White Paper published in 2005 called China's Peaceful Development Road notes that, "China's road of peaceful development is a brand-new one for mankind in pursuit of civilization and progress, the inevitable way for China to achieve modernization, and a serious choice and solemn promise made by the Chinese government and the Chinese people, " adding that "China's development will never pose a threat to anyone. "

The Quadrennial Defence Review states that "shaping the choices of major and emerging powers requires a balanced approach, one that seeks cooperation but also creates prudent hedges against the possibility that cooperative approaches by themselves may fail to preclude future conflict. "

According to the US National Security Strategy of 2006, "as China becomes a global player, it must act as a responsible stakeholder that fulfills its obligations and works with the United States and others to advance the international system that has enabled its success: enforcing the international rules that have helped China lift itself out of a century of economic deprivation, embracing the economic and political standards that go along with that system of rules, and contributing to international stability and security by working with the United States and other major powers." The NSS adds that "our strategy seeks to encourage China to make the right strategic choices for its people, while we hedge against other possibilities."

China's military modernization is a function of its phenomenal economic growth, which has averaged 9. 5% for more than two decades. The dependence of China on foreign trade and investment for its economic modernization means that any disruption of the regional security environment in Asia will have adverse consequences for its objective of development which is still a long way away.

China's rising dependency on energy imports is leading it into an aggressive pursuit of overseas energy assets, which could lead to confrontation with the US over its links with regimes that are opposed to the US.

US policies towards Japan and India can be seen in the light of its stated desire to hedge against the possibility of the emergence of China as a revisionist power. However the US will have to be careful not to make the latter possibility self-fulfilling through its actions. For its part China would like to prevent a balancing coalition against it that could constrain its ability to prevent Taiwan breaking away to independence. China is aware that in its quest to achieve a moderately well-off society during the next two decades, it will remain vulnerable to external pressures.

Other Powers in the Region

Russia, the successor state of the erstwhile Soviet Union, is yet to play an international role in line with its size and military power, but its huge resources of energy underline its claim as a major player. Russia's relationship with the West remains tense in the light of Western efforts to bring democracy to countries in Russia's sphere of influence and US attempts to build missile defence sites in Eastern Europe. While Russia is wary of becoming a junior partner to China, its current friction with the West has led it towards a tactical embrace of China. The two countries held unprecedented joint military exercises in 2005 and have also joined hands to keep the US out of Central Asia, which they view as their backyard.

Ever since the end of World War II, Japan's status as a close ally of the US under the US-Japan Mutual Security Treaty has remained unchanged. The end of the Cold War did not have an immediate fallout on the division of labour within the US-Japan alliance, with the US continuing to bear the bulk of the responsibility for Japan's security. However Japan's inability to provide any military support towards the first Gulf War in 1991 came in for criticism and it responded by passing legislation that enabled the SDF to take part in UN peacekeeping operations. As the 1990s progressed, developments in the East Asian strategic neighbourhood gradually caused Japan to reassess its defence posture. The Taiwan Straits incident of the mid-1990s was an eye opener to Japan of China's military capabilities and intentions, while North Korea's withdrawal from the NPT and its missile tests had a direct bearing on Japan's security.

With frequent calls also coming from the US for Japan to take on an equal share of responsibility and to contribute towards collective security, Japan revised its defence doctrine and the guidelines of its defence cooperation with the US to provide logistical support for US military operations within the region. After 9/11, the nationalist government of Prime Minister Koizumi passed special legislation that allowed for Japanese forces to be sent to the Indian Ocean to provide logistical support for the US operation in Afghanistan. In 2003 Japan even approved a contingent of ground troops for the Iraq war although their mandate was to participate in humanitarian operations in a non-combat role, which restricted their effectiveness. These were the first signs that Japan was finally on the road to becoming a normal nation. In 2004, the New Defence Policy Outline institutionalized these changes in the realm of policy by making it part of Japan's defence doctrine to undertake a role outside East Asia in association with the international community and its alliance partner, the US.

Australia is a major regional power which has contributed to security in the region by maintaining peace and promoting state building in East Timor, Fiji and the Solomon Islands. Under Prime Minister Rudd, Australia is following a multilateral approach while preserving its traditional ties with the US. Although Australia invoked the ANZUS treaty for the first time after 9/11, it has indicated that this does not extend to a US-China conflict over Taiwan, apparently influenced by the benefits it could derive from China's economic growth. China is going ahead to improve ties with Australia as the agreement on the sale of Australian uranium to China showed. The US, Japan, Australia and India had initiated a quadrilateral dialogue in 2007 on the sidelines of the ARF summit in Manila. This had caused concern in China, which went to the extent of serving a demarche on all four countries seeking an explanation for the meeting.

GLOBAL POWER BALANCE 2020

The global power balance has been in a churning state ever since the turn of the millennium. The disintegration of the Soviet Union enabled the United States global strategic predominance to be unrivalled and unquestioned. Concerned by United States unilateralism., Russia and China as the two nations most strategically affected set in motion two significant initiatives to offset the US predominance. Russia under the dynamic leadership of President Putin set Russia on a course of strategic and military resurgence. This was facilitated by rising Russian oil revenues. China with significant economic resources at its disposal embarked on a strategic build-up of its strategic assets and military upgradation. The United States decade-old strategic global predominance was now to be under challenge by Russia and China. This strategic challenge by these two nations became further accentuated as a result of United States getting inextricably tied down militarily in Afghanistan and Iraq.

The current global economic turbulence has prompted many strategic analysts to re-examine the short-term global balance of power perspectives with 2020 taken as a more identifiable time frame. Some would like to believe that the current economic melt-down could affect the global power balance and the inter-se strategic equations between USA, Russia and China. They would like to suggest that the United States as the strongest economy in the world could weather the storms, but Russia and China, and especially Russia's resurgence and its strategic challenge to the United States could be diluted.

This Author would like to maintain that the economic meltdown today is globalised in its dimensions and would therefore affect USA, Russia and China without any exception. However, Russia and China's strategic programs directed at altering the global power balance would not be diluted. This besides other reasons, is valid, because Russia and China are not involved in any costly strategic distractions like the United States in Iraq and Afghanistan, requiring a significant outlay of financial resources.

Otherwise too, it is conceded by many economists that economies of the world surface more strongly after economic depressions. Strategically, the historical evidence cannot be ignored that the Second World War took place within a decade of the Great Depression in which the United States was the most vitally affected.

Therefore, in strategic analysis such economic depressions may act as "speed breakers" but definitely do not bring global strategic power rivalries to a "dead end".

With the above as an introductory background, this Paper attempts to analyse "Global Power Balance 2020: Perspectives" under the following heads:

- Global Power Balance 2020 Will be Bi-polar in Nature
- Multi-polarity is a Political and Strategic Myth
- United States Would Have Strategic Edge Over Russia in a Bi-polar World
- A New Cold War is Inevitable.

Global Power Balance 2020 Will be Bi-polar in Nature

Assertions of this Author in this direction stand examined in fair detail in earlier SAAG Papers and particularly those dealing with Russia's resurgence. This Author firmly believes that the global power balance in 2020 would be bi-polar in nature with the United States and Russia as the two poles.

Russia is being dismissively discussed in US and Western think-tanks and Russia's resurgence is de-emphasised and devaluated. This dismissive attitude is not born out of realistic strategic analysis but wishful thinking that Russia does not emerge as a strategic challenge to United States global predominance. The moot question that needs to be considered is that who amongst Russia and China is more strategically potent to challenge United States global predominance? Even on current analysis the following strategic realities suggest that Russia is the foremost candidate to challenge USA and not China (1) Russia's existing strategic nuclear weapons arsenal outnumbers the United States whereas China's nuclear arsenal at about 400 warheads is a remote comparison (2) Russia's existing power projection capabilities extend far beyond its immediate neighbourhood, in all dimensions – land, sea and air. China's power projection is limited to her periphery and limited to ground forces dimensions only (3) Russia is an "energy self-independent" state and this is an essential pre-requisite of national power. Japan and Germany lost the Second World War because they were not "energy self-reliant" (4) Russia has existing strategic partnerships with many countries across the globe. China has no "natural allies" to boost her strategic power (5) Russia's resurgence has been welcomed in many regions and more importantly in the Middle East. China is not viewed as a credible strategic challenger to the United States.

More importantly Russia has been a practitioner of global power politics in the bi-polar environment of the Cold War and successfully provided countervailing power to the United States for 45 years. Further, it needs to be noted that Russia was not defeated by the United States in the Cold War; it was Russia that defeated itself.

Russia's current strategic and political resurgence is precisely aimed in this direction once again, namely, to reclaim her former superpower status. It has won recognition in Europe, Middle East, Central Asia and South East Asia too. Reading between the lines one gets a sneaking feeling that the United States may prefer China as a manageable strategic rival rather than Russia. But the strategic realities indicate that the United States would in 2020 have to accept a bi-polar world with Russia as the second pole.

Multi-polarity is a Political and Strategic Myth

Multi-polarity as a desirable state in the global power balance was forcefully enunciated by China to begin with in the immediate period following the demise of the Soviet Union. To begin with, in the early 1990s, China advocated a multi-polar world incorporating China, India, Iran and Syria with Pakistan added. Later inducements were to include France and Germany. This enunciation never took off though being repeated periodically.

So the initial Chinese model of multi-polarity comprised Asian nations with no strong strategic linkages with USA as the unipolar power. China then as the only nuclear weapons state in this grouping may have been led to believe that it would emerge as the natural leader of its proposed multi-polar grouping.

Russia today also talks of multi-polarity but one suspects that it is more for political reasons in favor of China than any strategic conviction. Russia would strategically prefer a bi-polar world at the global level and without frowning on multi-polarity at the regional level.

China, Japan and India even with the full development of their strategic strengths cannot hope to equal the strategic potential of being super-powers in the classical sense of definition of the term.

They can sit on the global powers high table as associate global players, but not as "super powers". China, Japan and India therefore are incapable of emerging as multiple poles to bring about a multi-polar world. Only the United States and Russia qualify to be superpowers. Available indicators suggest that the United States and Russia would be the two super-powers in 2020 and no scope exists for any of the other global players intruding into that league.

INDIA'S GROWING SOFT POWER

The drivers triggering a shift in China's India posture can be placed under the rubric of India's *hard power*. However, India's (re)rising *soft power* has also contributed to this shift in China's outlook a country's ability to alter the behavior of others through attraction rather than sticks or carrots. India has been a democracy right since its birth as a modern nation-state in 1947. However, its sluggish economic growth and weak military profile that led to its defeat in 1962 seriously tarnished this aspect of India's soft power. With the rising India story, its democracy as an important component of its soft power has again come into the global limelight. India has more than 1 billion people. It is linguistically, culturally, racially, and religiously diverse, and it is growing economically at an enviable pace under democratic governmental institutions (except for the emergency period of 1975-77 when civil liberties were undermined). Its culture values peaceful coexistence, nonviolence, and religious tolerance. All of these factors, combined with the largest pool of English speakers outside the US, has increased India's power of attraction without need for coercion or persuasion, a fact not lost on an envious, hard power-minded China.

The country to which India has projected most of its soft power is the US, through the export of highly skilled manpower, consisting mainly of software developers, engineers, and doctors. China has been keeping a close watch on the rising influence of the Indian community in the United States, especially over the last decade. In order to improve its own soft power in the United States, China has sent far more students to the United States than India. As per the Institute of International Education's annual report in the academic year 2009-10, out of 690,932 international students in the United States nearly 128,000 of them, or more than 18 percent, were from China while India sent only 107,897 students in the same academic year. However, with Oct 2011, educational exchanges between India and the US would rise much faster in the future.

INDIA'S SOFT POWER ADVANTAGE

During Prime Minister Tony Abbott's recent visit to India, he was asked to justify Australia's signing of a deal to sell uranium to the country. In response, the prime minister said, "India threatens no one" and "is the friend to many." This was no mere diplomatic nicety, but a carefully chosen answer based on India's international image. It is an image that is rare amongst great powers of India's size and strength, and will give Delhi a unique soft power advantage in the future multipolar world.

Much of the globe sees India as a relatively non-violent, tolerant and pluralistic democracy with a benign international influence. Its values are seen as largely positive.

The U.S., with its Indo-U.S. nuclear deal, accorded India special treatment in nuclear cooperation. The deal provided benefits usually reserved for Non-Proliferation Treaty (NPT) signatories. Washington justified cooperation with India by highlighting Delhi's impeccable non-proliferation record. This stance was replicated by other states, including the Nuclear Suppliers Group (NSG) member states who allowed India's participation in international nuclear commerce and supported the Indo-U.S. deal. The NSG decided to re-engage with India following an India-specific safeguards agreement with the International Atomic Energy Agency (IAEA). The IAEA's Board of Governors endorsed a nuclear safeguards agreement with India by consensus that would permit Delhi to add more nuclear facilities to be placed under the IAEA safeguards framework. India did not have to have an Additional Protocol like the non-nuclear weapons states who are NPT signatories. India also received favorable treatment from Canada (which agreed to supply "dual-use items" that can be used for civilian and military applications), Japan and South Korea.

This cooperation was not merely driven by these states' strategic relationships with the U.S. Russia has long cooperated with India on nuclear technology. Even China, as a member of the NSG, did not oppose the group's decision on India. Today, India is the only known nuclear weapons state that is not part of the NPT but is still permitted to engage in nuclear commerce globally.

India's reputation extends beyond its nuclear posture. Since independence, the country has been viewed as a neutral and harmless power by most foreign audiences, particularly in Africa, the Middle East, South America and Southeast Asia.

This is in part due to its prominent role in the Non-Aligned movement. Whilst Delhi's reputation in its own neighborhood is quite different, South Asian states do not see India as a threat in the way that many of Russia or China's neighbours view those powers.

Even long-time nemesis Pakistan is unlikely to have been as adventurous in its dealings with its much larger and more powerful neighbor had it not had firsthand experience of Delhi's restraint – even before Islamabad had nuclear capability.

So what is behind India's benign image? In part, it is self-created. For 60-plus years Delhi has favored cultivating the impression of a non-violent India. This is particularly clear in the realm of nuclear posture. Despite having tested weapons in 1974 and 1998 and being a non-signatory to the NPT and Comprehensive Test Ban Treaty, India has been one of the most vocal advocates for global disarmament. It has arguably been the most passionate anti-nuclear campaigner amongst the world's nine known or suspected nuclear weapons states, with one of the world's most notable pleas for global disarmament made by Prime Minister Rajiv Gandhi at the U.N. in 1988.

The pursuit of this image continued a decade later, even after the Pokhran II nuclear tests. BJP Prime Minister Vajpayee stated that the tests were not a repudiation of the disarmament goal. In the Draft Report on Indian Nuclear Doctrine, the very first sentence of the first paragraph describes the use of nuclear weapons as the "gravest threat to humanity and to peace and stability." The paragraph goes on to criticize the virtual abandonment by states of the goal of disarmament.

Delhi sought to avoid labels of hypocrisy by positioning itself as the "reluctant nuclear power." India argued that the bomb was a last resort in a world of threatening nuclear states who make no pledges to refrain from first strikes and the use of nukes against non-nuclear states. Somewhat legitimately, Indian leaders asserted that the country's nuclear weapons could act as bargaining chips to support its global disarmament agenda. India was said to have more credibility as a nuclear weapons state with itself having something to sacrifice in order to usher in global disarmament. India declared that its security would be enhanced and not diminished in a nuclear free world.

Delhi also sought to project an image of non-violence in other areas of foreign policy. In relation to the norm of "Responsibility to Protect," India voiced support for those aspects of R2P that encouraged and supported states to protect their own populations, and expressed extreme caution at R2P's coercive side. When some of the world's greatest debates over intervention occurred at the U.N., Indian ambassadors drenched their speeches with the language of non-violence.

This preciously guarded national image is not merely a strategic ploy to increase India's soft power. Policymakers wish the country to be seen as non-violent, pluralistic and tolerant, because India genuinely holds these values. Within the nuclear realm the influence of non-violence is seen through the foot-dragging in relation to integrating nuclear weapons into military strategy and in relation to serial production of weapons. A further sign of this influence is the long public debate before going nuclear – a rarity amongst nuclear powers. We have seen repeatedly that India's leaders find it morally inconceivable that nukes could ever be useable tools of war. Delhi's disarmament pleas were not merely PR: they consumed valuable diplomatic resources including precious stage-time in international forums. More broadly, non-violence affected for India's relatively restrained conduct in several conflicts with Pakistan.

When it came to humanitarian intervention, over the last 25 years India's opposition or support was directly related to the level of intrastate violence entailed in intervening. This was true regardless of who was intervening in whom, for what reason, and whether there were strategic gains in it for Delhi. This included interventions in Iraq, Libya and Syria. India's opposition to intervention was compounded by its pluralistic worldview, with acceptance of all regime types.

It would seem that India's values of non-violence, pluralism and tolerance stem from the independence era, when the country's foreign policy and modern identity was crafted.

Mahatma Gandhi made India's independence movement synonymous with non-violence. First Prime Minister Jawaharlal Nehru imbued morals into his external relations. But if the values influencing India's foreign policy took shape only then, they would have fizzled when Congress lost power. Instead the values have remained, as has the resultant global persona.

This is because the values that help guide Indian foreign policy and underpin its image are rooted deep in the country's cultural history. These values attained dominance during the formative stage of Indian civilization – the period between the Vedic era and medieval times when the greatest empires arose. India and China are the only modern great powers that have held a largely continuous culture for several millennia. Ancient India's cultural connection to its present-day manifestation is far stronger than ancient Greek, Roman or Anglo-Celtic culture is to present-day Western states, or the ancient Middle Eastern civilizations are to today's Arab world.

It remains to be seen how India's international reputation will fare as its strategic interests expand throughout the Indo-Pacific and beyond. With some diplomatic craftsmanship, Delhi can convert its somewhat ethereal values-based soft power advantage into hard strategic and economic gains. Modi's government seems to have recognized this and is building on Congress' initiatives to enhance India's public diplomacy toolkit.

India's soft power has rare characteristics when compared with the other great powers of the emerging multipolar world: U.S., China, Russia, Japan and Europe (as a unified entity). Its relatively neutral, non-threatening image will make India a uniquely attractive great-power partner for countries looking to hedge against future fallout between the U.S. and China, and not wanting to antagonize either superpower. Australia has chosen a wise time to solidify ties with one of the world's most dynamic rising powers.

INDIA'S RISE AS A GREAT POWER

In considering India's rise as a great power, this chapter focuses specifically on India's relations with its strategically significant neighbours, Pakistan and China. Though India's increasing projection of influence may change the regional dynamics, the fundamental balance of power among India and its neighbours will not change dramatically in the near future. Pakistan is already overwhelmed by the military strength of India, thus its strategic outlook will remain unchanged, while China and India have increasingly intertwined relations and evenly-matched conventional and nuclear forces, ensuring relative regional stability.

Analysis

The Problem of Pakistan

India's geographically closest and most frequently problematic relationship is with its neighbour and prodigal twin, Pakistan. India's rise as a great power will have its most immediate impact on the extremely dangerous stalemate which exists between the two states. Many security concerns converge in Pakistan, as: the state has been a key supporter of the Taliban in Afghanistan, factions of which the Pakistani Army is now fighting in a de facto civil war; elements within the state support Islamic terrorist organisations that periodically attack India, provoking regional crises; and, the Pakistani Army has a growing nuclear arsenal, which could be vulnerable to misuse by malicious elements within the state. India and Pakistan engaged in wars in 1965 and 1971, with crises about continuing Pakistani support for insurgents in the disputed Indian state of Jammu and Kashmir erupting periodically, and threatening war in 1990. Following Indian and Pakistani nuclear tests in May 1998, Pakistani incursions across the Line of Control in the Kargil region of Kashmir led to another limited war, and the veiled nuclear threat by Pakistani Foreign Secretary Shamshad Ahmed that, 'We will not hesitate to use any weapon in our arsenal to defend our territorial integrity.' Major terrorist attacks in Jammu and Kashmir on 1 October 2001 and in the Indian capital Delhi on 13 December 2001 again threatened war, though merely resulted in major military manoeuvres by India, code-named *Operation Parakram*. The lack of military retaliation by India despite grave provocation seems to suggest that India is successfully deterred by Pakistan's nuclear capability, and this in turn only fuels the eagerness of some elements within Pakistan to provoke India. Pakistan has adopted an "asymmetric nuclear escalation posture", which has deterred Indian conventional military power and thus enabled Pakistan's 'aggressive strategy of bleeding India by a "thousand cuts" with little fear of significant retaliation.'

India is four times larger and seven times more populated than Pakistan. As Pakistan averages only 300 miles in width, it is susceptible to a central assault that would split the country in two. A number of important Pakistani cities also lie close to the international border in the Indus River basin. As Pakistan is thus extremely vulnerable to conventional attack by India's larger military, it defines such an attack as an existential threat to the Pakistani state. Pakistani Lt. Gen. Khalid Kidwai thus outlined that Pakistan would use its nuclear weapons if: India attacks Pakistan and conquers a large part of its territory; India destroys a large part of Pakistan's land or air forces; India blockades Pakistan in an effort to strangle it economically; or, India pushes Pakistan into a state of political destabilisation. This asymmetric escalation posture is designed for a rapid first use of nuclear weapons against conventional attacks, thus leaving India without the ability to punish terrorist attacks through conventional retaliation. As elements within Pakistan continue to provoke India, this creates an extremely dangerous imbalance reliant on India's restraint to maintain peace.

India and Pakistan escalating to the use of nuclear weapons within the first 12 days. New analyses of this eventuality reveal that a conflict between India and Pakistan, in which 100 nuclear bombs were dropped on cities and industrial areas within the two countries, would kill more than 20 million people from the blasts, fires and radioactivity. In addition, the explosions could produce enough smoke to cripple global agriculture. Smoke generated by burning cities could create a climatic response that immediately reduces sunlight, cools the planet, and reduces precipitation worldwide. This "nuclear winter" would reduce or eliminate agricultural production over vast areas, simultaneously decreasing crop yields nearly everywhere. Approximately one billion people worldwide today live on marginal food supplies and would be directly threatened with starvation. While some analysts maintain that nuclear weapons would be used in only a measured way, the chaos, fear and interruption of communications that would follow nuclear war's commencement leads some to doubt that attacks would be limited in any rational manner. Additionally, Pakistan could face a decision to use its entire nuclear arsenal quickly or lose it to Indian forces which seize its military bases. Thus, unrestrained nuclear war in South Asia potentially has cataclysmic regional and global consequences.

Following the terrorist attack by Kashmiri militants in December 2001 and the subsequent military standoff with Pakistan in *Operation Parakram*, the Indian Army announced a new limited war doctrine in April 2004 called the Cold Start doctrine, which aims to allow conventional retaliation without posing an existential threat to Pakistan. Under Cold Start, the Indian army would avoid delivering a catastrophic blow to Pakistan, and instead make shallow territorial gains, 50-80 kilometres deep, that could be used in post-conflict negotiations. This doctrine aims to deny Pakistan the justification of "regime survival" for employing nuclear weapons in response to a conventional Indian attack. However, Walter C. Ladwig III foresees that, 'An operational Cold Start capability could lead Pakistan to lower its nuclear red line, put its nuclear weapons on a higher state of readiness, develop tactical nuclear weapons, or undertake some equally destabilising course of action.' The danger of escalation is further compounded by the relatively immature "command and control" and early warning systems of both the Indian and Pakistani nuclear arsenals. There also remains the danger of nuclear accident as, if one nation accidentally detonates a nuclear warhead on one of its own military bases, it probably will not have adequate surveillance intelligence to know that it has not been attacked by its enemy, and thus may falsely "retaliate" against the other country.

Meanwhile, in the context of the continuing conflict in Afghanistan, Pakistan believes that the United States would intervene to prevent war, as it relies on Pakistani troops along the Afghan border and supplies for American forces are transported through Pakistan. Thus, Pakistan believes the only potential military action available to India is air-strikes against Islamist training camps, which itself is not a serious problem, and may actually help Islamabad by killing destabilising jihadists while generating massive support among Pakistanis for their government. The dual problems of nuclear escalation and American reliance on Pakistan for counter-insurgency meant that following terrorist attacks in Mumbai by Pakistani group Lashkar-e-Taiba on 26 November 2008, which killed 163 people, India was unable to respond with conventional military strikes. Any attack by India might either destabilise the Pakistani Government, or escalate the conflict to nuclear exchange. In the event of state disintegration, Pakistani nuclear weapons could fall into the hands of militant elements who would attempt to use those weapons against India or the West.

Unfortunately, there is no easy path to stabilising reform within Pakistan. Pakistan essentially has a feudal political establishment, run by a civilian aristocracy of wealthy agricultural landowners and industrialists, and the Army. The civilian political parties primarily function as patronage networks, without deep-seated ideological differences, and merely struggle to control state resources. As a key aim of the agricultural and industrial élites is to avoiding paying income taxes, the Pakistani Government is also chronically in debt. The Army is seen by most Pakistanis as the primary defender of the nation and the ultimate guarantor of domestic stability. The ever-present threat of India is used to justify the Army's disproportionate share of national resources, and the Army itself also owns and manages a large agricultural and industrial empire. Domestically, the Army is the ultimate power-broker between the political parties, and has acted on several occasions to remove the party in power. As successive governments have received bailouts from international financial institutions, neither the civilian political élites nor the Army have felt any real incentive to institute fundamental change. For the time-being, the Army is objectively the most stable and responsible force to control the country. The Pakistani military is the only state institution that works effectively, and without it Pakistan would probably have disintegrated long ago. The dire alternatives are representatives of the rising wave of radical Islam who arose from the madrassas under the patronage of General Zia ul-Haq, and gained their training in the US-backed *mujahedeen* struggle against the Soviet occupation of Afghanistan. These elements, and more recent jihadist recruits, are currently involved in Kashmiri terrorist organisations like Jaysh-e-Mohammad, and Lashkar-e-Taiba, as well as in the Afghani and Pakistani Taliban which occupy Pakistan's border provinces. While the Pakistani Army and intelligence services are often unwilling to directly challenge these forces (and, indeed, currently cultivate relations with the Kashmiri groups and the Afghani Taliban), and external (and, particularly, American) attempts to move forces into Pakistani territory would almost certainly make things worse, this unstable situation is likely to continue.

As India's power increases, so will its ability to strategically encircle Pakistan, through relations with Iran and Afghanistan, and via naval power. At the same time, India's patience for Pakistan's continuing terrorist provocations will probably lessen. Nevertheless, Pakistan's deterrent capabilities remain, as attacks on the Pakistani state – either unsuccessful or successful – are likely to result in either nuclear exchange or widespread chaos and bloodshed. If India continues restraint, however, and reaches out to more moderate elements within the military and civilian political parties, it could leverage its growing economic strength to gradually help a more moderate Pakistani state develop.

The Challenge of China

On a grander strategic level, relations between India and China will be highly significant as India emerges as a great power. There is a growing interdependence between the two

Asian giants, as China is now India's number-one trading partner, with more than $52 billion in bilateral trade, and estimates are that China-India trade will surpass US-China trade by 2020. China's powerful manufacturing sector complements India's combination of a raw materials and cutting-edge technology economy. Strategically, a strong and influential India helps to create a more multipolar world, consistent with Chinese interests, although China increasingly regards India as its main Asian rival. China is thus involved in a complex game of encirclement with India. China has armed Pakistan with nuclear weapons and ballistic missile technology, and has built 'strong military-to-military ties with Burma, Pakistan, Nepal, Bangladesh, and Sri Lanka as part of what Indians see as a strategy to tie India down, Gulliver-like, in its region.' China is also developing deep-water ports throughout the Indian Ocean to support its projected blue-water naval capacity.

Meanwhile, on the border, China continues to press its claims to vast tracts of Indian territory. Over the past years, increased friction in the border area between India and China has led to incursions by Chinese troops, the wounding of several Indian border police, and a build-up of military forces on both sides, as Beijing has been uncharacteristically assertive in its claims to sections of India's Arunachal Pradesh state. The Indians responded by moving 30,000 troops and their latest warplanes into the area, leading some analysts to predict a China-India war within five years.

China rejects the McMahon Line that forms the border, and places the traditional Sino-Indian border at the base of the Himalayan foothills. Stratfor's George Friedman argues that, for China, control of Tibet is of vital strategic importance, providing a barrier against its populous and economically and militarily-advancing neighbour. The high mountain passes of Tibet provide virtually impenetrable terrain which is easy to protect militarily. Along the frontier directly south of this border, in India, is one of the largest population concentrations in the world. If China were to withdraw, Beijing fears that this population could migrate into Tibet, and Tibet could gradually turn into a beachhead for Indian power that would directly abut Sichuan and Yunnan provinces. The Chinese thus see control of Tibet as a matter of fundamental national security. They also see the 1959 decision by Indian Prime Minister Jawaharlal Nehru to give asylum to the Dalai Lama, and the continuing support for the Tibetan government-in-exile, as perpetuating this threat. Thus, 'Beijing's price for a border settlement and for normalisation of ties with India, appears to be that India dismantle the Tibetan settlement in Dharamshala and request the Dalai Lama take up residence in another country.'

On a broader front, 80 per cent of China's oil and gas supplies transit the Indian Ocean and South China Sea, so the Chinese navy is increasingly making its presence felt in the area in order to secure its lines of supply. For China, like India, the steady flow of imported resources is not just an issue of economic growth, but also of the longevity of the Chinese Communist Party. Chinese leaders increasingly fear that adversaries could blockade sea lanes and strategic bottlenecks such as the Strait of Malacca, and are thus moving to an offshore defence policy that will include "distant ocean defence". China's actions, however, may impinge upon India's interests and destabilise relations.

Jason Blazevic argues that, following "defensive realist" strategies, each nation will attempt to gain power for self-preservation and other nations will see this move as a strategic threat, thus decreasing collective security. As part of this competition, China has been developing a so-called "string-of-pearls" strategy, expanding influence into ports in Burma, Sri Lanka and Pakistan. According to a report by US defence contractor Booz Allen Hamilton, 'China is building strategic relationships along the sea lanes from the Middle East to the South China Sea in a way that suggests defensive and offensive positioning to protect China's energy interests.' China emerged as the biggest military spender in the Asia-Pacific in 2006, and now has the fourth-largest defence expenditure in the world. Its navy is also considered the third-largest in the world behind only the US and Russia, and is superior to the Indian Navy. In this context, India perceives Chinese actions as power maximisation, and fears that China's forward-basing strategy will be used to contain India and rapidly achieve hegemony in the Indian Ocean.

Meanwhile, China and India have adopted nuclear "assured retaliation" postures (what they sometimes refer to as "credible minimum deterrence"), which rely on a small but secure and survivable nuclear force that assures a retaliatory strike against a primary opponent. In many ways, this seems like the most stable aspect of the competition between India and China, though it is yet to be seen what reaction a new generation of *Surya* missiles might provoke in China. Meanwhile, analysts like Stephen Walt expect that China will follow a consistent but non-provocative build-up of its military capabilities and diplomatic alliances over the long-term, aiming to gradually edge the United States out of a hegemonic position. India is likely to mirror this build-up and thus tension, and possible low-level confrontation, may result on the India-China border and in the Indian Ocean region.

GOALS UNDERLYING INDIA'S GREAT-POWER QUEST

To India and other rising powers, the material might and political influence that define great powers are not simply teleological *ends*—they are *means* by which governments pursue their interests and foreign policy objectives. India has sought to build capabilities and influence not simply for the sake of being strong, but also to advance more specific national aims. In some respects, India has sought to become a great power for "defensive" reasons, as officials in New Delhi seek to protect their state against external domination or intimidation. In other respects, India has sought to revise the existing regional and international orders to enable it to play a more prominent role.

This section argues that despite significant shifts in tactics, four broad goals have provided much of the motivation for

India's great-power quest over the past several decades. These include increasing policy autonomy, securing the state from internal and external threats, raising the living standards of its vast population, and winning diplomatic recognition as one of the world's leading nations. Individually, none of these objectives is unique, but taken together they give India's quest its particular character.

In a 2004 speech on India's great-power quest, Minister of External Affairs Yashwant Sinha specifically outlined three of the four goals above. He acknowledged his country's efforts to build military and economic "hard power," as well as political and ideational "soft power," but emphasized that "India's search for great power status is not an end in itself." Rather, "India's power capabilities are a guarantee of the freedom and security of its people…a means of advancing the welfare of our people and a tool for preserving and consolidating the autonomy of our foreign and domestic policy." The same day, Prime Minister Atal Bihari Vajpayee referred to the fourth goal by saying that India sought to secure "a meaningful role in world affairs," partly by promoting a "cooperative multipolar order" that would restrain existing powers and give India a louder voice.

The aims that Sinha and Vajpayee expressed were not new. All of these goals have strong roots in the period immediately following India's independence in 1947 and remain important today. They certainly cannot explain all of the Indian government's specific foreign policy decisions. As in any state, domestic pressures and the need to respond to periodic crises often provide powerful alternative explanations for short-term policy trends and shifts in tactics. Moreover, the four goals above have sometimes been in tension with one another, requiring trade-offs and reconciliation. The argument advanced here is that these goals have nevertheless provided important guideposts for Indian policymakers and that they help illuminate the motives for the country's great-power quest. Understanding the core elements of India's foreign policy aspirations is an important precursor to constructive policy engagement with New Delhi.

Promoting Autonomy

Autonomy has long been one of the most important goals of Indian foreign policy. Modern India took shape in the shadow of British colonial rule, and the country's great-power quest is inextricably linked to the effort to avoid subservience to the United Kingdom or other external masters.

In 1946, amid the struggle for independence, Jawaharlal Nehru invoked the concept of a great power in an apparent effort to boost the confidence of his audience of Indian army officers. He declared that "India is today among the four great powers of the world: [the] other three being America, Russia, and China." That statement, of course, was more rhetorical than realistic.

India had a large army and population but was far from possessing the material capabilities or political influence to fit under any reasonable definition of a great power. Even after breaking free of British rule, India's new government was militarily and economically weak, confronted daunting domestic challenges, and faced the real possibility of continued external domination. India's tactics evolved throughout the Cold War era, but autonomy remained a mainstay of the country's foreign policy.

Although India is stronger today than it was in the early Cold War era, autonomy remains central to its foreign policy. Over the past several years, as India sought to strike a controversial civil-nuclear deal with the United States, the most common domestic criticism of the plan was that it would compromise the country's hard-earned sovereignty and independence. Interestingly, the governing Congress Party suffered criticism from both the left and right, showing the appeal of the independence theme across the political spectrum. The Communist Party of India and nationalist BJP were the most vocal critics of the plan. The memory of colonial subjugation still exerts a strong influence in New Delhi and in the minds of many Indian voters, encouraging the cultivation of power that will help ensure the country's political independence.

Securing the State

To India's governing elites, a second key foreign policy goal—and a second reason to build greater national capabilities and influence—has been to improve internal and external security. India's status as a developing country in a dangerous neighborhood has meant that the country's security dilemmas have been somewhat more complicated than they have been for other rising or established powers. One priority has been to develop the ability to deter or ward off stronger foes. India's modern history has been marred by frequent reminders of its military vulnerability and circumscribed position. The disastrous 1962 war against China in the Himalayas broke Nehru's faith in Third World solidarity and reinforced India's vulnerability to external giants. China has since been a frequent security concern for India, and many Indian officials continue to see China as a bona fide external threat to their interests, contributing to a "defensive" motivation for great-power capabilities. Contemporary concerns focus partly on maritime security. Chinese naval ties with Pakistan, Sri Lanka, Bangladesh, and Myanmar are one source of concern. The People's Republic of China's (PRC) bases or installations in those countries threaten to encircle India with a Chinese "string of pearls"—points from which China can exert naval influence along the Asian littoral from the Straits of Malacca to the Persian Gulf. The unresolved border disputes over Aksai Chin and Arunachal Pradesh also motivate Indian interest in a stronger military. Like the leaders of any budding great power, Indian officials seek, at a minimum, to avoid being bullied along their borders and in their own neighborhood.

On land, India has also faced serious impediments to achieving what it regards as its rightful role as the dominant regional power. Pakistan has posed the most vexing obstacle. Despite the 1971 war, which cleft Pakistan in two and solidified India's military advantage, Islamabad has issued frequent provocations and has refused to acquiesce to a South Asian security order predicated on strong Indian leadership. The campaign against Islamist militants and separatists in Kashmir has been a particularly painful thorn in India's side, tying down troops in a conflict that has been doggedly resistant to resolution. Frequent American remain acute, with the and Chinese military and economic *movement* support for Pakistan has reinforced the nexus between great-power politics and India's frustrated regional aspirations.

In Several states, and International relations theory usually focuses on the external security dynamics associated with rising *Islamic radicals that* powers, but India's bid for great-power status also reflects internal security concerns. Nehru inherited a state with a vast, mostly indigent, and dauntingly diverse population. Instilling a sense of national pride and identity has been crucial to uniting that population behind a single national government. Even today, with a much healthier economy and well-established democratic norms and institutions, Indian leaders face the perennial challenge of managing social unrest that springs from poverty, inequality, and ethno-religious cleavages. Centrifugal threats remain acute, with the leftist Naxalite movement challenging the government in several states, and continued clashes involving Hindu nationalists and Islamic radicals that contribute to tensions in the general population.

Pursuing Economic Development

India's internal security concerns relate closely to the goal of economic development. Since independence, Indian governments have confronted the challenge of mass poverty in both urban slums and the countryside. India is unusual (though not unique) as a state approaching great-power status while most of its population remains poor. This places significant political (and perhaps moral) constraints on New Delhi's ability to expend national resources on military buildup, economic liberalization, and other policies that may involve trade-offs between aggregate national capabilities and absolute or relative poverty in the country. Politically, Indian parties risk punishment for policies seen to neglect or downplay concerns of the poor—by voters, opposition parties, and sometimes coalition partners, as in the case of leftist members of the ruling

United Progressive Alliance, led by the Congress Party. After launching a major liberalization program as finance minister in the 1990s, Manmohan Singh argued that India would become "free from poverty" by "becoming a major global power in the world economy." India has indeed grown and become more active in international trade; robust growth has given India a total GDP approaching Japan's on a purchasing-power parity basis. However, poverty and inequality remain major problems. India's nominal per capita GDP lags behind even poor countries like Mongolia and Cameroon, and much of the country's wealth accumulation has accrued to the benefit of the urban middle class, leaving many in the countryside behind. In 2009, the Indian Planning Commission issued a report indicating that the country has more than 400 million people living on less than USD 1.25 per day—the World Bank and United Nations benchmark for absolute poverty. For that reason, some Indians, especially on the political left, continue to question the wisdom of a great-power quest that features military expansion and liberalization.

Achieving Social Status and Respect

A fourth aim of Indian foreign policy has been to achieve added social status and influence in international diplomacy. India's size, status as the hub of a major world civilization, and anti-imperial credentials all contribute to a sense of entitlement to regional leadership and to a major role on the world stage. However, wealthier states have tended to deny it treatment as a major player. India has not been a member of any of the official or unofficial clubs that have mostly defined great-power status since the end of the Second World War. It has not been a permanent member of the UN Security Council, a member of the G-7 or G-8, or a leading shareholder in the International Monetary Fund (IMF) or World Bank. By these institutional measures, India has been decidedly denied recognition as a great power.

Status is closely related to respect. India's exclusion from the great-power club has produced a deep sense of what Baldev

Raj Nayar and T.V. Paul call "status inconsistency." Even outside formal institutions, India has often been snubbed. In diplomacy, states' perceived pecking order is evident in the phone logs and travel schedules of great-power leaders and the schedules of sideline meetings at the margins of multilateral conferences. Indian diplomats have not been shy about jockeying for diplomatic position but have found it difficult to earn recognition as representatives of a major power. India's economic growth and military expansion have only just begun to change that situation.

The Challenge of Pursuing Multiple Goals

The goals have provided important ballast for Indian officials over time and have served as motives for seeking great-power capabilities and influence. They also help account for some of the broad outlines of Indian foreign policy behavior. Nevertheless, it is important not to exaggerate the extent to which these goals have dictated its foreign policy in specific situations. Indian leaders have rarely had the benefit of operating from a neat strategic roadmap. Like all policymakers, they have been constrained by myriad short-term political pressures and the need to respond to periodic crises. India's complex multi-party democracy, numerous externaland internal challenges, and material weakness relative to established great powers have made it difficult to articulate and follow a clear strategic plan. A number of scholars have therefore emphasized the "reactive" aspects of Indian foreign policy.

The following section outlines the difficult path that Indian leaders have trodden as they have tried, through various means, to acquire the great-power capabilities and influence that would help deliver autonomy, security, development, and respect. It draws attention to key strands in India's foreign policy practice and how its leaders have tried to adapt amid the shifting tectonic plates of international politics and in the face of periodic crises.

4

Globalised Arms Industry in India

The ongoing ninth Defexpo at Goa, the biennial event that assembles the arms merchants and arms producers from all over the world is being held for the first time outside Delhi, saw the defence minister Manohar Parrikar, a native Goan, announcing the latest Defence Procurement Procedure (DPP).

Predictably, the DPP has evoked mixed reactions. Critics have a point when they say that it is not a complete document as yet since the chapter on the much-talked about strategic partners in the private sector who could join the public sector undertakings that dominate the arms productions is still being written by the defence ministry. It seems that major private Indian players like the Tatas, L&T, Mahindras and Ambanis who have entered the defence industry of late want to be strategic partners in multiple areas (ranging from manufacturing fighter plane to building warships and submarines), something the government will like to be restricted to one field only.

This differing perception may be the reason for the delay on determining criteria for being a strategic partner.

However, the other features of the latest DPP (the last one was made in 2013) have been welcomed by the industry and foreign companies, an impression that I gathered by attending various seminars being held at defexpo venue Naqueri-Quitol,

South Goa. While encouraging foreign companies to come to India with their capital and technology to produce and develop arms along with their Indian partners, the DPP makes it clear that that the Modi government's topmost priority will be on Indian designed, developed and manufactured (IDDM) category.

For this writer, the overall evaluation of the new DPP should wait, since the defence minister himself says that "This is not a perfect policy document. It is not full-proof. We will reexamine it after six months, during which I will keep my eyes and ears open for suggestions to improve and remove difficulties, if any". What is more important, therefore, is the clarity on the part of the Modi government that India must be a major arms manufacturing nation by developing an indigenous military-industrial base in line with the idea of "Make in India", whose products will not only meet the domestic demands but also cater to the needs of the global market. In other words, from being the world's largest importer of arms, India should transform itself in such a manner that it will be a major exporter of arms. This is the point, made by both Parrikar and Dr. S Christopher (Secretary, Department of Defence Research & Development and Director General, DRDO), that caught my attention over the last two days. Let me dwell with this theme.

Parrikar says that "India can export LCA aircraft like Tejas, Akash and Brahmos missiles after meeting the 90 percent demands of our own forces." Dr. Christopher says that while many DRDO products may not be up to the expectations of our forces, but surely, they can meet the expectations elsewhere outside the country and can be easily exported. He gave the example of the Pinaka missiles(rejected by our armed forces), which are in demand in countries of West Asia. "I am all for exporting our products abroad after meeting the domestic demands. We also can export items that do not have domestic demands. We have demands for our Brahmos and Akash missiles, small arms and many other products".

As has been pointed out, India is the world's largest importer of arms. China is also a big importer of arms; in fact, it is the fourth largest. But China is a big exporter of arms, too, at the same time. The latest estimate says that China has replaced Great Britain as the world's fifth largest exporter of arms. That bulk of the Chinese arms supplies goes to Pakistan is a different matter altogether. The point is that while importing arms is unavoidable in the life of a nation while developing, the real strength in the ultimate analysis will come from a sound indigenous defence base, which, apart from working towards self-sufficiency or self-reliance in arms, generates wealth for national exchequer by exporting some of its products.

In other words, the bigger the gap between its exports and imports, stronger a country is. It is not that India does not export arms at all. It does.

However, there is a tremendous difference between the quantum of its imports and exports, whereas ideally this gap should have been between its exports and imports. We are number one in importing arms, but as far as arms exports are concerned, our rank is as low as 26th. An estimate says that in the year 2014015, India imported Rs. 36,900 worth of arms, ammunition and related goods. In contrast, its defence exports last year were worth of about only Rs.2000 crore, a figure given by none other than Parrikar himself on the inaugural day of the defexpo.

Of course, it is to the credit of Parrikar that last August he formally allowed the Defence Research and Development Organisation (DRDO) to export defence equipment in 16 categories that included armoured vehicles, ammunition, rifles and small arms, military training equipment, electronic warfare devices, software, bombs and torpedoes. In fact, the DRDO has now shortlisted missiles for being the centerpiece of India's arms exports, within the framework of the missile technology control regime that bans exporting missiles with ranges above 300 km. Overall, the military hardware shortlisted for export includes Astra beyond-visual-range air-to-air missile, Prahar surface-to-surface missile, Akash missiles, light combat aircraft (LCA), supersonic cruise missile Brahmos, sonars, Arjun Mk-2 tanks, airborne early warning and control system, a variety of unmanned systems and battlefield radars.

Of course, it is too early to say what impact the decision to export arms will make on the potential arms-buyers. That will be known when DRDO gets concrete orders from international orders for its indigenously designed military hardware. The usual criticism of the DRDO's functioning over the years have been that it promises more but delivers less and that while designing the products it does not take into account the views and concerns of the end-users, that is, the Indian military. That India still imports nearly 70 percent of its defence needs means that the DRDO and other defence public sector undertakings have not been able to overcome serious challenges that inhibit their growth and effectiveness.

Broadly speaking, India's defence industrial policy (DIP) has so far been marked by three principal features. First, India intends to maximize its indigenous production through its own efforts - quality personnel/scientists/technologists and production centers. Second, if indigenously not feasible then the country will go for licensed production of what could be obtained abroad. This obviously involves transfer of technology from the foreign vendors so that over the years the country gains required knowledge and expertise to develop arms on its own. Third, if the situation so warrants then the country will for direct purchases. But it has so happened that the third feature has over- dominated the DIP as a whole.

The most fundamental flaw in our DIP is that we have not spent enough on our research and development (R&D). It is very easy to criticize the DRDO, but the fact remains that the DRDO's share in our defence budgets is not much to talk about if one compares the sums that the major arms exporters invest in R&D. Our brightest students do not go for R&D. There is a tremendous shortage of qualified engineers and scientists in our defence sector. And this explains why the second feature of our DIP is equally poor. You may frame enough provisions or rules for technology transfer and offsets with regard to the foreign vendors. But what use they are they if you fail to utilize them because of the essentially faulty personnel policy? Besides, whatever one may say, the sad reality is that no foreign vendors or original equipment manufacturers (OEM) will like to part with their intellectual property rights; even if they want to, their respective governments will not allow that to happen all that easily.

That precisely is the reason why we have taken inordinately long time to develop Tejas or Arjun. And that is also the reason why foreign direct investment (FDI) in our defence sector will not rise beyond a point.

Secondly, it is to be learnt from the examples in the major arms-exporting countries that defence technology often involves long term investment as obsolescence here is high.

The production of the next generation of an equipment or of a different variant always increases the cost of the equipment, involving, as it does, the integration of various sub -systems. Similarly, you cannot expect your indigenous products to be as good as, let alone superior to, the similar foreign products that are available in the international market.

After all, making arms indigenously is a learning curve. China is exactly undergoing this process. Its home-made weapons are qualitatively inferior to foreign products. But the important point is that it is one the right course. China-made weapons will be infinitely better 10 years hence because China is climbing up that curve.

Of course, India is not China. Ours is mixed economy, a fact which should have added to our strength. Because, unlike in China, our challenge can be met by a partnership between the public and private sectors.

Unfortunately, the government in the past did not encourage the participation of the private industry in the defence sector. But things are changing now, evident from the fact a record number private players - 1055 companies from India and 47 other countries - are participating in this edition of the defexpo; and what is more important, they all are unanimous in joining hands with the Indian government and public sector undertakings to build "together" a "globalized military industry" in India but for not only India but also the whole world.

INDIA DESIGN AND BUILD OF MILITARY KIT

On an industrial estate in Hyderabad in south India, work is underway on developing advanced technology that replicates the experience of driving a tank through a war zone or using firearms against enemies in jungle terrain.

Zen Technologies is a two decade-old Indian company that designs and manufactures training equipment used by the country's armed forces, including flight, combat vehicle and hand grenade systems.

But India is keen to see firms designing and building more home-grown military equipment beyond simulators.

India is one of the world's largest importers of weapons and manufacturing is still at a nascent stage, but there are strides being made in the defence sector as the country finally starts to try to break away from its dependence on imports.

"For the first time in the history of Indian defence procurement the importance of design and development has been recognised by the ministry of defence," says Ashok Atluri, the managing director of Zen Technologies, who is very optimistic that India can transform itself into a top producer of weapons. "This is going to ensure huge inflow of funds into research and development and will ensure that the scientific talent in India is engaged in developing cutting-edge technologies in defence. India can become a hub for trail-blazing defence exports from being a destination for outdated defence equipment."

He says Zen has its own plans to "grow its exports business and emerge as a reliable indigenous defence player for supplying products to the Indian and global market".

New Delhi has hugely ambitious targets to reduce its defence imports. Narendra Modi, the prime minister, has said that its aim is for India to manufacture 70 per cent of its weapons at home by 2020. Currently, it relies on imports for about 70 per cent of its equipment, which is extremely costly for the country.

Mr Modi is pushing for India to become a global manufacturing centre under his "Make in India" campaign, and the defence and aerospace industry is a key part of this. Two years ago, India opened up the defence sector to 49 per cent foreign direct investment (FDI) from a previous limit of 26 per cent. In June this year, the government liberalised the rules even further, permitting FDI of 100 per cent in the sector.

The role of the private sector in India's defence industry is growing and Indian firms are eager to cash in the opportunity.

"Tata, Mahindra, Hero and Reliance are spending a lot on enhancing the defence manufacturing in India, bidding for big contracts and partnering with foreign companies to assemble or manufacture in India," says Ajay Pal Singh, who used to work as a scientist for India's Defence Research and Development Organisation before becoming an entrepreneur. Larsen and Toubro (L&T) and Godrej are other Indian firms that have entered into weapons manufacturing.

But Mr Singh says that for the time being at least Indian armed forces need to keep buying from abroad to "stay modern".

Over the next eight to 10 years, about US$200 billion is to be spent on defence capability expansion, and a further $150bn on ramping up homeland security capability, according to Roland Berger Strategy Consultants.

"India is seeing significant growth in the aerospace and defence opportunity currently," says Wilfried Aulbur, the managing partner for India at Roland Berger. "On an extremely broad level, this growth is due to the combination of three major factors, which are sustained geopolitical threats, increasing internal security threats and significant spends needed to address the need for new equipment as well as for addressing obsolescence related issues."

SIGNIFICANCE OF THE ARMS TRADE TREATY FOR INDIA

Despite existing legislation in India, the problem of gun violence from illicit small arms has grown instead of abating. It is thus evident that the national laws and procedures prove inadequate to control the problem. An international agreement would help by helping states to review the loopholes within respective national legislations relating to SALW marking, recording and tracing methods. In the South Asian context, there is a need for dedicated attempts by states to prevent losses from government armouries and recover illicit weapons. Security sector bureaucracies tend to assume that problems of illicit SALW will go away once the problem of insurgent movements are solved. In a way, it explains a lack of political mobilization for victims of gun violence in India; it further explains why the problem of illicit small arms manufacture has grown in the country. To assuage concerns of states that the ATT may impinge on their sovereign rights, the treaty should obligate the governance structures of the states to carry out accountability checks and stockpile verification procedures to prevent flow of illicit small arms from and across the nation's borders. This should make up for the ressistance to effective international verifiable processes for the recovery of illicit small arms or stockpile monitoring and verification. India is located in an unstable region where controls on small arms proliferation by other states in the neighbourhood are weak. Considering there is easy availability of illicit small arms from across the border, and the fact that small arms are being manufactured in illegal factories in the region, provisions for a strong ATT will converge with India's long-term security and political interests in creating a stable regional order, by helping to address the problem of illicit weapons and armed political violence. This would also have application elsewhere in the region, given that smaller countries such as Nepal and Sri Lanka have faced much stronger threats from insurgent movements, i.e., Maoists and Liberation Tigers of Tamil Elam, respectively.

In terms of India's arms exports to countries with poor human rights records, such as Myanmar and Sudan, its compliance with ATT principles could be open to question. For countries where the application of international human rights and international humanitarian law has been found wanting, continuation of such could become a problem.

If the ATT includes adequate requirements for transparency and accountability, it will benefit India in two ways: one, it will improve its own processes for security sector accountability for stockpile management; and two, it will reduce the risk of diversion to NSAsfrom arsenals in those neighbouring countries that do not have strong, democratic control of their military sectors.

Indian security concerns relating to small arms and ammunition are primarily three-fold:

- risks of diversion of such arms to NSAs by centres of domestic production;
- illicit manufactures in neighbouring countries and illegal diversion from their arsenals; and
- sales by arms-exporting countries to intermediaries which are then re-transferred to third parties without proper end-user verification or accountability.

The ATT must identify action to be taken by or against the state parties that fail to control the abovementioned risks. India should urgently engage the international community to address these concerns. And, if India continues to engage with the ATT perfunctorily, then in all likelihood the ATT will come into force without having Indian concerns on board.

According to a representative of the Indian delegation in July 2011, the ATT is indicative of India's shifting position: "...the draft paper seems somewhat vague, to my delegation, in addressing the question of the illicit trade of conventional arms." 5

Thus the question is: what have the Indian representatives done to gather informed Indian opinion and develop India's position to advance progressive solutions to our country's problem from rising illicit trade of conventional arms?

Indian officials may also be concerned that allegations of human rights violations against its armed forces operating in disturbed areas could prevent transfer of technologies required for the design and manufacture of a new generation of SALW, from being acquired by its military from international sources.

A way around this would be for the Indian armed forces and para-military forces being trained in programmes to address these issues: compliance with humanitarian and human rights laws and introducing human security concerns and those of victims of gun violence as well as security sector governance reforms.

Citizen-centric Considerations for Drafting of ATT

It is an accepted norm that states have sovereign rights to acquire weapons from international sources for their territorial defence. But they also have an obligation to ensure that such weapons that are acquired by their security forces, or are in transit, are not diverted to illicit markets or put to illegitimate use against any other state. In this regard, all states should actively co-ordinate international initiatives to identify and track violations of legitimate arms trade.

In pursuit of the abovementioned obligations, weapons-exporting countries, whose weapons are found in illicit trade, must share responsibility and compensation provided to the victims of gun violence irrespective of the territory in which the crime has occurred. In that regard, states which neglect compliance with provisions of the treaty, after having joined the ATT, should be deemed to be trading in illicit weapons and, therefore, debarred from international arms trade.

In order to achieve the objectives of arms acquisition transparency and responsibility, state parties should submit comprehensive national annual reports on international transfers of all arms and ammunition covered by the treaty to an international register, which should

a) analyse the data and publish comprehensive annual report on losses, diversions or thefts from national weapons stocks and arsenals;
b) publish assessments given by the state authorities on illegal manufacture of weapons in their territories;
c) enable legislative provisions for nationalverification of weapons stockpile security; and

d) provide international support and guidance to state parties in the form of regional training programmes for production of their national reports.

It is extremely important to have an international reporting and regulatory mechanism so as to standardise weapons markings, remove ambiguity and different interpretations in state practices as far as possible. Variations in implementation of the provisions of post-manufacture and imported weapons marking must be reduced to the minimum. This could be done by acceptance of best practices related to post-manufacture and import marking technologies.

A general lack of information and capacity in developing countries could impair such states from implementing provisions of the reporting, marking and regulatory mechanisms. Considering that the need for technical assistance is met through international organisations, more developing countries could be willing to undertake practical measures to implement the ATT markings and reporting requirements. This would help to maintain national arms sales registers that record and check all small arms and weapons held in the public sector as well as those held by private individuals, and their sales and gifts. If there is pilferage from state arsenals or from the state's stocks of de-commissioned weapons, data on such illicit weapons must be recorded in national registers and made available to the neighbouring states upon formal request. In this regard, the legal sales to individuals holding weapons licences can be abused if such individuals sell weapons to non-licence holders. States should be obliged to register all transactions between private individuals. For this purpose, all state parties should maintain a national contact point.

In addition, states should organise specialised agencies to proactively trace, track and seize illicit transfers of weapons to detect and prevent illegal manufacture of weapons on their territory, and to recover weapons lost by individuals and state agencies. All states must organise specialised police bureaus dedicated to these tasks with SALW control task forces deployed in areas that have a high incidence of illicit weapons.

Such a dedicated agency could be in shape of a specially-trained constabulary to investigate, recover and destroy illicit weapons and their manufacturing facilities and prevent unauthorised sales of weapons to and from former security forces personnel. Arming of civilians in border areas and disturbed districts must be banned. The state must maintain its monopoly over use of force in its territory.

Regional Cooperation Centres for prevention of illicit weapons transfers must be created to train and build capacities for detection, seizure and reporting mechanisms within the executive branches and the national security sector. The need for this can be gauged by the fact that the problem of illicit weapons proliferation varies in scale and scope from region to region and from province to province within states. For example, in the India-Pakistan sub-region, some districts/provinces are more notorious for manufacture of illicit weapons which end up across the borders in other states, and which contribute to high incidences of gun violence and illicit weapons proliferation.

As Pakistan has been more explicit in its call to prevent, combat and eradicate the illicit trade and trafficking in conventional arms, particularly small arms and light weapons, it behoves India to join its neighbour to the west in its quest to find practical solutions to address this problem. Whenever an importing state transfers imports weapons from government stocks to another government or civilian end user for re-sale, the re-assignment marking should be reported to the Central Register to be maintained at the arsenals of the original manufacturer as well as at the ATT Secretariat.

The compliance obligation for original markings should be on the seller and not on the buyer or importer. If a weapon is re-transferred to a third party, then the marking obligation should rest with the re-exporting state. India should move from its current method of engraving markings for the weapons it manufactures to non-erasable marking technologies.

As international assistance is required to develop standardised stockpile security management and verification procedures, its absence allows theft and pilferage to remain unverified within the state's security sector. To ensure compliance, penalities must be identified against states which neglect to check transfers of illicit small arms across their borders. This practical step is important for inclusion from India's perspective as large-scale illicit small arms are being transferred to insurgent groups in India through third countries.

The ATT should have provisions for verifiable destruction of old or de-commissioned weapons as these are likely to leak out of stocks or be sold without adequate end-use control.

SALW Marking, Recording and Tracing

Considering that weapons continue to be manufactured illicitly, whether in, for example, Landi Kotal, Darra Adam Khel in Pakistan or smuggled through other countries in the region add to the burden of problems in local policing and local security. 8 Illicit manufacturing in India or in Pakistan can have as much destabilising effect within their respective territories as they would have across borders. If the states are unable to comply with their public safety obligations, there is a need for international initiatives to be mobilised to address limitations in domestic processes relating to illicit gun manufacture at small-scale industrial facilities in a large number of small towns.

Ammunition Lot Markings, Recordings and Tracing

Even though it is very difficult to assign ownership of ammunition to a stock or group when recovered at the scene of crime, ammunition markings, when combined with thorough international verification of the chain of sales contracts (even if ammunition lots are re-transferred), should be enough to launch an enquiry into the leakages in sources of illicit arms proliferation. Methods for tracing of ammunition lots must begin from markings by the original manufacturer being standardised and made mandatory. Standardised international practices must be designed and adopted to help to identify and follow ammunition lots right from the place of recovery to its original source of manufacture in order to discourage illicit trafficking.

It is important that larger countries in South Asia—India and Pakistan—should lead the way to develop national legislation that obligate the original ammunition manufacturer to mark the identity of the first export recipient of ammunition; thereafter, subsequent re-sales must be recorded in an international tracing registry. Alongwith online book keeping procedures, lot numbering will make it possible to trace the movement of ammunition.

There are two preconditions essential for tracing: (a) the ammunition has been marked according to standardised international practices, and (b) the information relating to the marked ammunition has been recorded and stored in a centralised database, thus enabling tracing to start and evidence can be collected to initiate legal proceedings against all participants insmuggling en route.

Ammunition markings are not the only means of tracing a weapon. Even a marked ammuni¬tion lot could be transferred several times after it was diverted from its original purpose. But markings, combined with thorough analysis of the sales or re-sales contracts, should be sufficient to start an enquiry into the sources of illicit proliferation.Combined with legislated obligations for national-level recording and book keeping, the state parties would be provided with a means of detecting diversions from national stocks. In countries, where surveillance of ammunition delivery personnel are weak, ammunition lot marking could be a valuable back-up method. Internationally binding and nationally-regulated management of ammunition stockpiles and SALW transfers must develop preventive and pro-active measures to check illegal di¬version. It is in India's interest to convince countries that oppose the international practice of marking of SALW and ammunition to strengthen their national stockpile management and verification practices. It is curious that the states that seem most affected by the non-regulation of ammunition also oppose any international controls measures most fiercely.

EDB Engineering , a Belgian company, has developed a process for laser-marking of ammunition. This technology is regarded as revolutionary for the efficient tracea¬bility of ammunition. The innovative technique is based on laser technology and can apply a marking after assembly, just before the cartridges are packaged and delivered to the customer. Such a procedure would be impossible with the stamping technique, which, in any case, can be defaced. The armaments industry views this technique as an effective ammunition marking process, which has since been developed for one of the world's leading ammunition manufacturers. EDB has proved that, technically, the identification of each piece of ammunition is a feasible operation and that financially too this laser process may be considered to be acceptable. However, the costs will come down once this technology gets widely spread.

CURRENT MILITARY SPENDING AND ARMS SALES

Despite their being locked into this poverty trap, poorer nations are still regarded as legitimate and profitable arms customers for Western states which helped create their situation. According to a report for the US congress, arms sales to developing countries together far outweigh arms sales to developed countries. According to their definition, countries of the South accounted for 66 per cent of the value of all international arms deliveries in 2000.

Social Impacts of Conflict

The servicing of debt for arms sales obviously affects health and education, and has other social impacts in the developing world. Money spent on arms, or money spent servicing debts, means less money is spent in social and developmental programs within the country. Countries are prevented by international trade rules from unfairly supporting their own industries above the industries of other nations. Caribbean countries are not allowed to give financial aid to their banana industry on which the region depends, because it is unfair competition for the American-owned banana industry in Central and South America. The Global Agreement on Trade and Services (GATS), which is currently being pushed through the WTO, intends to extend these kinds of rules to other areas such as water, healthcare and education provision.

But at the WTO, and in all other global agreements, the military is specifically excluded from the rules governing global trade. The main WTO governing document, the General Agreement on Tariffs and Trade (GATT), states that a country cannot be prevented from taking any action 'it considers necessary for the protection of its essential security interests... relating to the traffic in arms, ammunition and implements of war and such traffic in other goods and materials as is carried on directly for the purpose of supplying a military establishment.'

In other words, the WTO GATT and other trade agreements do not apply to the arms trade. There are no international restrictions on what munitions a country can buy or sell, how much these should cost, how much a country can spend, who they buy weapons from or to what extent they subsidize their own arms industry. This process has contributed to the pattern of rich countries becoming richer, and poorer nations staying poor, or becoming poorer. Western nations are not prevented by WTO rules from subsidizing their own arms industries, and so are able to acquire military equipment at artificially low knock-down prices, while keeping the finance within the country. Moreover, the exclusion from WTO regulations means they can buy arms domestically, even when other countries are offering better products more cheaply.

Developing nations rarely have established arms industries and so buy their weaponry from abroad at a cost often way above what the equipment is worth, draining yet more money out of the country. Even when there is a local arms industry, this is usually so small that buying abroad remains cheaper. Developing nations pump cash into their own arms industries too, in attempts to improve their economies, because it is the only industry they can legally support in this way.

When seeing how trade rules benefit the rich countries, especially in the arms arena, it is not surprising that airplane and arms manufacturer Boeing was the prime sponsor of the

WTO meeting in Seattle in 1999. Global agreements to break down barriers to trade are having the effect of preventing developing and middle income countries from exploiting the resources they do have to trade on the world market, keeping those countries financially subordinate to the rich West.

The argument that the arms trade creates or sustains jobs, or brings money into the national economy, is one of the most difficult arguments campaigners face. These arguments have strong political currency-people don't vote for governments that threaten their livelihood-but they are based on a fallacy which is only now becoming fully apparent.

The arms trade is an immoral business that cause death, maiming, human rights abuses and suffering around the world. It is also a business that does not bring huge economic or employment benefits to the biggest arms-exporting countries. In many cases, high government subsidies, tax breaks, insurance schemes and promotion for arms manufacturers cost governments more money than weapons producers generate for them. Countries are artificially propping up their arms industries while refusing to explore fully the potential for diversification into areas that are not only more productive and socially positive but also economically viable.

The Extent of Government Subsidies

Governments subsidize their arms sector in a number of ways. The difficult job for campaigners and academics is to show by how much, and why it is a bad thing. Information, such as how much a government spends on its own armed forces, what procurement decisions it makes, how much it spends on military research and development and how much export credit insurance it provides for arms companies, is usually secret or difficult to obtain.

Strong, well-informed estimates based on obtainable information are usually the best that campaigners can muster before issuing the challenge to governments: if we are wrong, it falls to you to prove how wrong. After all, if arms exports are big earners for state economies, wouldn't politicians be shouting it from the roof tops? With that proviso in mind, valiant attempts to look at this issue have been made. In the US, the defence and foreign aid budgets are the largest single source of federal funding to private corporations. According to the World Policy Institute, more than half of all US weapons sales are financed by taxpayers instead of by foreign arms purchasers. During the fiscal year of 1996 (the last year for which figures were available) the US Government spent more than $7.9 billion to help companies secure just over $12 billion in agreements for new international arms sales.

Direct Subsidies

Governments' direct financial support for their arms exports can be roughly placed into a few distinct categories. Each of these subsidies results in taxpayers' money being spent, or risked, helping foreign governments to buy arms.

Export promotion-The major arms-exporting countries each year spend huge amounts of money all over the world promoting and marketing their domestic arms companies' products. Export promotion ranges from diplomatic visits by politicians to the provision of advice and support for companies marketing their systems, to regular attendance and promotion at arms exhibitions and conferences. At the US Pentagon, nearly 6,000 people were employed in 1996 to promote, broker, administer and finance arms sales abroad, at a cost of $378.2 million. In the State Department a further 75 personnel were employed, part of a defence export promotion budget of $3.7 million. And the US commerce department also plays a role, publishing 'defence market assessments' such as How to do business in Indonesia, and mounting US presence at foreign arms exhibitions. During 1996, the US Government sent equipment and personnel to 19 overseas weapons shows, at a cost of more than $5.1 million.

Export credits-Government insurance schemes to compensate arms companies when their foreign clients default on payment generally make up the bulk of the government direct subsidies. They also provide financing support for deals.

Governments then attempt to recoup the cost from the defaulting nations, with usually only limited success. Often the companies insist on some kind of insurance or guarantee from their home government before embarking on large weaponry export deals. Arms sales make up, large proportions of the export credits extended in many major arms exporting countries.

The US Export-Import Credit Bank, which could be seen as the equivalent of an export credit organization, is usually prohibited from guaranteeing arms deals (though not always-Congress occasionally makes exceptions). However the US more than makes up for it in other loans and funding programs which subsidize US arms exporters.

The US Foreign Military Financing Program (FMF) received $3.35 billion in 1999 to support grants and loans for the provision of US military equipment and services to more than 24 countries. Recipients of FMF grants in recent years have included Egypt, Israel, Jordan, Turkey and the Ukraine. More funds were allocated for Africa. Another $16 million of subsidy is granted through the US Defence Export Loan Guarantee fund. Spending distortions-governments also artificially support their arms industries by distorting their own spending on domestic military purchases. They buy more arms from domestic suppliers than really needed, they pay more than these ought to cost, and they choose domestic arms suppliers even if foreign-made equipment is cheaper and better. In any other industry, World Trade Organization rules and other free-trade legislation would prevent such spending distortions as unfair competition. But as we have seen earlier, the military is exempt from international agreements on trade. In a report by the World Policy Institute, William Hartung decries this kind of spending in the US, which he calls 'defence pork'. He argues that politicians add unnecessary and expensive military equipment purchases to the Pentagon's budget in order to please arms companies, secure or create jobs and so gain campaign donations and votes. In 1998, $3.8 billion was added by senators and officials to the amount that the Pentagon had said it needed to meet its own defence plans. While most 'defence pork' is US-bought-so not an arms export subsidy-the example shows how political pressure distorts procurement decisions.

Other Subsidies

The above are just three direct financial subsidies which governments provide for their arms industries. But there are many different ways that governments indirectly financially support their arms industries, and while it is more difficult to quantify this kind of support in concrete terms, the benefits to arms companies can be quite considerable.

Research and development (R&D)-Governments spend large portions of their defence budgets on research and development of new weapons systems, which they contract arms companies to carry out on their behalf. In 1998/99, the three big US weapons manufacturers received over $8 billion in R&D funding. Commissions and bribes-According to one World l Bank estimate, the sums distributed worldwide each year as pay-offs and bribes total $80 billion. Campaign group Transparency International (TI) has surveyed attitudes to corruption in business, and found that arms and construction companies were perceived to be the most likely to pay bribes.

Jobs in the Arms Industry

Off-set deals and joint procurement aside, a further argument-that the weapons business is a thriving employer-is also false.... the global arms industry has been gradually shrinking since the end of the Cold War.

Linked to this, the number of people employed in the sector has also fallen. Moreover, the argument that a government should spend huge amounts of money propping up an industry to safeguard a relatively small number jobs is one that only has so much credibility. Governments should no more subsidize their arms business than any other industry to safeguard jobs. Sir Samuel Brittan, the British economist and journalist, has written extensively on the weakness of the employment argument. He says the argument is based on the myth that there is a 'lump of labour' that is engaged in making specific products, that cannot be deployed elsewhere. If defence orders are lost, those people become unemployed and unemployable, runs the line. Brittan points out that millions of people change jobs, find jobs or leave jobs every year. 'Indeed, it is almost certainly easier for arms workers, many of whom have a wide range of valued skills, to find new jobs... Where will the new jobs come from to replace those lost in exporting weapons? Other jobs, on a much greater scale, arose to take the place of handloom weavers [and] drivers of horse-drawn carts. A report by the British Ministry of Defence and York University, published in 2001, revealed that 40,000 arms export jobs would be replaced by 67,000 civilian posts if arms exports were cut in half, albeit at a lower average salary per job.

Mercenaries: The Dogs of War

Selling arms is one side; purchasing people to use them is another. The use of privately hired might is nothing new. The Romans used mercenaries, and the practice probably went back even before them. Italian merchants in the 16th century hired muscle to protect their assets and control trade routes. Colonial explorers were accompanied by hired fighters. From the mid-20th century, Western firms setting up mines and oil exploration in Africa, Asia and Latin America protected their assets by hiring armed heavies.

Mercenaries come under a number of guises, but all include the provision of military might or advice for a profit. Under the guise of 'security' for example, private military companies, consultants, advisors or training outfits, all manner of services to both governments and companies are supplied, including full participation in conflicts, the provision of arms, and armed protection of royal families and industrial plants.

Former members of security services often run modern mercenary companies, exploiting their contacts in the arms and political world. They hire disaffected, unemployed former soldiers wherever they win contracts, and source second-hand weapons and equipment for them to fight with. They will often provide whatever services are required, in exchange for hard currency or interests in mining and oil exploration. UN Special Rapporteur Bernales Ballesteros was appointed by the UN General Assembly in 1996 to report on 'the use of mercenaries as a means of violating human rights and impeding the exercise of the rights of peoples to self-determination'.

Child Soldiers

At least mercenaries can usually make their own l choices; it is different for children. There are more than half a million children (under 18s) serving in armed forces, in more than 87 countries. At least 300,000 children are actively fighting in 41 countries, including Colombia, Sri Lanka, Sierra Leone, Uganda and Chechnya.; In some countries, very young children are used as messengers, spies and equipment carriers, but by the age of 10 they are given rifles, or rapid repeating machine-guns and set to fight in conflicts they cannot possibly understand. As members of armed forces, children become lawful targets for attack, but the use of child soldiers also increases the danger faced by civilian children who come under suspicion from warring parties. Within armed forces, children are often treated brutally, suffering physical, emotional and even sexual abuse. But it is not only faraway nations mired in internal conflicts that use child soldiers. The US is the country most opposed to setting 18 as the minimum age limit for recruiting and participation in armed forces. One in every 200 of its armed personnel is 17, while many more become temporary members as part of youth military training programs.

The UK continues to recruit 16-year-olds leaving school, and the recruitment process begins even while they are still at school. British soldiers under the age of 18 fought-and died-in both the Falklands/Malvinas conflict and the Gulf War. Other countries that recruit under-18s to the armed forces, via conscription or voluntary enlistment include: Australia, Bangladesh, Belgium, Brazil, Burundi, Canada, Chile, Croatia, Cuba, Denmark, El Salvador, Estonia, Finland, France, Germany, Honduras, India, Indonesia, Iran, Iraq, Ireland, Israel, Italy, Japan, Jordan, Libya, Luxembourg, Mexico, Namibia,

Netherlands, Aotearoa/New Zealand, Norway, Pakistan, Peru, Portugal, Republic of Korea, Sudan, Switzerland, Uganda and Yugoslavia.

A number of factors lead to the use of children as soldiers. Technological advances have made semi-automatic rifles light enough to be used and simple enough to be operated by a child, while rabid proliferation has made them cheap and easily obtainable. The longer a conflict goes on, the more likely children are to be 'recruited' as manpower becomes short-both young girls and boys are recruited-and new soldiers are needed to replaced the killed and injured.

Children are perceived to make obedient soldiers, they are cheap and are easy to manipulate. Children 'volunteer' or are coerced to join-up in order to survive, to prove their 'adulthood' or because it is a natural step in a culture of violence. In the Revolutionary United Front in Sierra Leone, children are held and trained for two or three months, threatened with death if they disobey orders or attempt to escape. In the Kamajors militias, they are initiated into secret societies and told they will gain magical powers and be immune to bullets if they join military forces.

Prevailing international law at the United Nations sets 15 as the minimum age for military recruitment and participation in armed conflict, though there is widespread agreement that this age is too low. The Coalition to Stop the Use of Child Soldiers is an international movement of organizations seeking the adoption and implementation of an Optional Protocol to the Convention on the Rights of the Child (CRC) setting the minimum age for all forms of military recruitment and use in hostilities at 18 years of age.

By the end of 2001, a total of 92 countries had signed or ratified the Optional Protocol, but implementation will take many years and a great deal of effort. Programs to prevent child recruitment, including monitoring, providing alternatives, and establishing proper procedures, as well as programs to ensure safe demobilization and integration of former child soldiers are particularly needed.

Landmines: The Legacy

Children, whether child soldiers or not, are often the main victims of landmines, perhaps the most vicious weapons brokered by the arms dealers. In the words of the International Campaign to Ban landmines, Put simply, anything that landmines can do to an enemy's army, they can do to a civilian population. What they cannot do is discriminate between the soldier and the civilian. Their impact cannot be confined to the duration of the battle. Thus, under the laws of war, they are an illegal weapon.'

More than any other weapon of war, landmines have received much public and legislative attention over recent decades. They are horrific because their effects on civilian communities, after battles have ended, are so long-term and devastating. Under internationally recognized definitions, landmines fall into two broad categories:

- Anti-personnel (AP) landmine-'A mine designed to be exploded by the presence, proximity or contact of a person and that will incapacitate, injure or kill one or more persons'.
- Anti-tank (AT) landmine-A device designed to detonate by more than 100 kilograms of pressure.

Whether anti-tank or anti-personnel, the effect of landmines on civilian communities is the same. They kill and maim indiscriminately, taking children just as easily as heads of households. Families are devastated not only because of the loss of a loved one, but also because their means of income or a future generation is destroyed. In the same way, those who are not killed when a landmine explodes are maimed or permanently disabled, becoming a long-term financial and emotional burden on families. Some landmines are designed to scatter thousands of shards of metal up to 50 meters, specifically to injure rather than kill.

Landmines also have devastating effects when they don't kill or maim, rendering thousands of acres of land unusable for farming or livestock. Families are forced to make a terrible choice between starvation or risking their lives on mined fields.

In Cambodia alone there are over 35,000 amputees as a result of landmines, and they are just the survivors. Mine deaths and injuries in the past few decades amount to hundreds of thousands. They are a daily threat in Afghanistan, Angola, Bosnia, Cambodia, Chechnya, Croatia, Iraq, Mozambique, Nicaragua, Somalia and dozens of other countries. In December 1997, following decades of pressure from campaigners, a total of 122 governments signed the Ottawa convention, officially titled 'The Convention on the Prohibition of the Use, Stockpiling, Production and Transfer of AntiPersonnel Mines and on their Destruction'. Less than one year later the treaty became international law when Burkina Faso became the 40th country to ratify.

It is the most comprehensive international treaty of its kind, and became law quicker than any other treaty of its kind in history. But despite worldwide support, and condemnation of the use, sale and stockpiling of anti-personnel landmines, a total of 53 countries still refuse to sign including China, Egypt, Finland, India, Israel, Pakistan, Russia and the US. The US's refusal has a devastating political influence, giving credence to other countries' refusal. The campaign continues to demand that these countries drop their opposition to the treaty, and to expand it to cover anti-tank mines and other 'area denial weapons'-a euphemism meaning they blow you up if you stray where you 'should not'-like cluster munitions and unexploded ordnance.

The 'trade' in landmines, as traditionally defined at least, is all but non-existent. Cuba, the United States, Russia, Egypt, Iran, Iraq, Burma, China, India, North Korea, South Korea, Pakistan, Singapore and Vietnam are still classified as producers of the weapons by the International Campaign to Ban Landmines, though some of them have only failed to prove written attestation to the contrary. Military monitor Jane's Mines and Mine Clearance 2000-2001 revealed there has been a 'virtual absence of mines-legitimate or otherwise-at arms shows and military equipment exhibitions this year'. Thirty-four countries are known to have exported anti-personnel landmines in the past. All but Iraq have attested that they no longer do so. The trade in anti-personnel landmines has been confirmed to exist only in a relatively small amount of illicit trafficking.

For a book on the arms trade, it could be argued the issue should stop there-the trade in anti-personnel landmines no longer exists, and the manufacture is nominal. Unfortunately, the step is not so easily taken. The Ottawa treaty covers only certain types of antipersonnel landmines, leaving vast loopholes where area denial weapons, including anti-tank weapons, remain available and traded.

The campaign against landmines concentrates now on encouraging the states who have so far failed to sign and ratify the Ottawa treaty to do so, but it has also broadened its outlook to the new and next generations of landmines and weapons that are landmines by any other name. The weapon causing most concern for campaigners is the cluster bomb. Usually dropped from a plane, it explodes just above the ground, scattering hundreds of miniature 'bomblets' over a wide area. Many of these bomblets fail to explode, remaining in the ground, just like anti-personnel landmines, until disturbed.

Like landmines, unexploded ordnance (UXO) poses a serious threat to lives and livelihoods. Between 1964 and 1973 the US dropped a huge number of cluster bombs over Laos. It is estimated that millions of unexploded bomblets remain. Cluster munitions were used in Kosovo and Vietnam, during the Gulf War, in the Falklands/Malvinas conflict, and during the recent attacks on Afghanistan. NATO admits to a failure rate of between 8 and 12 per cent in Kosovo, leaving as many as 35,000 live bomblets on the ground. The campaign against landmines is far from won. Many countries, having signed Ottawa, pour money and research into mine clearance programs-an expensive and time-consuming business. But while taking mines away with one hand, the landmines of the future are being created and delivered across war zones all over the world. The arms companies which are earning millions from developing mine clearance equipment are also at the forefront of developing new generations of weapons, laying the foundation of devastation in the future. The International Campaign to Ban Landmines is calling for a moratorium, banning the use of cluster weapons because of their devastating and long-lasting effects.... government ministers, advisers and senior members of the armed forces frequently move into the employment of arms companies and vice versa. The supposed wall between government and the industry has a huge gaping hole in it, in which a constantly revolving door has been established.

In Frank Vogl's Earth Times article on bribery and corruption in the arms trade, he outlines how the George W Bush regime in the US takes 'this game of political pressure to an unprecedented new level'. 'Rarely before has US business taken such total charge of the Pentagon. Not only does the Secretary of Defence [Donald Rumsfeld] come from big business, but so too do the new heads of the Army, Navy and Air Force... President Bush has nominated James Roche a vice president at military aircraft seller Northrop Grumman, to become Secretary of the Air Force; Gordon England from arms and naval vessel manufacturer General Dynamics to become Secretary of the Navy.

For good measure, US Vice President Dick Cheney's wife, Lynne, serves on Lockheed Martin's board, a company which is a major contractor to the US Government and its allies.

Purchasing Power

Donations from private companies to political parties and candidates are nothing new, and have been the foundation of many scandals for governments across the Western world. Not surprisingly, because there are lucrative domestic contracts to be won, and restrictive legislation to be challenged, the arms business is a major player in the cash-for-influence money-go-round. As Lumpe and Donarski note in The Arms Trade Revealed, 'Whenever and wherever arms export policy is being made, financially self-interested representatives of the arms corporations are present. Generous campaign contributions from the weaponeer's political action committees (PACs) open doors, providing access and influence on the policy making process. According to the World Policy Institute, the 25 leading weapons-exporting companies contributed a record $10.8 million during the 1995-96 general election cycle in the US. Of this, $6.6 million came in regulated PAC donations and $4.2 million in unregulated 'soft' money-donations theoretically targeted for party-building activities, but often used to benefit specific candidates. Lockheed Martin was the leading arms corporate donor during this time. The Republican Party, more military-minded than the Democrats, received the bulk of donations.

A US Code of Conduct?

Although the US has relatively strict legislation governing the involvement of its citizens in arms brokering the world's largest arms-exporting country has comprehensively stalled on drawing up its own code of conduct on arms exports. Progressive Congress representatives have been attempting for nearly a decade to introduce a Code of Conduct on arms exports into US legislation. In 1995 International Relations Committee member Cynthia McKinney (Democrat) introduced the 'Code of Conduct on Arms Transfers Act' into the 104th Congress.

Campaign for an International Code | Finally, the US President has now been instructed by Congress to pursue multilateral steps for controlling and monitoring the arms trade. There is a real possibility that within a generation, perhaps even before, an International Code of Conduct on Arms Transfers could be introduced, building on the EU Code. In 2000 the US and the EU signed a declaration to work towards a common vision on the question of arms export controls. In May 1997, 14 Nobel Laureates met in New York to launch their own International Code as a first step to persuade arms exporting countries to adopt standards: 'Today, we speak as one to voice our common concern regarding the destructive effects of the unregulated arms trade. Together, we have written an International Code of Conduct on Arms Transfers, which, once adopted by all arms-selling nations, will benefit all humanity, nationalities, ethnicity, and religions.

Their proposed Code requires that arms transfers are only granted if transfer would complement and comply with international human rights standards, international humanitarian law, respect for international arms embargoes and military sanctions, promotes peace, security and stability, promotes human development and opposes terrorism. It calls too for public accounting of the Code's implementation, and transparent international co-operation through the UN and other bodies to improve and adjust the code as appropriate. While the proposal needs updating to account for recent changes in the international arms trade, it is a bold attempt to set in motion some international moves to curb the arms export business. It is perhaps the best tool arms trade campaigners currently have to effect change on a global scale.

A Broader View of Campaigning

From Seattle onwards, politicians and executives of the biggest and richest transnational corporations realized that wherever they went, and whatever they did, an inspired, passionate group of united people was watching, criticizing and acting for social justice and equality. Also for the first time, campaigners on widely diverse issues, from gay rights to third-world poverty, from peace and nuclear disarmament to environmental activists, joined together.

They realized their concerns overlapped in many different and complex ways. They discovered that united campaigning, using the concerns they shared as a foundation, was more effective than disparate, isolationist campaigns along strictly issue-based lines. The campaign against arms trading cannot, and should not, be considered in isolation from other concerns of social justice, except perhaps for convenience' sake. In almost every area of global injustice, the arms trade plays its deadly role. It was revealed how the trade exacerbates conflict, promotes human rights abuses and worsens poverty in developing countries. The trade is also intimately connected to environmental destruction, inequality, immigration and asylum, gender and cultural rights, privatization and worker exploitation-in fact, most of the world's evils have their roots in the fighters, tanks, mines, guns and bullets that corrupt individuals and destroy lives.

THE ETHICS AND ECONOMICS OF THE ARMS TRADE

Every sensible market economist should accept that a market must operate within a framework of law and moral convention.Investment Bankers are not permitted to finance firms that sell poison and there are strong constraints on the emission of lead into rivers or on pollutants into the chain of foodstuffs.My contention is that exports of arms to dubious regimes should come within the sphere of what is out of bounds – and more decisively so than at present. Would we have to pay a heavy economic price for such restraint? There is indeed sometimes a conflict between national self-interest and ethical actions, just as there can be a conflict between personal self-interest and moral behaviour. But in both cases this is often exaggerated. In the national case it is exaggerated by an inflated view of the role of arms and export promotion in the British economy.

The promotion and *de facto* subsidisation of arms sales is – like most other industrial subsidies – wealth destroying; there would be very little, if any, sacrifice involved in doing away with the whole effort. Behind the arms promotion lobby is the primitive belief that if one source of overseas sales dries up, the workers and other resources involved would waste away. This is rubbish in view of the millions of people who change jobs every year. If other countries want to compete with us in foolish subsidies, let them.

The Ethical Case

It might be best to examine the ethical case before the economic arguments. It is not my intention to argue against all arms sales. It would be absurd for each member of an alliance to try to make a full range of weapons, simply out of *amour propre*, when specialisation would pay far better. In

1998-99 the Ministry of Defence spent 13% of its equipment budget on 64 co-operative equipment programmes involving 19 partner nations. The most important of these, by far, were France, Germany, the USA, Italy and the Netherlands.

Subsidised credit for exports of arms or major capital goods have far worse effects than just the economic ones. Western nations are undoubtedly rich enough to waste some resources. As Adam Smith said: 'There is an awful lot of ruin in a nation.'

The worst effects are political and moral. They are both illustrated by the instance of the Pergau Dam in Malaysia in the mid 1990s when the Conservative government overturned a publicly minuted reservation by the Permanent Secretary of the Department of Overseas Development and insisted on supporting credits for this dam. One of the unstated arguments for going ahead was that this would act as a sweetener to persuade the Malaysian government to buy other goods, including arms, from Britain. On the other hand arms sales are justified because they are supposed to persuade governments that buy them to use British equipment in their capital projects. Thus one bad consequence is called in aid to support another; and Third World despots are encouraged to devote still more resources to military spending on prestige projects of dubious value.

More recently, the Labour Prime Minister was said to have overruled the Foreign Secretary when he authorised a statement by Stephen Byers on 21 December 1999 that he was 'minded', subject to certain conditions, to grant export credit for the Ilisu dam project in Turkey, which will flood several valleys with sites of unique cultural and religious value to the Kurds. You can imagine what this will do to promote ethnic harmony inside Turkey. In the spring of 2001 we were still waiting for a decision.

We cannot leave out of account the enormous part that bribery plays in this trade. A forthcoming study by Joe Roeber concludes that: 'Because of the structure, complexity and capacity of the market, and above all, because of the secrecy that surrounds every aspect of its activities, the international arms trade is the most corrupt of all legal trades.' He finally asks: 'Can we justify bribing people to buy arms they may not need with money their taxpayers cannot afford, simply to inflate the number of jobs in a declining industry?'

All these follies are supported by the myth that exports are valuable for their own sake, however small the return the British nation gets from them. Business lobbyists are able to persuade a succession of prime ministers, ranging from ultra-dry Conservatives to New Labour that, if the government does not support them, their overseas rivals will win the contracts instead.

Orders of Magnitude

The official estimate for British arms sales is that they amounted in 1999 to about £4bn or appreciably less 0.5% of GDP. A great part consisted of aircraft and aerospace parts. A good academic estimate of the direct cost of government support is about £400m per annum. This does not cover the arms promotion aspects of many royal, political and military visits and activities, which are ostensibly for other purposes. Indirect support for what is known as the Defence Industrial Base is a good deal larger. The number of workers employed is put at 90,000 or just over 0.33% of UK employment. There are two practical inhibitions that limit official export promotion. The first and obvious one is the Exchequer cost. Secondly there is the fear that official promotional activities will be self-defeating, and still more expensive, if all governments follow them in a competitive race. Accordingly, international organisations such as the European Union, the World Trade Organisation, the OECD and the Berne Credit Union have set rules to limit – but not stop – government support. Unfortunately these agreements do not prevent the never-ending procession of royalty, ministers and ambassadors who promote arms sales abroad, to say nothing of the military and trade attachés. Then there is the Defence Export Services Organisation, which provides marketing and military assistance. Above all, arms sales are often backed by the Export Credits Guarantee Department (ECGD), which provides 'insurance and finance packages for exporters of capital goods and services and political risk insurance' – in other words, taxpayer support for sales that would not pass muster on purely commercial terms. While public enterprises are set a target real rate of return of six per cent, the ECGD has to do no more than break even on average. The ECGD covers medium to long-term capital goods exports from three years up to 16 years duration. In a typical year it underwrites about £7bn of cover. The business is concentrated almost entirely on civil engineering projects and military and civil aerospace. The largest recipient is China. The military share of ECGD business has averaged over 25% in the most recent five years. The much-maligned Treasury tends to fight many ECGD deals, but is often defeated. Huw Evans, a former Treasury deputy secretary, has said that the ECGD is too vulnerable to intensive lobbying of ministers by large corporations and that it should become an independent agency. As Andrew Tyrie MP, a former adviser to Conservative chancellors has written, 'It is illogical to indulge in a competition to give away our own exports through an auction of subsidies.'

SMALL ARMS AND LIGHT WEAPONS MARKINGS

As micro-stamping and laser marking technology will become widely available, it will enable manufacturers to stamp all the information needed to mark the origin, registration and tracing of am¬munition, right from the time of manufacture. The same technologies, with due modification, can used for marking and tracing of SALW.

International cooperation is required to facilitate access to state-of-the-art technology for un-erasable and unique/standardised markings. There is a need to facilitate developing countries to fully implement provisions on post-manufacture non-erasable marking of weapons to establish the place and date of manufacture of weapons as part of their production process. These non-erasable markings should be of three kinds:

- Proof marking, which should indicate links with an ATT Central Register that must be maintained at the factories of its original manufacture and at the ATT Secretariat.

- Import marking, for identification of the country and year of import.
- Weapons assignment and export marking, which should identify weapons designed for the country's armed forces, weapons designed for security forces of foreign states, or weapons assigned for sale to private individuals.

The un-erasable laser markings that are required to verify diversion of SALW should describe the year of manufacture, original manufacturer, weapon number, and the identification of the recipient of the arms. The units of armed police and the military also need to have access to facilities of markings as weapons get transferred from one unit to the other. The information must be inscribed deeply enough to prevent erasure of marking history. It should be inscribed at such places on the weapon where average wear and tear would not deface the history of re-transfers. Recording of these markings must be available in national databases and records maintained for a period of 50 years for SALW. The data should be transferable officially to the elec¬tronic register kept by the national authorities and specific querries must be responded to if formally requested by international parties to the treaty.

With these developments in standardised international marking of SALW and ammunition, it would be possible to identify leakages and trace illicit transfers as never before. It will plug loopholes in illicit transfers and reduce the burden on weapons recovery policing. In South Asia, it will release resources and increase confidence in the police system to go actively after illicit manufacture within small villages and towns of the country. Once national legislations are made and enforced, it is likely to make the technology cost-effective through a wider international spread and obligatory standardisation of weapon's marking norms.

International Traceability Instruments

Improvements in domestic legislation and controls on SALW and ammunition would help in identification of illicit delivery and smuggling networks.

In absence of a legally binding in¬ternational traceability instruments, countries that export SALW and ammunition can avoid responsibility when their arms or ammunition are seized overseas in the hands of criminal gangs or insurgent groups. Related domestic legislation, control and prevention instruments in different countries will lead to effective marking to check illicit arms transfers and smuggling.

Many states have an irrational fear of having to account in front of international jurisdictions, little realising the larger benefits to public safety in their countries.

The Indian state should actively engage to encourage promotion of international processes that obligate arms and ammunition manufacturing countries to frame their legislation on marking, recording of data, and a tracing me¬chanism based on active international cooperation and changing political habits.

These steps should be the basis of the Internatio¬nal Instrument for the traceability of SALW and lead to its effective implementation. Even though there would be a political-bureaucratic battle to build up regional consensus in South Asia to abide by regional and internatio¬nal instruments, our diplomats owe this to thousands of innocent victims of firearms in India.

Thereafter, the armed forces and armed police, as part of obligations of the state parties, must annually report losses and recoveries to their respective parliaments. This should include methods of effectiveness of management of marking, recording and tracing for verification of ammunition stocks. The report should explain responsibilities of personnel for marking (on principles of uniformity and clarity) and tracing by recording in a data base. Recording of movement of ammunition (including re-location of stocks, sales and transfers within or between stocks) and independent cross-checking of stock holdings is essential for tracing of illicit trafficking.

International Experience

There are useful examples of counter-measures against illicit proliferation of SALW from Brazil, where a compulsory electronic connection between the databases of the armed force establishments is required with the offices controlling manufacture, imports and exports of weapons and the Brazilian Federal Police, which maintain a centralised information and data on confiscated weapons and ammunition.

Previously, a lack of communication and information exchange between these institutions prevented efficient action against diversion and trafficking. The new law also provides for a centralised ballistic information system run by the Brazilian Federal Police, which contain samples of bullets fired from each small arm and light weapon manufactured in Brazil. This should make it possible to identify light weapons used during crimes as well as identifying the origin of ammunition which was legally transferred but since been diverted to the illicit market.

The new Brazilian law on ammunition makes it obiligatory for the police and the armed forces to have their stampings on bullets and cartridges to be included in their lot numbers. This measure should improve the security of military and police stockpiles, and would enable the police to identify the leakages of ammunition from each of the two institutions towards organised crime. The penalties provided in the law should be sufficiently dissuasive towards arms trafficking, diversion of ammunition, theft and illicit stockpiling of ammunition, illicit manufacture and trading in firearms, and activities related to international arms trafficking.

Recommendations

India needs to take a progressive approach to address the problem of illicit small arms which takes into account humanitarian concerns. This approach aims to provide state parties with a means of detecting diversions from national stocks or from points in transit. In states where the control and surveillance of ammunition-handling personnel are inadequate, ammunition lot markings could also serve as a valuable tool for back-up surveillance against diversion or theft.

In addition, if in due course of time, all countries are

obliged to have electronically connect their weapons database and ammunition manufacturing entities, the details of losses by units under their Minstries of Defence and the armed police units under the Ministry of Home Affairs; traceability of diverted weapons will then be easier. But the Indian paper is conspicuously silent on much needed aspects of public safety. Fortunately, there is a view that advocates ATT to take humanitarian concerns into account. The least Indian diplomats can do in New York is not to obstruct such advocacy and abstain from criticising progressive ideas, as the Indian public certainly does not want a still-born or an ineffective arms trade treaty.

INDIA ABSTAINS AND EXPOSES THE ARMS TRADE TREATY

Once again India has been forced to abstain from voting in favour of a discriminatory global Arms Trade Treaty (ATT) – after its unpleasant experience with the NPT and the CTBT in the past. The treaty, aimed at laying down common international standards and limiting the illicit sale of conventional arms, was passed by the UN General Assembly with an overwhelming majority of 154 votes on April 3, 2013. Iran, North Korea and Syria voted against the treaty while China, India and Russia abstained.

As the largest importer of arms in the world, India objects to the ATT on several counts. First and foremost, India finds it difficult to accept that the treaty will enable arms exporting countries to impose unilateral conditions on the countries that import arms. The treaty has failed to address Indian concerns about the illegal transfer of arms to terrorist organisations, insurgent groups and other non-state actors who oppose democratically elected governments. The treaty also does not ensure a "balance of obligations" between arms exporting states and the importers of arms.

As a country with a pacifist strategic culture, India has traditionally abhorred the export of arms and itself refrained from doing so for several decades after independence. India has

39 Ordnance factories, which are wholly government owned, and eight Defence Public Sector Undertakings (DPSUs). India's defence exports are less than two per cent of the total production of weapons and equipment and were valued at USD 191 million (Rs 859.60 crore) in 2008-09. These are mainly indigenously produced surplus small arms and light weapons that have been supplied to some of India's neighbours as a goodwill gesture. However, the new Defence Procurement Policy (DPP) and the new Defence Production Policy (DPrP) are encouraging the formation of joint ventures with 26 per cent foreign direct investment (FDI). This is expected to go up to 49 per cent, gradually resulting in an increase in arms exports as MNCs will begin to use their Indian joint ventures as hubs for sourcing weapons and equipment components for their factories abroad.

India is likely to spend approximately USD 100 billion for the import of weapons and defence equipment over the next 10 years. The DPP stipulates an offsets commitment of 30 per cent of the total value of a contract if it exceeds USD 66 million (Rs 300.00 crore). In fact, the offsets obligation specified for the multi-mission, medium-range combat aircraft (MMRCA) is 50 per cent of the total value, which is estimated to exceed USD 12 billion. Assuming that 60 to 70 per cent of the import contracts will exceed USD 66 million, defence MNCs exporting to India will be required to procure items worth approximately USD 18 to 21 billion from Indian companies over the next 10 years by way of direct and indirect offsets. Even though the items that may be exported by these MNCs and joint ventures will be mainly components and not fully assembled weapons system, India needs to ensure that the stipulations of the ATT do not bar such exports.

South Asia is arguably the second most dangerous global hotspot after West Asia and radical extremism in the Af-Pak area is making the region further dangerous. One of the major reasons for this is the large-scale proliferation and easy availability of small arms and light weapons (SALW). India has witnessed around 152 militant movements since independence, of which 65 are believed to be still active in one form or the other. Pakistan is still the primary source of small arms that are India bound. It uses SALW as political and military tools against New Delhi and facilitates smuggling of SALW both through sea and land routes to ISI-supported terrorist organisations and sleeper cells across India. Funding for SALW proliferation can be accredited to money laundering and safe havens abroad organised through hawala channels. The transfer of small arms takes place mostly through clandestine routes and the grey market.

The Chinese angle to SALW proliferation in South Asia also cannot be ignored. Chinese weapons gained immense popularity among the insurgent groups in the region as they were competitively priced and low-level officials offered counter-trade agreements. The Chinese weapons pipeline soon permeated into Myanmar's underground markets along the Thai border. Beginning with the Type 56 rifle, China produced and offered for sale five different varieties of rifles (Type 56, 68, 79, 81 and 5.56 Type CQ), allied light machine guns and sub-machine guns. China also became the prime official supplier to Sri Lanka, Myanmar and Pakistan (including anti-aircraft and anti-tank weapons). Significantly, large numbers of weapons of Chinese origin have been seized in Cox's Bazaar in Bangladesh.

The Chinese supplied small arms to Indian insurgent groups in Manipur, Mizoram, Nagaland and Tripura for many years up to the late-1970s. In a statement with far reaching consequences, India's Home Secretary, G K Pillai, said on November 9, 2009, that the Maoists in India were receiving small arms from China, "Chinese are big suppliers of small arms..." Earlier, then Union Home Minister P Chidambaram had said in an interview in October 2009 that the Maoists were acquiring weapons through Bangladesh, Myanmar and possibly Nepal since the Indo-Nepal border is a porous border.

Since 1989-90, Indian security forces have seized huge stocks of arms and ammunition along the LoC in J&K alone. It has been documented that between 1990 and 2005, as many as 28,000 assault rifles of the AK-47 series; 1,300 machine guns; 2,000 rocket launchers; 365 sniper rifles; 10,000 assorted pistols; 63,000 hand grenades; seven million rounds of ammunition; 6,200 land mines and IEDs and 37,000 kg of explosives were recovered from various hideouts in J&K during counter-proxy war operations. Large-scale recoveries are still being made. Large numbers of illegal arms also comes into the country through the north-east and from the Khyber-Pakhtoonkhwa province (NWFP) on Pakistan's Afghan border. India finds itself at the centre of two major international weapons warehouses—the NWFP and the Southeast Asian arms market comprising Thailand, Cambodia and Myanmar, with approximately 13 identified gun-running routes close to India's north-eastern border areas and the Chittagong hill tracts.

Countries exporting arms have a responsibility to ensure that they do not provide weapons without strict end user verification or else SALW may be diverted to wage intra-state conflict by non-state actors. The ATT should have refrained from imposing new norms; it should have reinforced the existing obligations and responsibilities of all countries under international law and should have provided a mechanism for their effective application to the trade in SALW.

The present treaty is also deficient on monitoring and verification. While initially monitoring may have to rely on the good practices of the member states, viable technical means need to be developed over time. Subsequently, the treaty must make provisions for intrusive international monitoring of sources, means of transportation of weapons and, where possible, their end use based on formal complaints being launched by affected state parties. Such a system can only be implemented by constituting an international body like the IAEA.

India accords immense importance to compliance with arms control, non-proliferation and export control regimes, even though India is not a signatory to some of them. Hence, an initiative like the ATT, that seeks to establish a global benchmark, would under normal circumstances have been welcomed and supported, but the treaty has turned out to be discriminatory. The government of India has instituted stringent controls for the export of arms, including the requirement of an end-user certificate from the country to which SALW are to be exported. Each request is thoroughly vetted before an arms export license is cleared by the government.

India ensures that no arms are exported to countries that are involved in conflict, or to non-state actors engaged in intra-state conflict. In fact, most arms exports out of India so far have been those of goodwill gestures towards friendly countries in India's neighbourhood. Despite repeated requests from Sri Lanka and at the risk of driving it into Chinese or Pakistani arms, India had steadfastly refused to supply offensive weapons when the Sir Lankan armed forces were engaged in fighting the LTTE. Only non-offensive equipment like air defence guns and radars were supplied.

Elaborating on the complexity of small arms proliferation, former UN Secretary General, Kofi Annan had stated perceptively, "Small arms proliferation is not merely a security issue; it is also an issue of human rights and of development." The moral argument for an ATT, one that underpins human security, social and economic development is overwhelming. However, if it is viewed through the prism of disarmament or arms control instrument, it will not find much support. While India has not voted in favour of the ATT, it will undoubtedly adhere to all its provisions, much as it has done in respect of the NPT and the CTBT.

5

Defense Reforms in Rising India

For the past decade, pundits and commentators have showcased India as another rising Asian power like China. India's growing economy, larger international profile, and particularly its increased military spending, are seen as proof of India rising from being a regional power to perhaps a new Asian or even global power. Will India correspondingly move its military posture away from internal security and territorial defense, to emphasize power projection?

Many commentators have pointed to India's large military purchases as evidence that India is moving toward power projection and rivalry with China. Whether this is really happening is hotly debated in India. This chapter will look at the debate over defense and security reform in India and the establishment of India's first joint theatre command (for the Andaman and Nicobar Islands) as a test case.

India took an unprecedented step ten years ago by setting up a joint regional command for the Andaman and Nicobar Islands. The establishment of the Andaman and Nicobar Command (ANC) was perceived as evidence that India is starting to balance against a larger China by reforming its defence organization (Posen, The Sources of Military Doctrine; Rynning, Changing Military Doctrine). Although the ANC is a strategic location, India has historically avoided building up forces there and it has resisted building up power projection capabilities. Moreover, India has been reluctant to build jointness and joint operational commands, even though India's development of hard power capabilities are receiving increased attention. India provides an interesting case to examine different theories about how militaries learn. Realism and internal balancing (Posen), constructivism (Kier), and organization theories (Nagl, Bickle) will be used to see if they can explain why some actors have proposed change and others have opposed it. This study will also look towards Michael Raska's framework of a Diffusion Dynamics Model to help structure its analysis.

INDIA'S GROWING SOFT POWER

The drivers triggering a shift in China's India posture can be placed under the rubric of India's *hard power*. However, India's (re)rising *soft power* has also contributed to this shift in China's outlook a country's ability to alter the behavior of others through attraction rather than sticks or carrots. India has been a democracy right since its birth as a modern nation-state in 1947. However, its sluggish economic growth and weak military profile that led to its defeat in 1962 seriously tarnished this aspect of India's soft power. With the rising India story, its democracy as an important component of its soft power has again come into the global limelight.

India has more than 1 billion people. It is linguistically, culturally, racially, and religiously diverse, and it is growing economically at an enviable pace under democratic governmental institutions (except for the emergency period of 1975-77 when civil liberties were undermined). Its culture values peaceful coexistence, nonviolence, and religious tolerance. All of these factors, combined with the largest pool of English speakers outside the US, has increased India's power of attraction without need for coercion or persuasion, a fact not lost on an envious, hard power-minded China.

The country to which India has projected most of its soft power is the US, through the export of highly skilled manpower, consisting mainly of software developers, engineers, and doctors.

China has been keeping a close watch on the rising influence of the Indian community in the United States, especially over the last decade. In order to improve its own soft power in the United States, China has sent far more students to the United States than India. As per the Institute of International Education's annual report in the academic year 2009-10, out of 690,932 international students in the United States nearly 128,000 of them, or more than 18 percent, were from China while India sent only 107,897 students in the same academic year. However, with Oct 2011, educational exchanges between India and the US would rise much faster in the future.

THE ORIGIN OF THE RISING INDIA STORY

Admittedly, India shifted its foreign and economic policies soon after the end of the Cold War in 1991 when it started broadbasing its diplomacy, initiated economic reforms by dismantling the economic model based on *import substitution,* and went for market friendly policies. The economic reforms did give India economic stability in the sense that India started growing at 6% annually ever since the economic liberalization of early 1990s, however, political stability remained fragile. Once P. V. Narasimha Rao's government completed its five-year term in 1996, there was political chaos from 1996 to March 1998. From 1989 to 1999 8 governments came to power in New Delhi, six of them lasting less than a year and the shortest lasting for only 13 days. In fact, one of the reasons why India's candidature for the Asia Pacific Economic Cooperation (APEC) was rejected was its hung parliament in 1997.

The country got much-needed political stability at the centre when the BJP-led NDA (National Democratic Alliance) government came to office in March 1998 and took a series of radical initiatives in quick succession beginning with the nuclear tests in the Pokhran desert of Rajasthan on May 11th and 13th 1998, which, the author opines, was a *grand strategic masterstroke* (emphasis added) by independent India.

India initiated Multi-aligned/Great power diplomacy for the first time in its independent history when it developed strategic partnerships with all the great powers simultaneously, especially its relations with the its national security when it set up the National Security Advisory Board, National Security Council, Nuclear Command Authority, developed a nuclear doctrine, and so on.

More importantly, India developed a much-needed strategic vision whereby it redefined its geo-strategic construct well beyond the mainland of South Asia. The extended geo-strategic construct included the Indian Ocean, the Middle East, Central Asia and the Asia-Pacific.

The Chinese Perception of *Rising India*

China's perception of India has come full circle in that it started off treating India as a peer competitor, then it wrote off India as one, and again China has begun to treat India as a main strategic threat in its regional grand strategy. To illustrate this, despite all the rhetoric of *Asian Solidarity, Hindi-Chini Bhai-Bhai, civilizational dialogue* and so on in the 1950s or even earlier, the *realpolitik*-minded Chinese security planners had realized in their long term calculations that India, given its political, geographic, cultural, diplomatic, and demographic attributes, is going to be their main rival in constructing Asia as the *neo-Middle Kingdom*.

This apprehension was justified as India, despite the partition, was on a natural course to emerge as the predominant power in Asia due to its centrality in the British Empire, its geostrategic location in the Indian Ocean, its competent navy, and its diplomatic and cultural links with the Middle East, Southeast, and Africa. Not surprisingly, the first Asian Relations Conference was held in New Delhi in Mar-Apr 1947 and not in Beijing.

While China, in a sharp contrast, was ostracized by the international community, India's democracy and its non-alignment policy was a far more acceptable political and diplomatic model for the fledgling Third Finally Nehru's reconciliatory policy of acting as a bridge between East and West enjoyed far greater international legitimacy in a world that was trying to recover from two World Wars in a short period, than the Maoist Agenda of deepening the polarization between the two super powers by exporting revolutionary violence and intensifying the class struggle.

What was more troublesome for Maoist China was that India was destined be the main intermediary in the US-Soviet strategic game. After 1949, democratic India began to be seen as the main interlocutor by the USSR under Stalin because he had come to the conclusion that the US could not be militarily defeated, and so the next best option was negotiations. At the same time Stalin had mistrusted Mao since 1927. Similarly, the US shared its core political value with India, which was democracy. In short, communist China was becoming increasingly edgy and even jealous of India's growing *soft power* in this phase. The net result of these internal and external Indian positives was that China singled out India as its main competitor to the top of the Asian mountain.

With its military victory over India in 1962, China grabbed the initiative from India and projected itself as *primus inter pares* in the developing world. A hard power-minded China institutionalized this victory with its policy to use Pakistan as a strategic spoiler against India in South Asia soon after the 1962 war and openly sided with Pakistan in the 1965 war, as argued by Subhash Kapila .

The second shift in China's perception of India started when China entered the super power rivalry following Henry Kissinger's secret visit to China to see Chairman Mao Zedong in July 1971, which was followed by U.S. President Richard Nixon's visit to China in Feb 1972. China accepted the US offer to ally with permanent seat in the U.N. Security Council in 1971 replacing the Republic of China on Taiwan.

This strategic partnership further deepened under President Jimmy Carter and his anti-Soviet advisor Zbigniew Brzezinski. Brzezinski rewrote the rules of China-U.S. rapprochement and offered all advantages to China in return for its promise to confront the Soviets in the East. Under the Reagan administration their relations followed Carter's policies. In the early 1990s under President Bill Clinton, FDI flows to China increased from about US$5 billion a year in 1989 to US$20 billion by the late 1990's. The huge inflow of FDI converted China into a manufacturing giant.

The high point in the U.S.-China relationship was the signing of a nuclear deal in 1997. It was Clinton's welcome gift to Chinese President Jiang Zemin. This agreement further strengthened a 1985 U.S.-China nuclear cooperation agreement, which allowed exports worth billions of dollars of nuclear technology into China without hindrance. China, as an original member of the Nuclear-5 or "nuclear weapons states," could import everything for the commercial exploitation of nuclear technology.

Meanwhile India, in sharp contrast, was facing a reversal in fortune. Just as China was an international pariah until 1971, India was ostracized from international nuclear commerce after its nuclear detonation in 1974. Washington tailored new rules to punish India economically and diplomatically too. The new rules, enacted in 1978, denied India economic aid and nuclear technology.

It was in this context, in which India was subjected to international sanctions and also was grappling with its internal issues, while China remarkably enhanced its political, diplomatic, economic, and military clout that the latter no longer treated India as a strategic rival in Asia. However, things took a turn a third time and China had to again reorient its India stance. After its military victory over India in 1962 and the subsequent South Asia and never think of challenging China's predominant role in Asia. However, India undertook an array of path-breaking initiatives in quick succession in late 1990s (and beyond) to herald its arrival as a great power in the unfolding 21st century that removed this Chinese (mis)perception.

The year 1998 was an eventful year in terms of China rediscovering the Indian threat. India's annual 6% GDP growth in the 1990s and *de facto* nuclear power status made China review its traditional perception of India. What really stunned the Chinese, however, was India's first-ever *Multi-aligned diplomacy*, or what the Chinese defense analysts call *Great power diplomacy*, under which it developed strategic partnerships with all the major powers of the world concurrently, especially with the United States and later with Japan. When an economically better-off and nuclear-armed India ventured into the South China Sea (with possibly the United States' support) in October-November 2000 and conducted naval exercises with Vietnam and South Korea , China could no longer afford to rely solely on its proxy Pakistan to keep India confined within South Asia. China's strategic attention which was traditionally focused on the Asia-Pacific suddenly found an emerging security nightmare in the growing Indo-United States strategic partnership in South Asia, somewhat similar to the one during the Cold War between India and then Soviet Union.

Why did the traditional Chinese strategic posture of India shift?

Jing-dong Yuan opines that China used to dismiss India as a peer competitor, citing India's handicaps, like poverty, poor infrastructure, and sluggish bureaucracy. However Beijing is now paying increasing attention to India's drive for great-power status through robust diplomatic initiatives, a military buildup, Indo-US relations, and new regional initiatives. Based on similar Chinese writings on India, the author argues that the interplay of four factors led China to reorient its strategic perspective on India. They included, India's rising military profile, its poly/multi-aligned diplomacy, growing economic clout, and rising soft power.

INDIA'S DEFENCE POLICY

India inherited some defence industries from Great Britain. They included Hindustan Aeronautics Limited (HAL), which is today India's largest defence public sector undertaking (DPSU), Mazagon Docks Limited (MDL), the largest shipyard in the nation, and more than half a dozen ordnance factories. The growth of the domestic defence industry has, however, been sporadic since Independence. It did not follow any definite plan though emphasis was placed on enhancing indigenous defence production capability.

Some analysts have also traced certain vigorousness in the Indian effort at developing an indigenous defence capability to the early 1960s spawned by the 1962 India-China war. The war is seen as having underscored the urgency of building a domestic defence industry through foreign assistance. It was also in consonance with Nehru's policy of building a strong industrial base patterned on the Soviet model. But while the war with China has been identified as the catalyst in the effort at developing a domestic defence base, there was no concerted, systematic and well-orchestrated effort towards the achievement of this goal.

There were many factors that stood in the way of India building a strong military-industrial base. India's comparatively easy access to various types of defence equipment from the former Soviet Union (FSU) and their purchase against deferred rupee payments and on "friendship" price were some of them. Sophisticated defence equipment was transferred to India under the favourable rupee-rouble arrangements from FSU. Some license production facilities were also established in India, for instance for the Mig-21 aircraft. The Cold War also ensured that India continued to have a favourable and preferred source of defence systems and equipment from FSU. It did not find the superpower wanting in any critical manner in fulfilling India's defence requirements. However, this had the unintended consequences of dampening any sense of urgency in India to develop an indigenous defence industry. Coupled with this was the reluctance of the US to help in India's effort to develop a domestic defence production base. Nevertheless, trudging along, India was able to develop the largest defence industry among developing nations.

However, with the collapse of the FSU, India lost easy access to sophisticated defence equipment at cheap prices. The problem was compounded by the absence of an alternate source of modern defence equipment. The situation became worse with the almost complete disruption in the supply of services and spare parts necessary to maintain the predominantly Soviet-equipped Indian armed forces. The navy was particularly affected, as it was dependent on Soviet designs and equipment for some of the ships that were under construction in India. This led to huge cost and time overruns in the indigenous construction programme of naval vessels.

Ironically, the need to service and maintain various kinds of equipment imported from FSU compelled India to seek ways and means to develop some level of indigenous capability. Towards this goal, certain technologies and know-how were obtained, both for the repairs and for the local production of some critical spare parts. These efforts were, however, largely case-specific and were not components of any systematic strategy for the comprehensive development of an indigenous defence industry. They were also service-driven in the absence of any coherent strategy to achieve self-reliance. However, the liberalisation of the Indian economy that almost coincided with the collapse of FSU and promised to unlock India's productive capabilities gave impetus to the goal of developing a domestic military-industrial complex.

It was, however, not until 2005 that India formulated a defence offset policy to contribute to the nation's goal of developing its domestic defence industry. This policy was incorporated in the Defence Procurement Procedure (DPP) 2005. The policy introduced a 30 per cent offset in contracts valued above Rs 3 billion under "buy" and 'buy and make" categories.

Under the policy, foreign vendors had the liberty to discharge their obligations either through the execution of defence exports of Indian items and services or through investments in India's defence infrastructure. They also had the option of selecting Indian firms in consultation with an industry associate of their choice to implement their offset obligations. The hallmark of this policy was its non-obligatory nature, or in other words, these offsets were non-mandatory. It was left to the Services Capital Acquisition Plan Categorisation Committee (SCAPCC) to recommend the incorporation of offset obligation in acquisition proposals. The offset policy was, however, in the nascent stage and it lacked clarity in many areas. It also suffered from the absence of any designated agency in the Ministry of Defence (MoD) for guiding, overseeing, executing and monitoring the implementation of the policy. In reality, confusion reigned in equal measure in the corridors of South Block as in the minds of the vendors on how to implement the offset obligations. Consequently, the offset policy did not yield any dividend.

The absence of any offset benefit to the Indian defence industry led the Government of India (GoI) to make significant changes in DPP 2006 and they included the following:

- offset was made mandatory in defence contracts of the size and nature as prescribed in the 2005 policy;
- foreign firms were allowed the flexibility of forming joint ventures (JVs) with Indian firms, and;
- a new organisation called the Defence Offset Facilitation Agency (DOFA) was established comprising of representatives of all stakeholders; the Services, DPSUs, Defence and Research Organisation (DRDO), etc.

Defence Offsets

Offsets have been variously defined. In essence, offsets in defence, as in civil trade, are compensations that a buyer seeks from the seller for the purchase of goods and/or services. The demand for offsets in defence has exhibited an upward trajectory since the 1950s. It gained further momentum in the 1980s and has been growing ever since. From around 20 nations about two decades ago, this practice has now been now adopted by more than 130 nations. European nations have been able to generate more offsets than others. During the period 1993-2004, European countries were able to obtain offsets valued at 99.1 per cent of their defence imports while non-European countries achieved 46.6 per cent of their imports. Significantly, 72.9 per cent of the offsets obtained by European nations were 100 per cent or more of the value of the weapon systems imported by them. The data on arms sales and offsets show that demands for offsets "are increasing over time in all regions."

India was, however, late in adopting an official offset policy though it had obtained some compensatory benefits since Independence through a series of bilateral arrangements. It was only in 2005 that the nation, through its Defence Procurement Procedure (DPP), announced an official policy to secure offsets for its defence imports. The policy was amended to give it greater clarity and direction in 2006 and again in 2008. Consequently, as a late entrant in the field, India's polices are yet to be fully tested against the complex process of managing offsets and it is yet to traverse the path of achieving its declared objective of creating a vibrant military-industrial base.

Objective of Paper

This paper seeks to critically examine the salient features of India's offset policy and answer the following questions.

- Will the policy outlined in DPP 2008 contribute substantially to the development of a military-industrial base in India?
- What are the shortcomings of the policy?
- What modifications are required in the offset policy and connected government procedures to maximise the benefits that can accrue to the nation from capital acquisition of defence equipment?

In order to understand the basic arguments contained in this paper, a few concepts relating to offsets in general and in defence trade in particular are explained.

Offsets Explained

Offset, as the term implies, is an element that counterbalances or compensates an act. It is a set-off from a development, in this case, military acquisition. However defined, the term offset primarily signifies an element of 'compensation' as the predominant import of the term. It occurs "when a supplier places work to an agreed value with firms in the buying country, over and above what it would have brought in the absence of the offset." As is commonly understood, in trade, offsets have been classified as direct or indirect offsets. Direct offsets are those that are directly connected with the item being sold by the seller and can take the form of co-production, component production, licensed production, etc. Indirect offsets are those not directly related to the product being imported and here compensations can be secured in any other area with the aim of obtaining for the economy what would otherwise have not been available to the buyer but for the purchase.

Though the above two forms characterise the two widely-accepted compensatory strategies, it is necessary to add a new terminology to describe a hybrid form of offsets that is between the direct and indirect offsets that India is seeking to obtain. This may be termed as quasi-direct offsets. It can be defined as compensation given in the sector under which the purchase falls, but is not directly connected with the product that is being imported. For instance, when tanks are imported, and the offset is obtained in the form of assistance for the co-production of a warship, then it will fall within this definition (quasi-direct) as it enhances the defence capability of the importing nation, though the compensatory arrangement is not directly connected with the item being imported. Therefore, though analysts have largely described India's policy as seeking direct offsets, it would be more accurate to describe it as quasi-direct offsets.

MAJOR TRANSITION IN INDIAN DEFENCE POLICY

Recently the US journal Defence News reported that the Indian government is working on a program whereby Israel would replace Russia as India's largest supplier of weapons and defence equipment by 2008. Since Russia now supplies some 70 percent of India's weapons imports, this report, if true, would mark a major transformation in Indian defence policy. Under the terms of the program, India would identify the products it wants and ask the Israeli government to negotiate with domestic firms on its behalf as Jerusalem does with regard to its own weapons. Israel is already the second-largest supplier of military systems to India, so this program could affect a major transformation in India's security relationships. The potential repercussions of this project, which would clearly show a serious break with Moscow's arms salesmen, are immense. Given the deep ties between the US and Israeli defence industries, if this program does materialize it will also probably enhance the United States' competitive position in the Indian defence market and result in further substantial increases in the already rising amount of US arms sales and security cooperation with India. Those sales could either be bilateral or brokered through Israel, such as weapons made jointly by Israel and the United States, including missile defence systems that India reportedly is interested in acquiring.

This program would then also strengthen the developing tripartite relationship among Israel, India, and the US in regard to defence sales. We can see this already occurring, because the United States has brushed aside Pakistan's objections to India's receiving the Israeli Phalcon radar, made with US technology and thus subject to US veto on its transfer to a third party.

Realization of the projected Indo-Israeli project would also simultaneously symbolize and express India's rising continental Asian status as a great power with interests and capabilities across the continent, allowing it to break free of its confining chains as merely a major South Asian power if not the regional leader, something that both Indian and foreign observers have labeled as a prerequisite for a full partnership with the United States. Not only would those trends strengthen Indo-Israeli ties, they would provide fuel to the oft-reported desire on the part of at least some US elites to create a tripartite alliance with India and Israel against terrorism (if not for other, broader objectives that would emerge later). Joint Indo-Israeli defence collaboration on a scale envisaged above would also, or so these advocates hope, tie into the US alliance and Israeli partnership with Turkey, creating a kind of pan-Asian bloc. The new program grows out of India's difficulty in negotiating a US$10 billion multi-year defence acquisition program with Russia. Three areas in particular seem to have caused some anxiety in New Delhi.

In March 2002, The Times of India reported that the Parliamentary Standing Committee had urged the government to avoid overdependence on Russia for armaments and spare parts. The committee reportedly acknowledged Russia's previous contributions and reliability as a provider of defence equipment to India but cautioned that the current dependence on Moscow for almost 80 percent of its arms imports is unhealthy. It also observed that Russia was not providing military hardware on the same beneficial financial terms that it had during the Soviet era. Therefore the committee also urged the Indian government to cease making advance payments for weapons acquisitions from Russia, and that in the future it seek to put more defence contracts up for competitive tender. Russia also has come under criticism because of India's difficulty in obtaining and negotiating speedy delivery of spare parts for these weapons systems. At the same time it became clear that given its worsening relations with Pakistan, India is seeking to diversify its foreign purchases and use foreign partners to develop its own defence industrial capability, eg by conditioning purchases on obtaining offsets from the sellers to develop its own indigenous capability. The alliance, if it were to materialize, would build on the already greatly improved Indo-Israeli relationship that has led to large-scale military sales from Israel and to India's rapprochement with the United States as well. As the Phalcon deal suggests, it could become possible to envisage tripartite collaboration among these states on missile defence, especially if India's great goal of securing the end to all US sanctions on the transfer of both civil and military technology is realized.

Moreover, the broadening of India's ties and reach in political-military terms through the acquisition of top-quality defence systems would enable it to play the kind of role that analysts in both India and the US postulate as being essential to any serious strategic partnership with the United States. And that role also accords very much with some of the deepest aspirations of India's foreign and defence policy elites, thus highlighting a congruence of visions concerning India's future international position.

In effect India's aspiration to play a major role "from Socotra to Sumatra" would have been both realized and blessed by the United States, as Secretary of State Colin Powell implicitly suggested in 2001. India would then become not just a South or even Central Asian power but a major player in the Persian Gulf, the Middle East, and Southeast Asia.

At the same time, India's search for new vistas in defence acquisition and production relates very much to its rising economic, technological, and military-industrial capabilities as well as to its desire to strengthen existing long-standing partnerships, eg with Russia. For example, beyond the existing $10 billion weapons sales from Russia to India, India is collaborating with Russia on joint production of a fifth-generation fighter that Russia feels vital to its military future. Both are also collaborating on research that is probably tied to missile defence and nuclear systems as well. More broadly, India is the only country with whom Russia is collaborating on joint production of sophisticated and futuristic weapons systems. Likewise India, not China, gets the best weapons currently being produced in Russia, systems that not even Russia's armed forces can obtain. Moscow offers offsets in the form of technology transfer of production skills and know-how to India, one of its largest customers. Although India obviously seeks to diversify its sources of foreign procurement, Russian producers have until now been confident of their ability to obtain the bulk of Indian defence contracts.

Whether or not this confidence is misplaced, time will tell, but diversification and strengthening of India's own capabilities surely would increase India's scientific-technological and manufacturing capabilities for weapons production. This objective also appears to be a major goal of the deals now being made with Russia, Israel, and presumably the United States. We see similar deals with Italian and French firms for joint manufacture of weapons systems.

India's leading defence firm, Hindustan Aeronautics Ltd (HAL), is also pressing an outsourcing program whereby it would help private Indian companies find and choose foreign partners to undertake such high-tech projects as avionics integration, weapons-system integration, and other related efforts to "lay the foundation for a credible domestic aerospace industry base that could meet the majority of India's military aerospace requirements in the next 10 years".

And it is no less logical to assume that India would be thrilled to duplicate this particular kind of relationship with Washington, especially as India already has a large space program with military applications and very much wants US conventional-weapons systems and technology transfer.

Indeed, a Pentagon-commissioned study of Indo-American perceptions reported that on the basis of many interviews, a uniform conclusion was reached that "for Indians, technology transfer from the United States is military cooperation's touchstone".

Other Indian assessments confirm the great importance that India attaches to transfer of both civil and defence technology as a critical and essential element in any partnership with the US. While India's aspirations in the defence industry are common to other countries that seek the capability for indigenous production of most, if not all of their weapons, it is nevertheless clear that this deal, if it materializes, would utterly transform defence relationships among major players in the defence business: India, the US, Israel, and Russia. The major transformations in Asian security that accelerated after September 11, 2001, have clearly not yet run their course. Nor is it clear when the overall Asian situation will stabilize or when also the rising tide of weapons sales will abate.

CHALLENGES IN DEFENCE PLANNING

Defence planning is essentially a subset of overall national level planning in the political, economic and social spheres and has to be evolved in the context of global and proximate factors affecting the nation.. It has also to take into account the philosophy and ethos animating the national psyche; in other words the historical and cultural forces which have shaped the collective memory and outlook of the people over the centuries. The Cold War, was a classic example of the factors stated above. There were fundamental philosophical differences between the adversaries – the western bloc, advocating the virtues of free enterprise and its own interpretations of democracy, and the Soviet bloc, equally strongly asserting the merits of the socialist system as the only one genuinely meeting democratic aspirations and assuring social equality and economic well-being of the people as a whole, rather than for a few. Fifty years of the Cold War could not conclude the capitalism-socialism debate, though, in the end, it did push the socialist forces into, perhaps temporary, retreat. This was because the struggle was really for power and domination.

"The evil empire" of Ronald Reagan's description may have withered away, but the necessity for the US to target the so called "rogue states" has not disappeared. Many examples can be found of philosophical differences leading to stand-offs, usually with the USA as one of the parties. The USA-Cuba divide is a long-standing one. USA-Venezuela stand-off is just developing and resonating in other Latin American countries. Sometimes the differences are couched in the language of anticipated threats, such as in US-North Korea, or US-Iran relations. The true reasons and underlying causes are buried in verbiage and obfuscation. A more serious rift has developed over the selective and poorly conceptualised US war on terrorism, launched for spurious reasons in Iraq, when the real source of terror was elsewhere and far more complex.

Differing religious beliefs and rigidities are often cited as causes but do not sufficiently explain conflicts within the same religion, as between Protestants and Catholics in Northern Ireland or the Shias and Sunnis in Iraq and elsewhere. Planning for the security and defence of a vast country like India with its particular geographic location, historical experiences and associations, social, ethnic, religious and cultural diversity, political and economic structure and a large, relatively poor, democratically governed population, is a complex and challenging task. It is rendered more so in the context of the national and international situation in the last sixty years or so, embracing post-World War II de-colonisation, partition, the creation of Pakistan and later Bangladesh, conflicts with Pakistan and China, the Cold War and its aftermath, the disintegration of the Soviet Union, the re-definition of NATO's role, and of most recent and decisive significance, the September 11, 2001 terror attack on the United States mainland. This last factor is significant because it resulted in a major re-orientation in US foreign policy.

Strategic Overview

Planning for defence pre-supposes identification of threats and contingencies. Until about five years ago, the strategic situation for India was difficult but relatively clear. Pakistan was a definite threat, conventional, clandestine and nuclear. China was a strategically reducing threat, though its international power, influence and economy were growing. Uncertainties in Bangladesh and Nepal required us to be vigilant for fall-out effects. There were problems in the north-east of insurgent groups exploiting the ethnic ties and jungles in Myanmar, and the destabilising spill-over effects of the activities of the Liberation Tigers for Tamil Eelam(LTTE) in Sri Lanka. The presence in our proximate waters, of non-littoral naval forces in substantial numbers, such as those of the US, which has been traditionally supportive of Pakistan, had to be taken cognisance of. Also the fact that warfare at sea, because of its distinctive characteristics of rapidity of concentration and dispersal of forces, mobility, flexibility and speed of execution, requires a different, longer term approach to threat assessment.

Strategically the global situation is now evolving in a manner less inimical to India's interests than in the preceding fifty years. Yet the end of the Cold War did not see any easing of pressures on India.

On the contrary, economic sanctions and technology denials were increased so as to coerce India to conform to norms of international behaviour prescribed by dominant world powers, led by the US and the European Union on the one hand and

China on the other. The reason was the desire of the P-5, the five permanent members of the UN Security Council, who are also the N-5, the self-certified nuclear powers, to preserve their monopoly power status in the face of India's challenge through the nuclear tests of 1998. Yet, the re-evaluation of foreign policies by leading powers set off by the September 11, 2001 terrorist attack on the USA, has initiated processes that are, by and large, beneficial to India. An indication of this is the US declaration of seeing India as a strategic partner for the 21st century, and its efforts to legislate exceptions to its domestic laws to allow supply of nuclear materials for peaceful civilian use to India by the cartel operated by the Nuclear Suppliers Group (NSG).

Nearer home, the pathological hostility of the Pakistanis establishment towards India is rooted in its quest for a national identity, which no novel interpretations, distortions or reinventions of sub-continental history seem able to provide. It will be a long time before there can be normal relations with Pakistan because they are influenced more by the internal contradictions and dynamics of the Pakistani state rather than considerations of mutual benefits through good relations. Since the Pakistan army is the self-appointed guardian of the undefined "ideology of Pakistan", normalcy will come when the Army decides it should be so; or the cost-benefit equation alters.

With China, there is perceptible progress on resolving disputes and fostering economic and cultural relations. As for Nepal, Bangladesh, Myanmar and Sri Lanka, there is no significant positive change, and because of shared borders, internal problems in those countries will continue to spill over into India. Instability in Afghanistan remains a cause of concern, especially because of Pakistan's dubious role, and this will have its impact on the pursuit of India's energy and strategic interests in Central Asia.

Non-littoral naval forces in significant numbers are still present in the Indian Ocean, but there is no coercive or inimical intent as in the past. Indeed, the Indian Navy holds regular friendly exercises with them on a routine basis. China's long term plans for a naval presence in the region have to be taken note of. There are ample signs of Chinese maritime interest, starting from building and operating communications facilities in Myanmar to financing and building Pakistan's Gwadar Port on the Makran coast, collaboration in building warships for the Pakistan navy at Karachi shipyard, as well as port building in Sri Lanka. On the western rim of the Indian Ocean, China is vigorously pursuing options in Africa, underlined by the meeting of 49 heads of state/government in Beijing in early November this year.

National Objectives in the Long Term

Planning for defence has to be in the framework of national objectives over a period of decades ahead, even if these are not publicly articulated. USA does not hesitate to state its intention to remain the dominant global technological, space and military power for the foreseeable future and tailors strategic policies accordingly. China has, by its actions, investments and developments over the years, demonstrated that it intends to be at least the equal of the USA, though with "Chinese characteristics". Pakistan makes no secret of its intention to be "different" from India, and to compete with and undermine India at every opportunity.

India too has shown in various ways that it intends to be in the forefront of nations in every sphere: economic, technological, industrial and human development. What about military capability? Does it wish to have only a capacity to ward off aggression by land and sea? Or does it aspire to play a larger role in the region? If it emerges as the world's third or fourth largest economy in a few years, would a commensurate military role follow? Or are national objectives to be largely achieved by a combination of diplomacy and economic policies? If it aspires for a permanent seat in the UN Security Council, is it prepared for the increased diplomatic and military responsibilities attached? Many of these seemingly philosophical issues require to be debated to facilitate meaningful defence planning for the future.

6

India's Rising Economic Power 2030

US intelligence has predicted that in 2030, India could be the rising economic powerhouse of the world as China is seen today and that it will continue to consolidate its power advantage over Pakistan.

"In 2030 India could be the rising economic powerhouse that China is seen to be today. China's current economic growth rate - 8 to 10 per cent - will probably be a distant memory by 2030," said the fifth installment of the 'Global Trends 2030: Alternative Worlds', of National Intelligence Council (NIC), released on Monday.

As the world's largest economic power, China is expected to remain ahead of India, but the gap could begin to close by 2030.

"India's rate of economic growth is likely to rise while China's slows," said the report which is aimed at providing a framework for thinking about the future. According to the report, the total size of the Chinese working-age population will peak in 2016 and decline from 994 million to about 961 million in 2030.

"In contrast, India's working-age population is unlikely to peak until about 2050," it said.

"Also of significance, India will most likely continue to consolidate its power advantage relative to Pakistan. India's economy is already nearly eight times as large as Pakistan's; by 2030 that ratio could easily be more than 16-to-1," the US report said. The NIC report said the diffusion of power among countries and from countries to informal networks will have a dramatic impact by 2030, largely reversing the historic rise of the West since 1750 and restoring Asia's weight in the global economy and world politics.

In a tectonic shift, by 2030, Asia will have surpassed North America and Europe combined in terms of global power, based upon GDP, population size, military spending, and technological investment.

China alone will probably have the largest economy, surpassing that of the United States a few years before 2030.

According to the NIC report, the World Bank assesses that India will join China as an "emerging economy growth pole" by 2025, which could help to strengthen the global economy.

"India's expected robust growth in the next 15-20 years means that its contribution to global growth will surpass that of any individual advanced economy except the United States," it said.

World Bank modeling suggests that together China and India will serve as nearly twice the engine for growth as of the United States and the euro zone combined by 2025, the report said.

India, however, faces many of the same problems and traps accompanying rapid growth as China: large inequities between rural and urban sectors and within society, increasing constraints on resources such as food and water, and a need for greater investment in science and technology in order to continue to move its economy up a notch, the report said.

India's democracy provides it with a safety valve for discontent in a way that China's one-party rule does not.

"At the same time, regional tensions between India and many of its neighbors could threaten India's rise should such tensions explode in conflict and confrontation," it said.

"As with China, a sharp economic downturn-particularly propelled by a political or military crisis-could quickly have broader regional and global effects," it added. NIC report said long-term forecasts show Indian economic power growing steadily throughout the 21st century and overtaking China at the end of the century because of China's maturing age structure.

"To maximize its advantage from the greater proportion of youths, however, India will need to boost its educational system, both attainment and quality at lower levels; make substantial governance improvements, particularly in countering corruption; and undertake large-scale infrastructure program to keep pace with rapid urbanization and the needs of a more advanced economy," it said.

The NIC report notes that the current, largely Western dominance of global structures such as the UN Security Council, World Bank, and IMF probably will have been transformed by 2030 to be more in line with the changing hierarchy of new economic players.

"Besides the large emerging powers like Brazil, India (who are not permanent UNSC members), and China (has a veto in UNSC, but not IMF voting rights commensurate with its economic power), many second-tier emerging powers will be making their mark-at least as emerging regional leaders," it said.

"Just as the larger G-20-rather than G-7/8- was energized to deal with the 2008 financial crisis, we expect that other institutions will be updated-most probably also in response to crises," the report said.

Meanwhile, the economies of Europe, Japan, and Russia are likely to continue their slow relative declines, it said.

According to the report, by 2030, no country - not even US, China - will be a hegemonic power.

"Enabled by communications technologies, power almost certainly will shift more toward multifaceted and amorphous networks composed of state and non-state actors that will form to influence global policies on various issues," it notes.

The NIC report believes that in the world of 2030 - a world in which the growing global population will have reached somewhere close to 8.3 billion people (up from 7.1 billion in 2012) - four demographic trends will fundamentally shape, although not necessarily determine, most countries' economic and political conditions and relations among states.

These trends are: aging both for the West and increasingly most developing states; a still significant but shrinking number of youthful societies and countries; migration, which will increasingly be a cross-border issue; and growing urbanisation, which will spur economic growth but place new strains on food and water resources.

Among the US Census Bureau's projections for South Asia, only Afghanistan is projected to remain youthful by 2030.

However, the aging that will occur among the large and growing populations in nearby Pakistan and India probably will mask youthful ethnic and regional populations that could remain a security concern, it said.

"In India, where the southern states and large cities have attained low fertility, youthfulness - which can contribute to instability in the absence of employment outlets - is likely to erode more slowly in the central northern states of Uttar Pradesh and Bihar," the NIC report said.

EFFECTS OF GLOBALIZATION ON MACRO-ECONOMIC BALANCES

Analyzing the data in pre-globalization and post-globalization periods, Olekalnsa and Cashin (2000) concluded: Indian government revenue and expenditure data indicates that adherence to the inter-temporal budget constraint has not characterized Indian fiscal policy. These results provide support for the moves towards fiscal consolidation, which occurred since the early 1990s. However, it is important to note that the reforms are unlikely to have led to a sustainable path for the debt stock. This is despite the fact that the size of the budget deficit as a proportion of GDP has fallen since 1991. Following the reforms, deficits have been financed through borrowings in a relatively less regulated financial market. As domestic markets have been liberalized, the cost of domestic borrowing has increased and concessional external financing has become a smaller proportion of total borrowing. This has led to a major increase in interest liabilities and to an increase in the debt-to-GDP ratio. Further fiscal consolidation may well be required if Indian public finances are to be consistent with debt sustainability.

Effects of Globalization on the Foreign Sector

The immediate cause to launching of NEP was the foreign sector, the foreign exchange reserve and trade imbalance. If we look at the statistical trends, we find that the post-globalization period exhibits a comfortable position of India.

Gold reserves jumped from 300 million US $ to around 4000 million US dollars. There was steep growth in foreign currency assets and foreign currency reserves, well near 1000 times. The outstanding repurchase obligations to IMF reduced steeply. Exports as well as imports shot up manifold; percentage of import to export reduced substantially. Trade in international sector as a percentage to the national income increased and became much more stable than what it was in the immediate past to globalization.

Some Macro-economic Indicators in the Domestic Sector

The foreign sector is as yet a tiny part (about 5-6 percent) of the national income of India. The growth of gross domestic product, although impressive, did not take up any significant acceleration. If we measure the logarithm of GDP against time, we observe a linear growth. Thus, the impact of globalization on structural changes so as to accelerate the growth rate of GDP has been meager. Contribution of agriculture to the GDP continued falling at the pre-globalization rate and thus we find a linear trend in the fall of the percentage contribution of agriculture. The percentage contribution of the secondary sector to the total GDP continued increasing at more or less constant rate, indicating that the post-globalization era did not bring in any structural change.

The statistical trends in gross savings and capital formation indicate that the traditional log-linear growth, set in the early sixties of the last century, continued. However, indications are there to structural changes as to the source of savings. Rate of savings (as percentage to GDP) in the household sector accelerated, while the said rate of savings (as percentage to GDP) in the public sector decreased. Savings in the Private corporate sector have shown an increase. Gross fixed capital formation has lagged behind the gross domestic savings.

Agriculture after Globalization: The statistics of area under 12 major crops in India covers about 95 percent of area under cultivation. The data indicate that after globalization, the area under cultivation has increased. However, the area under food crops as percent to the total area under cultivation has decreased. More so, the area under coarse (food) crops as percentage to total area under cultivation (as well as the total area under food crops) has decreased. This trend indicates a shift of the Indian Agriculture to cash crops and in the food grain sector to the finer crops. As pointed out by Swaminathan (2002), such changes have affected the poorer section of the society adversely.

Components of Agricultural Growth

We use Minhas-Vaidyanathan decomposition scheme with 1991-92 prices (Wi) of major crops for decomposition analysis of agricultural growth. Among the percentage contributions of different components of agricultural growth, the contribution of area under cultivation after globalization remains as prominent as before globalization.

INDIA'S MODI ARTICULATES VISION FOR ECONOMIC CHANGE

India's government is moving away from the populist approach of previous administrations that used handouts to win over different groups and generate voter support, Prime

Minister Narendra Modi said. "This has become an almost settled way of doing politics in India," Mr. Modi said in a speech at the Council on Foreign Relations on Monday. "But India's young people don't want to live on dole-outs anymore. They want to be treated differently." Mr. Modi, who came to power in a landslide victory in May, articulated a broad vision for economic change, saying he was determined to rise above "small interests to focus on good governance."

His statements point to a shift in political thinking in a country governed for most of its post-independence history by the Congress party, which in the past decade expanded entitlements for the poor and farmers. It is unclear how far Mr. Modi will be willing to go to reorient economic policies. He is unlikely, for instance, to reduce food subsidies,which benefit a majority of Indians. Nor has he indicated how quickly he wants to enact change.

While saying he didn't subscribe to a "populist approach to economic management," Mr. Modi underscored the limits of reform in a country that is still plagued by abject poverty. When asked about his government's widely criticized blocking of a trade agreement at the World Trade Organization over a separate discussion on food security, Mr. Modi said, "I can't keep my people hungry."

India told the WTO in July that it won't sign on to a trade-facilitation agreement unless a deal is reached on the issue of stockpiling food grains. Steps like this and an underwhelming budget have led critics to accuse Mr. Modi's four-month-old government of sending mixed messages about reform and not moving boldly enough to retool India's sputtering economy.

Government ministers say they don't want to push policies bound to be opposed or get stuck in Parliament. Their approach, they say, is to gradually create consensus and support for economic change. Mr. Modi said his government had already started working on some politically difficult decisions, such as amending labor laws blamed for restraining the manufacturing sector. He said the federal government welcomes initiatives by state-level administrations to start amending the laws that burden companies with many regulations, including those that make it difficult to fire workers. He must also tackle a land-acquisition law that has been a major concern among businesses.

"We are moving forward with responsibility on even those issues that may not be seen as politically expedient," Mr. Modi said. "Ultimately, those steps will benefit everyone."

He is seeking to woo U.S. businesses to invest in India to help kick-start growth. Before speaking at the Council on Foreign Relations, Mr. Modi had meetings with executives of U.S. businesses, including Boeing , IBM and MasterCard , in which he promised to get rid of bureaucratic delays and make tax policies more stable.

In a number of speeches on his U.S. visit, he has pitched India as a provider of labor for an aging world and a potential manufacturing hub, saying India was uniquely positioned for exponential growth.

"India has three D's: democracy, demographic dividend and demand," Mr. Modi said. "No other country in the world has all these three things."

WILL NARENDRA MODI'S ECONOMIC DIPLOMACY WORK?

Driving around Lutyens' Delhi these past few months has been a commuters' nightmare and a Vexillologists' delight - the city has seen hundreds of flag changes to honour visits by heads of state who have trooped in and out of the city (it's protocol to display the flag of the visiting country head along-side the Indian flag on the road leading up to Rajpath, South Block, airport, and at all meeting venues).

The historic city dotted with its mausoleums, architectural relics, forts has resembled a fortress on several occasions - with heightened security, traffic checkpoints and choked roads as Prime Minister Narendra Modi, huddled in meetings, realigns India's passage to the world.

The most recent visitor to the capital was the President of China, XI Jinping, who gave a commitment to realise $20 billion investment from China in the next five years and a reduction in the awfully skewed trade balance. China's exports to India were at a paltry $3,019 million, whilc India imported Chinese goods worth $13,744 million between April-June 2014/15.

India's current account deficit has been and continues to be a reason of enormous worry for economists - CAD is a measure of a country's trade - while the deficit narrowed to 1.7 per cent of GDP in the first quarter of 2014/15 to $7.8 billion from $21.8 billion a year earlier, as exports rose 10.6 per cent compared with a 1.5 per cent decline a year earlier, imports fell 6.5 per to $116.4 billion on the back of a 57 per cent fall in gold imports. Non-gold imports, however, rose 1.3 per cent as against a decline of 0.6 per cent in corresponding quarter of 2013/14.

"Effectively, nothing has changed. A lot of gold is coming through the hawala route, it has shifted from visible to invisible. Industry has grown quite import dependent. We should be able to push exports and explore newer markets. We have been talking about it, we have to match talk with concrete actions," observes Biswajit Dhar, Director General of Research and Information System of Developing Countries.

Professor N.R. Bhanumurthy of National Institute of Public Finance and Policy terms a current account deficit of 1.7 per cent with 4.5 per cent growth "a major concern". "This is despite negative growth in imports. Imports are still high and IIP (Index of Industrial production) is low. A CAD of one per cent would be comfortable with a below five per cent growth rate," he adds.

Successively, over the years, India's leadership has inadvertently pushed services over manufacturing , and reclaiming India's position as a manufacturing hub, as articulated by the Prime Minister on several occasions, to increase the share of manufacturing from 15 per cent to 25 per cent of GDP will also entail reducing industry's dependence on imports, apart from a host of other factors centred around facilitating ease of doing business in a nation where businesses spend anything between 19 and 29 per cent of their total expenses on meeting regulatory requirements, as compared to

10 per cent in business friendly countries. "From agarbatis (incense sticks) to Ganesha idols, everything is coming from China, because it is cheaper to import than manufacture here. Traders are making money selling these things cheap. In the last decade about two million jobs were lost in the handicraft sector," laments former home and commerce secretary G.K. Pillai. "He (PM) has to take much tougher decisions against those who are only importing, somebody has to feel the pinch," he adds.

While Chinese lights decorate Indian homes during Diwali and Chinese apples deluge Indian fruit marts, China is yet to allow import of India's basmati rice.

It is India's ability to wrestle such nitty-gritty that will form the basis of success or failure of Modi's big economic diplomacy push. India is not new to capitalise on foreign relations to further economic interest, but to say that the last few years in particular saw foreign-economic policy hang in a limbo will not be an exaggeration.

Accelerating a foreign-economic policy that had been static for too long has been a job well done. The sequencing of Modi's engagements starting with immediate neighbours, followed by Japan, China and the United States gives out several messages - it's clear that Modi has established India's immediate neighbours as number one priority -a move crucial for India to further its geopolitical-economic interest. Defining an economic policy with our neighbourhood is perhaps something we are doing for the first time.

"The message to Nepal and Bangladesh that we also want to be partners is very significant. Our future lies in how we are able to harness the markets in our neighbourhood, for potential the sky is the limit, the entire East Asian region is very important," adds Dhar.

Observers say that sequencing of the visits is an effort to create competition among superpowers to compete for investment in India. "He has reached out to everyone equally (Japan, China, US), they will be forced to wait and watch which way will India tilt," adds Bhanumurthy.

India's investment in Nepal and Bhutan's hydropower sector would mean that Nepal will be in a position to send surplus power to India, but something can really concretise after Nepal has a constitution in place. With Bangladesh, the Prime Minister will have to change his stance and move forward on the Teesta water sharing agreement rather quickly. Normalisation of trade relations between Sri Lanka, Pakistan and Nepal will remain tricky for border tensions.

Moreover, the Modi-led National Democratic Alliance will also have to clean up after the largesse of the UPA's free trade agreements signed between India and Korea, Japan and ASEAN. Almost with all the countries, FTAs have meant that India has become a net importer. A review of how India has benefited from these FTAs has been called for by the new administration and some of these issues can be addressed through dialogue.

What adds to the worry of whether India will be able to go beyond talk are doubts on intellectual bandwidth of the government. While Modi during his campaign had highlighted the need to take the states along, he is yet to call a meeting with state chief ministers who will play an integral role in facilitating and enabling cross-country and cross-border trade. The previous government, economists and policy observers say, was quick to call experts to voice their opinions but this government has been rather frugal with sourcing of expertise in such matters of detail and significance.

But Modi has the rest of the year to convince the naysayers that words do translate into action. Many suspect that the PM will get moving on the reform agenda after state elections in Maharashtra. "He is the first PM born post partition. He is not from a land-locked state, which really frees up India's economic diplomacy agenda," says an optimistic Executive Director of Gateway House, Manjeet Kriplani.

"Mr. Modi as CM also would do a lot of economic diplomacy, his was one state which would attract foreign investors. He is a master of art of economic diplomacy-and the beauty of this is that here nobody is a loser," says BJP's Vice President and General Secretary of Bharatiya Janata Party, Ram Madhav, echoing the view of Modi believers. The spectacle at the legendary Madison Square Garden in the US also drove home the point that the stage is set for India to perform and now is as good a time as any for the PM to get off the rotating stage and get down to nuts and bolts. For instance, details of how's of economic diplomacy could emerge from the new administration's foreign trade policy whose release has been delayed twice.

INDIA'S ECONOMIC DIPLOMACY

WITHOUT MUCH ado, a new trend is quietly transforming the nation's foreign policy — economic diplomacy. The reforms initiated in 1991 and some intensive recent efforts have begun to have an impact on our external relations that few could have visualised. Negotiation of liberal trading arrangements with key nations, large-scale national investments in the hydrocarbon sectors of other countries, focus on developing transport infrastructure in the neighbourhood, India's new role as an economic donor, and the focus on mega projects such as natural gas pipelines cutting across our borders have significantly transformed our foreign policy template.

The popular debate on foreign policy, however, remains focussed on the political. Since the nuclear tests of 1998, much of India's diplomatic energy had gone into managing the fallout. War and peace with Pakistan, addressing the political differences with China, handling the unending tensions with the smaller neighbours, the concerns with cross-border terrorism, and creating strategic partnerships with major powers have been the stuff of India's recent diplomacy. While these issues continue to dominate the agenda, issues of trade, access to markets in the region and beyond, energy security, and the imperatives of regional economic integration have opened up unprecedented prospects for a recasting of India's external relations.

The Indian discourses on foreign and economic policies tended to be compartmentalised in the past, although the latter was not completely absent in the conduct of the former. Economics played a different role then. The quest for hard currency was a major foreign policy concern. Indian missions in the developed world had to ensure that there was enough aid flowing through bilateral and multilateral channels to bridge the foreign exchange gap. Negotiating cheap and reliable oil contracts with producer countries was another task. Within the Non-Aligned Movement and in the Group of 77 at the United Nations, India took the lead in articulating the need for "collective self reliance" and raising the demand for a restructuring of the international economy to suit the needs of the developing countries. This multilateralism however came to a nought thanks to India's relative decline in the global economy. Despite talk of collective self-reliance, there was very little commercial activity between India and the developing world in general. Even historical economic links within the neighbourhood got disconnected in the first few decades of Indian foreign policy.

But all that is changing. A look at India's current position at the World Trade Organisation might suggest the opposite. While India remains loathe to opening up its markets under pressure at the WTO, it certainly has been willing to loosen control over its economic space through a variety of bilateral free trade arrangements. India is aware that opening up its own markets to the outside world is inevitable over the long term. New Delhi hopes that bilateral free trade arrangements will let this happen in a controlled manner and give Indian industry time and space to compete in markets around the world in the coming years. While maintaining a tough posture at the WTO, India is negotiating a rash of preferential and free trade agreements with a number of countries.

To the east, PTAs with Thailand and Singapore are in an advanced stage of negotiation. India has also promised to work out trade liberalisation with the Association of South East Asian Nations over the next decade. India has agreed to initiate a study on comprehensive economic cooperation with China. As the ASEAN itself negotiates free trade agreements with China, Japan and South Korea, the idea of a larger framework that includes India presents itself. It is not impossible to visualise an Asian economic community built around Japan, ASEAN, China, India and South Korea (JACIK), an idea that is already floating around. While Asian unity has long been a dream for Indian foreign policy, there is an opportunity for the first time to give it concrete economic shape. JACIK could emerge as an economic bloc that can be compared with the expanded European Union and the North American Free Trade Area.

India's trade and economic cooperation initiatives are by no means limited to East Asia. To its west, India already has a PTA with Afghanistan and another is under consideration with Iran. The countries of the Gulf Cooperation Council (GCC) are looking at creating a trading bloc and are interested in working out common trade liberalisation with India. When the South African President, Thabo Mbeki, arrives in New Delhi in October, India will be signing a framework agreement on trade liberalisation with the South African Customs Union, a regional grouping led by Pretoria. India is also engaged in trade talks with Latin American regional groupings, where Brazil is the dominant player. In a recent initiative, India, South Africa and Brazil decided to explore common economic interests through mutual cooperation as well as develop a united front in multilateral organisations. With South Africa and Brazil close to a PTA, the triangular economic cooperation among three large emerging powers has an exciting future.

But nowhere is the geopolitical significance of emerging economic diplomacy more significant than in the subcontinent and the extended neighbourhood. The highly successful Free Trade Agreement with Sri Lanka could become the trendsetter for future economic cooperation in the subcontinent. Commercial flows between the two have increased nearly threefold since the agreement was signed in 1998. That there is a long way to go is reflected in the fact that Sri Lankan trade with the United States is larger than it is with India. By reducing Sri Lanka's import-export ratio with India from 16:1 in 1998 to 5:1 in 2002, the FTA has demonstrated that trading with the larger neighbour would not be inimical. India is all set to expand the FTA with Sri Lanka and hopes to begin discussions on free trade with Bangladesh shortly.

The Indo-Sri Lankan trade experience shows that the economic integration of the subcontinent is at hand, if India is willing to be more creative in its policies towards the neighbours. With massive trade surpluses in India's favour, it is in New Delhi's interest to offer greater market access and facilitate investment in the neighbourhood. India, which thunders against the protectionism of the developed world, remains a relatively closed market to its neighbours despite the recent changes. Our neighbours have genuine complaints about tariff and non-tariff barriers in accessing the Indian market. India can take a leaf out of Brazil's book in making a strategic decision to allow trade surpluses in favour of its neighbours. The political benefits of such a move are indeed immense.

As trade flows expand in the region, the focus has inevitably turned to transport infrastructure. India has begun to invest in road-building in Myanmar that will link it to South East Asia. New Delhi has also committed resources to building a transport corridor through Iran to Afghanistan, in a bid to overcome the political barrier that Pakistan has been to regional economic integration. Iran will also become the gateway to Russia and Europe through the North-South Corridor that is being developed. The historic Silk Route between India and China will be opened shortly to link Sikkim and Tibet. Sri Lanka has been interested in building a land bridge to India that can move people and goods. At the same time, transport links with Nepal and Bangladesh are in an awful shape and demand immediate political attention.

Energy security considerations have moved India from being a mere buyer of petroleum products to a major investor in "equity oil" around the world from Sakhalin to Sudan. And the size of its petroleum market has given it a powerful card in shaping the politics of natural gas pipelines in the region. Sections of the Indian establishment have begun to see the strategic value of economic diplomacy but it is yet to spread across and filter down to the operational level. India is in a position today to leverage access to its big market to bring down barriers within the subcontinent and between South Asia and the extended neighbourhood. The story of India's economic diplomacy has barely begun. For generations of Indians, the begging bowl has been an important symbol of Indian diplomacy. It is refreshing to see New Delhi now offer large credit lines across the world and help others make progress. To derive the full political benefits of economic diplomacy, the leadership will have to act decisively to break the old mindset, which defines national security and trade policy in separate and narrow terms. If the Government can bring together the disparate strands of its economic diplomacy and give it bureaucratic coherence and political purpose, India would dramatically enhance its standing in the region and beyond in the coming years.

ECONOMIC DIPLOMACY

Economic diplomacy is a form of diplomacy. Economic diplomacy is the use of the full spectrum economic tools of the state to achieve its national interest. Economic diplomacy includes all the economic activities, including but not limited to export, import, investment, lending, aid, free trade agreements etc.

Economic diplomacy is concerned with economic policy issues, e.g. work of delegations at standard setting organizations such as World Trade Organization (WTO). Economic diplomats also monitor and report on economic policies in foreign countries and give the home government advice on how to best influence them. Economic diplomacy employs economic resources, either as rewards or sanctions, in pursuit of a particular foreign policy objective. This is sometimes called "economic statecraft".

Background and Definitions

Economic diplomacy is traditionally defined as the decision-making, policy-making and advocating of the sending state-business interests. Economic diplomacy requires application of technical expertise that analyze the effects of a country's (Receiving State) economic situation on its political climate and on the sending State's economic interests.

The Sending State and Receiving State, foreign business leaders as well as government decision-makers work together on some of the most cutting-edge issues in foreign policy, such as technology, the environment, and HIV/AIDS, as well as in the more traditional areas of trade and finance. Versatility, flexibility, sound judgment and strong business skills are all needed in the execution of Economic Diplomacy.

a. Scope: International and Domestic economic issues – this includes the "rules for economic relations between states" that has been pursued since the World War II. And owing to the increased globalization and the resultant interdependence among state during the 1990s obliges "economic diplomacy to go deep into domestic decision making" as well. This covers "policies relating to production, movement or exchange of goods, services, instruments (including official development assistance), money information and their regulation" (Bayne and Woolcock (eds) 2007)

b. Players: State and non-state actors – As all government agencies that have economic mandates operate internationally and are players in economic diplomacy though they do not describe them as such. Further, non-state actors such as NGOs that are engaged in economic activities internationally are also players in economic diplomacy (Bayne and Woolcock (eds) 2007). Businesses and investors are also actors in the process of economic diplomacy, especially when contacts between them and governments are initiated or facilitated by diplomats.

Berridge and James (2003) state that "economic diplomacy is concerned with economic policy questions, including the work of delegations to conferences sponsored by bodies such as the WTO" and include "diplomacy which employs economic resources, either as rewards or sanctions, in pursuit of a particular foreign policy objective" also as a part of the definition.

Rana (2007) defines economic diplomacy as "the process through which countries tackle the outside world, to maximize their national gain in all the fields of activity including trade, investment and other forms of economically beneficial exchanges, where they enjoy comparative advantage.; it has bilateral, regional and multilateral dimensions, each of which is important".

Senkaku Islands Dispute

After the widely reported incident near the Senkaku Islands in 2010, over which Japan, China and Taiwan all claim sovereignty, China engaged in coercive economic diplomacy. In response to the dispute, China blocked all shipments of rare earth minerals to Japan, harming their economy.

2010 Nobel Peace Prize

In response to the 2010 Nobel Peace Prize going to Chinese dissident Liu Xiaobo from the Norwegian Nobel Committee, China froze free trade agreementnegotiations with Norway and imposed new veterinary inspections on imports of Norwegian salmon. This caused the volume of salmon imports fromNorway shrunk 60 percent in 2011.

2012 Incident with the Philippines in the South China Sea

Recently, China has become more assertive in its claim that the South China Sea is part of its territory. This has caused several disputes with the seven sovereign states who also claim part of the South China Sea as their own territory. In one such dispute, China and the Philippines engaged in a standoff over the Scarborough Shoal in which Navy vessels were sent in. In retaliation to this territorial conflict, China engaged in coercive economic diplomacy by blocking Philippine bananas from entering Chinese ports, as well as slowing down the inspections of apayas, mangoes, coconuts, and pineapples from the Philippines. Philippine businessmen pressured their government to stand down. According to Manila, Chinese Vessels now block the entrance to the lagoon, preventing any Philippine ships from entering, in another example of China using coercive economic diplomacy.

United States

The United States has a long history of economic diplomacy dating back to the dollar diplomacy of William Howard Taft. The United States was also central to perhaps the most important economic diplomacy event, the Bretton Woods Conference where the International Monetary Fund and International Bank of Reconstruction and Development were created. The United States was involved in one of the more notable acts of economic diplomacy in history with the Marshall Plan. Though it has always played an important role, Economic diplomacy has took on increased importance during the first term of President Barack Obama under the leadership ofSecretary of State Hillary Clinton.

During a major policy speech as Secretary of State, Clinton stated that economic statecraft is at the heart of (the American) foreign policy agenda. Secretary of State Clinton sees economic development and democratic development as inextricably linked. In her speech she stated explained the importance of its success: "we happen to believe that our model is not only the best for us; we think it embodies universal principles, human aspirations, and proven results that make it the best model for any country or people. Now, there can be variations on how it's implemented, but we are in this competition to win it. We want to make clear that it's not only good for America but it's good for the rest of the world to pursue democratic and economic reform." Clinton laid out the stakes as such: "If people don't believe that democracy and free markets deliver, then they're going to be looking elsewhere for models that more readily respond to their daily needs." Secretary Clinton saw pursuing mutually beneficial trade between the United States and other areas of the world as central to the American diplomatic agenda. She went on to detail the American strategy for several significant regions.

Secretary of State Clinton's regional economic diplomacy strategies

On Russia: "Even in a U.S.-Russia relationship dominated for decades by politics and security, we are now focused on helping Russia join the World Trade Organization, and we are putting a special premium on protecting freedom of navigation and a rules-based approach to resource development in places like the South China Sea and the Arctic Ocean."

On Europe: "Together, America and Europe account for half of the world's economic output, but just one-third of global trade. We can and we should be trading more. At theTransatlantic Economic Council, too often we re-litigate regulatory differences when we ought to be resolving them and avoiding new ones. And this frustrates companies on both sides of the Atlantic. The Transatlantic Economic Council is the forum where we try to resolve these differences, and I believe harmonizing regulatory schemes between the United States and the EU is one of the best ways we can both enhance growth, enhance exports, and avoid duplicative costs. But if you spend weeks arguing about the size of a jar for baby food, that's not exactly facing up to the potential of the payoff that comes from resolving these issues."

On China: "We also need to promote the free flow of capital, too. Investment in both directions, backed by well-enforced rules, is vital to creating growth and jobs here at home. For example, last year, the Kentucky-based company that owns KFC and Pizza Hut, two iconic American brands, actually made more money selling pizza and fried chicken in China than in the United States.

But this creates jobs at headquarters in Louisville and it creates jobs as well in China. When Tom Friedman warns that the Chinese will "eat our lunch," I'm not sure that's what he had in mind."

On the Middle East: "Consider the transitions underway in Egypt, Tunisia, and Libya. If we want to see democracy take root, which we do, we have to bring advanced tools to bear to help countries reform economic systems designed to keep autocrats and elites in power. And we know that aid alone, no matter how generous, is not enough. We need a sophisticated effort to integrate the region's economies, to promote investment, and to assist in economic modernization. This is the logic behind the Middle East proposals that the President laid out in May, which I have been urging Congress to support. To succeed, the Arab political awakening must also be an economic awakening."

On Latin America: "we are also making it a priority to engage with the Latin American jaguars, if you can call them that, which grew by more than six percent last year. Our free trade agreements with Panama and Colombia move us closer to our ultimate goal of a hemispheric trade partnership reaching from the Arctic to the tip of Argentina."

On the Pacific Basin: "...we will continue to use the Asia Pacific Economic Cooperation Forum, which President Obama will host next month in Hawaii, to push the envelope on open, free, transparent, and fair trade across the Pacific basin."

India

India has engaged in economic diplomacy primarily through the use of trade and aid. For example, in order to build a stronger, more stable relationship with Bangladesh, India granted it an $800 million soft loan, and provided $200 million in aid. India set up a development wing in its government in January 2012. The Development Partners Administration (DPA), is a primary way India uses economic diplomacy, in this case development aid, as a way to engage diplomatically. The DPA is building 50,000 housing units in Sri Lanka, a large transmission line in Puli Khumri, Afghanistan, and extends Lines of Credit projects globally, particularly in Africa.

Economic diplomacy and the DPA are very important to Indian foreign policy. As the former Indian foreign secretary Lalit Mansingh stated: "The fact that the DPA division is located in the ministry of external affairs shows it is in sync with our foreign policy objectives of transforming India into a global player".

IMPACT OF GLOBALIZATION ON INDIAN ECONOMY

Indian economy had experienced major policy changes in early 1990s. The new economic reform, popularly known as,

Liberalization, Privatization and Globalization (LPG model) aimed at making the Indian economy as fastest growing economy and globally competitive. The series of reforms undertaken with respect to industrial sector, trade as well as financial sector aimed at making the economy more efficient. With the onset of reforms to liberalize the Indian economy in July of 1991, a new chapter has dawned for India and her billion plus population. This period of economic transition has had a tremendous impact on the overall economic development of almost all major sectors of the economy, and its effects over the last decade can hardly be overlooked. Besides, it also marks the advent of the real integration of the Indian economy into the global economy.

This era of reforms has also ushered in a remarkable change in the Indian mindset, as it deviates from the traditional values held since Independence in 1947, such as self reliance and socialistic policies of economic development, which mainly due to the inward looking restrictive form of governance, resulted in the isolation, overall backwardness and inefficiency of the economy, amongst a host of other problems. This, despite the fact that India has always had the potential to be on the fast track to prosperity.

Now that India is in the process of restructuring her economy, with aspirations of elevating herself from her present desolate position in the world, the need to speed up her economic development is even more imperative. And having witnessed the positive role that Foreign Direct Investment (FDI) has played in the rapid economic growth of most of the Southeast Asian countries and most notably China, India has embarked on an ambitious plan to emulate the successes of her neighbors to the east and is trying to sell herself as a safe and profitable destination for FDI.

Globalization has many meanings depending on the context and on the person who is talking about. Though the precise definition of globalization is still unavailable a few definitions are worth viewing, Guy Brainbant: says that the process of globalization not only includes opening up of world trade, development of advanced means of communication, internationalization of financial markets, growing importance of MNCs, population migrations and more generally increased mobility of persons, goods, capital, data and ideas but also infections, diseases and pollution.

The term globalization refers to the integration of economies of the world through uninhibited trade and financial flows, as also through mutual exchange of technology and knowledge. Ideally, it also contains free inter-country movement of labour.

In context to India, this implies opening up the economy to foreign direct investment by providing facilities to foreign companies to invest in different fields of economic activity in India, removing constraints and obstacles to the entry of MNCs in India, allowing Indian companies to enter into foreign collaborations and also encouraging them to set up joint ventures abroad; carrying out massive import liberalization programs by switching over from quantitative restrictions to tariffs and import duties, therefore globalization has been identified with the policy reforms of 1991 in India.

THE IMPORTANT REFORM MEASURES

Indian economy was in deep crisis in July 1991, when foreign currency reserves had plummeted to almost $1 billion; Inflation had roared to an annual rate of 17 percent; fiscal deficit was very high and had become unsustainable; foreign investors and NRIs had lost confidence in Indian Economy. Capital was flying out of the country and we were close to defaulting on loans. Along with these bottlenecks at home, many unforeseeable changes swept the economies of nations in Western and Eastern Europe, South East Asia, Latin America and elsewhere, around the same time. These were the economic compulsions at home and abroad that called for a complete overhauling of our economic policies and programs. Major measures initiated as a part of the liberalization and globalization strategy in the early nineties included the following:

Devaluation: The first step towards globalization was taken with the announcement of the devaluation of Indian currency by 18-19 percent against major currencies in the international foreign exchange market. In fact, this measure was taken in order to resolve the BOP crisis Disinvestment-In order to make the process of globalization smooth, privatization and liberalization policies are moving along as well. Under the privatization scheme, most of the public sector undertakings have been/are being sold to private sector

Dismantling of The Industrial Licensing Regime At present, only six industries are under compulsory licensing mainly on accounting of environmental safety and strategic considerations. A significantly amended locational policy in tune with the liberalized licensing policy is in place. No industrial approval is required from the government for locations not falling within 25 kms of the periphery of cities having a population of more than one million.

Allowing Foreign Direct Investment (FDI) across a wide spectrum of industries and encouraging non-debt flows. The Department has put in place a liberal and transparent foreign investment regime where most activities are opened to foreign investment on automatic route without any limit on the extent of foreign ownership. Some of the recent initiatives taken to further liberalize the FDI regime, inter alias, include opening up of sectors such as Insurance (upto 26%); development of integrated townships (upto 100%); defense industry (upto 26%); tea plantation (upto 100% subject to divestment of 26% within five years to FDI); enhancement of FDI limits in private sector banking, allowing FDI up to 100% under the automatic route for most manufacturing activities in SEZs; opening up B2B e-commerce; Internet Service Providers (ISPs) without Gateways; electronic mail and voice mail to 100% foreign investment subject to 26% divestment condition; etc. The Department has also strengthened investment facilitation measures through Foreign Investment Implementation Authority (FIIA).

Non Resident Indian Scheme the general policy and facilities for foreign direct investment as available to foreign investors/

Companies are fully applicable to NRIs as well. In addition, Government has extended some concessions especially for NRIs and overseas corporate bodies having more than 60% stake by NRIs.

Throwing Open Industries Reserved For The Public Sector to Private Participation. Now there are only three industries reserved for the public sector.

Abolition of the (MRTP) *Act,* which necessitated prior approval for capacity expansion.

The removal of quantitative restrictions on imports.

The reduction of the peak customs tariff from over 300 per cent prior to the 30 per cent rate that applies now.

Wide-ranging financial sector reforms in the banking, capital markets, and insurance sectors, including the deregulation of interest rates, strong regulation and supervisory systems, and the introduction of foreign/private sector competition.

IMPACT OF THE GLOBAL FINANCIAL CRISIS ON INDIA COLLATERAL DAMAGE AND RESPONSE

The global economic outlook deteriorated sharply over the last quarter. In a sign of the ferocity of the down turn, the IMF made a marked downward revision of its estimate for global growth in 2009 in purchasing power parity terms – from its forecast of 3.0 per cent made in October 2008 to 0.5 per cent in January 2009. In market exchange rate terms, the downturn is sharper – global GDP is projected to actually shrink by 0.6 per cent. With all the advanced economies – the United States, Europe and Japan-having firmly gone into recession, the contagion of the crisis from the financial sector to the real sector has been unforgiving and total. Recent evidence suggests that contractionary forces are strong: demand has slumped, production is plunging, job losses are rising and credit markets remain in seizure. Most worryingly, world trade – the main channel through which the downturn will get transmitted on the way forward – is projected to contract by 2.8 per cent in 2009.

Policy making around the world is in clearly uncharted territory. Governments and central banks across countries have responded to the crisis through big, aggressive and unconventional measures. There is a contentious debate on whether these measures are adequate and appropriate, and when, if at all, they will start to show results. There has also been a separate debate on how abandoning the rule book driven by the tyranny of the short-term, is compromising medium-term sustainability. What is clearly beyond debate though is that this Great Recession of 2008/09 is going to be deeper and the recovery longer than earlier thought.

Emerging Economies

Contrary to the 'decoupling theory', emerging economies too have been hit by the crisis. The decoupling theory, which was intellectually fashionable even as late as a year ago, held that even if advanced economies went into a downturn, emerging economies will remain unscathed because of their substantial foreign exchange reserves, improved policy framework, robust corporate balance sheets and relatively healthy banking sector. In a rapidly globalizing world, the 'decoupling theory' was never totally persuasive. Given the evidence of the last few months – capital flow reversals, sharp widening of spreads on sovereign and corporate debt and abrupt currency depreciations- the 'decoupling theory' stands totally invalidated. Reinforcing the notion that in a globalized world no country can be an island, growth prospects of emerging economies have been undermined by the cascading financial crisis with, of course, considerable variation across countries.

Questions that will be Addressed

India too has been impacted by the crisis – and by much more than it was suspected earlier.

What I propose to do in the rest of my speech is to address the following four questions:

i. Why has India been hit by the crisis?

ii. How has India been hit by the crisis?

iii. How have we responded to the challenge?

iv. What is the outlook for India?

Why has India been Hit by the Crisis?

There is, at least in some quarters, dismay that India has been hit by the crisis. This dismay stems from two arguments.

The first argument goes as follows. The Indian banking system has had no direct exposure to the sub-prime mortgage assets or to the failed institutions. It has very limited off-balance sheet activities or securitized assets. In fact, our banks continue to remain safe and healthy. So, the enigma is how can India be caught up in a crisis when it has nothing much to do with any of the maladies that are at the core of the crisis.

The second reason for dismay is that India's recent growth has been driven predominantly by domestic consumption and domestic investment. External demand, as measured by merchandize exports, accounts for less than 15 per cent of our GDP. The question then is, even if there is a global downturn, why should India be affected when its dependence on external demand is so limited?

The answer to both the above frequently-asked questions lies in globalization. Let me explain. First, India's integration into the world economy over the last decade has been remarkably rapid. Integration into the world implies more than just exports. Going by the common measure of globalization, India's two-way trade (merchandize exports plus imports), as a proportion of GDP, grew from 21.2 per cent in 1997-98, the year of the Asian crisis, to 34.7 per cent in 2007-08. Second, India's financial integration with the world has been as deep as India's trade globalization, if not deeper. If we take an expanded measure of globalization, that is the ratio of total external transactions (gross current account flows plus gross capital flows) to GDP, this ratio has more than doubled from 46.8 per cent in 1997-98 to 117.4 per cent in 2007-08.

Importantly, the Indian corporate sector's access to external funding has markedly increased in the last five years. Some numbers will help illustrate the point. In the five-year period 2003-08, the share of investment in India's GDP rose by 11 percentage points. Corporate savings financed roughly half of this, but a significant portion of the balance financing came from external sources. While funds were available domestically, they were expensive relative to foreign funding. On the other hand, in a global market awash with liquidity and on the promise of India's growth potential, foreign investors were willing to take risks and provide funds at a lower cost. Last year (2007/08), for example, India received capital inflows amounting to over 9 per cent of GDP as against a current account deficit in the balance of payments of just 1.5 per cent of GDP. These capital flows, in excess of the current account deficit, evidence the importance of external financing and the depth of India's financial integration.

So, the reason India has been hit by the crisis, despite mitigating factors, is clearly India's rapid and growing integration into the global economy.

How has India been hit by the Crisis?

The contagion of the crisis has spread to India through all the channels – the financial channel, the real channel, and importantly, as happens in all financial crises, the confidence channel.

Let us first look at the financial channel. India's financial markets-equity markets, money markets, forex markets and credit markets-had all come under pressure from a number of directions. First, as a consequence of the global liquidity squeeze, Indian banks and corporates found their overseas financing drying up, forcing corporates to shift their credit demand to the domestic banking sector. Also, in their frantic search for substitute financing, corporates withdrew their investments from domestic money market mutual funds putting redemption pressure on the mutual funds and down the line on non-banking financial companies (NBFCs) where the MFs had invested a significant portion of their funds. This substitution of overseas financing by domestic financing brought both money markets and credit markets under pressure. Second, the forex market came under pressure because of reversal of capital flows as part of the global deleveraging process. Simultaneously, corporates were converting the funds raised locally into foreign currency to meet their external obligations. Both these factors put downward pressure on the rupee. Third, the Reserve Bank's intervention in the forex market to manage the volatility in the rupee further added to liquidity tightening.

Now let me turn to the real channel. Here, the transmission of the global cues to the domestic economy has been quite straight forward – through the slump in demand for exports. The United States, European Union and the Middle East, which account for three quarters of India's goods and services trade are in a synchronized down turn. Service export growth is also likely to slow in the near term as the recession deepens and financial services firms – traditionally large users of outsourcing services – are restructured. Remittances from migrant workers too are likely to slow as the Middle East adjusts to lower crude prices and advanced economies go into a recession.

Beyond the financial and real channels of transmission as above, the crisis also spread through the confidence channel. In sharp contrast to global financial markets, which went into a seizure on account of a crisis of confidence, Indian financial markets continued to function in an orderly manner. Nevertheless, the tightened global liquidity situation in the period immediately following the Lehman failure in mid-September 2008, coming as it did on top of a turn in the credit cycle, increased the risk aversion of the financial system and made banks cautious about lending.

The purport of the above explanation is to show how, despite not being part of the financial sector problem, India has been affected by the crisis through the pernicious feedback loops between external shocks and domestic vulnerabilities by way of the financial, real and confidence channels.

How have we Responded to the Challenge?

Let me now turn to how we responded to the crisis. The failure of Lehman Brothers in mid-September was followed in quick succession by several other large financial institutions coming under severe stress. This made financial markets around the world uncertain and unsettled. This contagion, as I explained above, spread to emerging economies, and to India too. Both the government and the Reserve Bank of India responded to the challenge in close coordination and consultation. The main plank of the government response was fiscal stimulus while the Reserve Bank's action comprised monetary accommodation and counter cyclical regulatory forbearance.

Monetary Policy Response

The Reserve Bank's policy response was aimed at containing the contagion from the outside-to keep the domestic money and credit markets functioning normally and see that the liquidity stress did not trigger solvency cascades. In particular, we targeted three objectives: first, to maintain a comfortable rupee liquidity position; second, to augment foreign exchange liquidity; and third, to maintain a policy framework that would keep credit delivery on track so as to arrest the moderation in growth. This marked a reversal of Reserve Bank's policy stance from monetary tightening in response to heightened inflationary pressures of the previous period to monetary easing in response to easing inflationary pressures and moderation in growth in the current cycle. Our measures to meet the above objectives came in several policy packages starting mid-September 2008, on occasion in response to unanticipated global developments and at other times in anticipation of the impact of potential global developments on the Indian markets.

Our policy packages included, like in the case of other central banks, both conventional and unconventional measures. On the conventional side, we reduced the policy interest rates aggressively and rapidly, reduced the quantum of bank reserves impounded by the central bank and expanded and liberalized the refinance facilities for export credit. Measures aimed at managing forex liquidity included an upward adjustment of the interest rate ceiling on the foreign currency deposits by non-resident Indians, substantially relaxing the external commercial borrowings (ECB) regime for corporates, and allowing non-banking financial companies and housing finance companies access to foreign borrowing.

The important among the many unconventional measures taken by the Reserve Bank of India are a rupee-dollar swap facility for Indian banks to give them comfort in managing their short-term foreign funding requirements, an exclusive refinance window as also a special purpose vehicle for supporting non-banking financial companies, and expanding the lendable resources available to apex finance institutions for refinancing credit extended to small industries, housing and exports.

Government's Fiscal Stimulus

Over the last five years, both the central and state governments in India have made a serious effort to reverse the fiscal excesses of the past. At the heart of these efforts was the Fiscal Responsibility and Budget Management (FRBM) Act which mandated a calibrated road map to fiscal sustainability. However, recognizing the depth and extraordinary impact of this crisis, the central government invoked the emergency provisions of the FRBM Act to seek relaxation from the fiscal targets and launched two fiscal stimulus packages in December 2008 and January 2009. These fiscal stimulus packages, together amounting to about 3 per cent of GDP, included additional public spending, particularly capital expenditure, government guaranteed funds for infrastructure spending, cuts in indirect taxes, expanded guarantee cover for credit to micro and small enterprises, and additional support to exporters. These stimulus packages came on top of an already announced expanded safety-net for rural poor, a farm loan waiver package and salary increases for government staff, all of which too should stimulate demand.

Impact of Monetary Measures

Taken together, the measures put in place since mid-September 2008 have ensured that the Indian financial markets continue to function in an orderly manner. The cumulative amount of primary liquidity potentially available to the financial system through these measures is over US$ 75 bln or 7 per cent of GDP. This sizeable easing has ensured a comfortable liquidity position starting mid-November 2008 as evidenced by a number of indicators including the weighted-average call money rate, the overnight money market rate and the yield on the 10-year benchmark government security.

Taking the signal from the policy rate cut, many of the big banks have reduced their benchmark prime lending rates. Bank credit has expanded too, faster than it did last year. However, Reserve Bank's rough calculations show that the overall flow of resources to the commercial sector is less than what it was last year. This is because, even though bank credit has expanded, it has not fully offset the decline in non-bank flow of resources to the commercial sector.

Evaluating the Response

In evaluating the response to the crisis, it is important to remember that although the origins of the crisis are common around the world, the crisis has impacted different economies differently. Importantly, in advanced economies where it originated, the crisis spread from the financial sector to the real sector. In emerging economies, the transmission of external shocks to domestic vulnerabilities has typically been from the real sector to the financial sector.

Countries have accordingly responded to the crisis depending on their specific country circumstances. Thus, even as policy responses across countries are broadly similar, their precise design, quantum, sequencing and timing have varied. In particular, while policy responses in advanced economies have had to contend with both the unfolding financial crisis and deepening recession, in India, our response has been predominantly driven by the need to arrest moderation in economic growth.

What is the Outlook for India?

The outlook for India going forward is mixed. There is evidence of economic activity slowing down. Real GDP growth has moderated in the first half of 2008/09. The services sector too, which has been our prime growth engine for the last five years, is slowing, mainly in construction, transport and communication, trade, hotels and restaurants sub-sectors. For the first time in seven years, exports have declined in absolute terms for three months in a row during October-December 2008. Recent data indicate that the demand for bank credit is slackening despite comfortable liquidity in the system. Higher input costs and dampened demand have dented corporate margins while the uncertainty surrounding the crisis has affected business confidence. The index of industrial production has shown negative growth for two recent months and investment demand is decelerating. All these factors suggest that growth moderation may be steeper and more extended than earlier projected.

In addressing the fall out of the crisis, India has several advantages. Some of these are recent developments. Most notably, headline inflation, as measured by the wholesale price index, has fallen sharply, and recent trends suggest a faster-than-expected reduction in inflation. Clearly, falling commodity prices have been the key drivers behind the disinflation; however, some contribution has also come from slowing domestic demand. The decline in inflation should support consumption demand and reduce input costs for corporates. Furthermore, the decline in global crude prices and naphtha prices will reduce the size of subsidies to oil and fertilizer companies, opening up fiscal space for infrastructure spending. From the external sector perspective, it is projected that imports will shrink more than exports keeping the current account deficit modest.

There are also several structural factors that have come to India's aid. First, notwithstanding the severity and multiplicity of the adverse shocks, India's financial markets have shown admirable resilience. This is in large part because India's banking system remains sound, healthy, well capitalized and prudently regulated. Second, our comfortable reserve position provides confidence to overseas investors. Third, since a large majority of Indians do not participate in equity and asset markets, the negative impact of the wealth loss effect that is plaguing the advanced economies should be quite muted. Consequently, consumption demand should hold up well. Fourth, because of India's mandated priority sector lending, institutional credit for agriculture will be unaffected by the credit squeeze. The farm loan waiver package implemented by the Government should further insulate the agriculture sector from the crisis. Finally, over the years, India has built an extensive network of social safety-net programmes, including the flagship rural employment guarantee programme, which should protect the poor and the returning migrant workers from the extreme impact of the global crisis.

RBI'S POLICY STANCE

Going forward, the Reserve Bank's policy stance will continue to be to maintain comfortable rupee and forex liquidity positions. There are indications that pressures on mutual funds have eased and that NBFCs too are making the necessary adjustments to balance their assets and liabilities. Despite the contraction in export demand, we will be able to manage our balance of payments. It is the Reserve Bank's expectation that commercial banks will take the signal from the policy rates reduction to adjust their deposit and lending rates in order to keep credit flowing to productive sectors. In particular, the special refinance windows opened by the Reserve Bank for the MSME (micro, small and medium enterprises) sector, housing sector and export sector should see credit flowing to these sectors. Also the SPV set up for extending assistance to NBFCs should enable NBFC lending to pick up steam once again. The government's fiscal stimulus should be able to supplement these efforts from both supply and demand sides.

When the Turn Around Comes

Over the last five years, India clocked an unprecedented nine per cent growth, driven largely by domestic consumption and investment even as the share of net exports has been rising. This was no accident or happenstance. True, the benign global environment, easy liquidity and low interest rates helped, but at the heart of India's growth were a growing entrepreneurial spirit, rise in productivity and increasing savings. These fundamental strengths continue to be in place. Nevertheless, the global crisis will dent India's growth trajectory as investments and exports slow. Clearly, there is a period of painful adjustment ahead of us. However, once the global economy begins to recover, India's turn around will be sharper and swifter, backed by our strong fundamentals and the untapped growth potential. Meanwhile, the challenge for the government and the RBI is to manage the adjustment with as little pain as possible.

A NEW POWER PLAY: ECONOMIC DIPLOMACY AND STATE AUTONOMY IN INDIA

India is seriously contemplating the export of electricity to Pakistan and Bangladesh in a bid to reach out to its neighbours through 'power diplomacy'. The Indian states of Punjab and Tripura played a pivotal role in convincing New Delhi to do so, which raises the issue of whether state governments in India should have greater autonomy when it comes to managing its economic affairs.

India has indicated it is willing to export 500 megawatts of electricity to Pakistan and Bangladesh to help alleviate their energy crises. But there has been considerable opposition to the power-selling scheme, particularly in Pakistan. Jamaat-ud Dawah leader Hafiz Saeed and other hardliners in Pakistan have attacked Prime Minister Nawaz Sharif for agreeing to the scheme, stating that are there is 'no need to beg India'. Sceptics in India also feel that this is not a pragmatic decision, arguing that the country should first address its own energy crisis before exporting electricity to its neighbours.

It remains to be seen how and when the power trade will actually kick off, since negotiations for the scheme have gone on for far too long without yielding much success. What is encouraging, however, is that Punjab and Tripura, which share borders with Pakistan and Bangladesh respectively, have indicated their enthusiasm for the power-selling scheme — more so than the central government.

Deputy Chief Minister of Punjab Sukhbir Singh Badal discussed the idea of Punjab selling power to Pakistan during his visit there in November 2012. In June, an Indian delegation headed by Indian Joint Secretary Rita Acharya put forward the proposal of selling 500 megawatts of power to Pakistan. Pakistan, which is facing a serious energy crisis, was quick to accept the proposal.

Tripura Chief Minister Manik Sarkar has also urged the central government to push forward the proposal to sell electricity to Bangladesh. India is currently supplying power to the northeastern region of Bangladesh, which borders Tripura, from its power plant in West Bengal. But this alone cannot meet the energy demands in the region. Interestingly, both Manik Sarkar and Bangladesh have agreed to the power-selling scheme. India will sell electricity generated from the ONGC Tripura Power Company (OTPC) at Palatana on the condition that Bangladesh transport heavy power gears through its territory to Tripura.

The recent 'power diplomacy' by Punjab and Tripura raises a significant policy question: is it time for the central government in India to delegate certain responsibilities to the states? Poor diplomatic relations between the Indian government and its neighbours, as well as the lack of coordination between the central and state governments in India, is partly responsible for India's failure to develop stronger economic ties with its neighbours. Giving Indian states the power to determine their own economic affairs could certainly improve economic developments in the region. While foreign policy obviously plays a central role in the issue, it is time India infuses foreign policy with pragmatic solutions. India should take a leaf out of the Chinese model of economic diplomacy, where states — especially border states — are given substantial leeway when it comes to trade and commerce. Results of the past few years clearly show that these states are more likely to benefit from closer economic relationships with neighbouring countries when they are given more flexibility and latitude.

Instead of allowing the Ministry of External Affairs to drive economic ties with the neighbourhood, greater autonomy must be given to not just the ministries in charge, but the concerned department in the state itself. Rather than getting embroiled in semantics as foreign ministries often do, the concerned department is in a better position to deal with the critical issues. The bilateral economic engagement between India and Pakistan that commenced in April 2011 was a strong reiteration of this point. Commerce Secretaries from both sides avoided entangling themselves in complex issues and focussed on doables, such as the setting up of the Integrated Check Post at the Wagah-Attari border, giving a boost to bilateral trade via this route.

Small steps could be taken to give India's state governments more autonomy. For example, the central government could give branch secretariats in each state the same responsibilities as the Provincial Foreign Affairs Offices in China. Rather than involving India's Ministry of External Affairs in every communication between states and India's neighbours, these branch secretariats have the responsibility of handling basic logistical issues and preliminary negotiation. This way, branch secretariats can act as intermediaries between state and central governments.

State governments of border states should be given greater autonomy when it comes to economic investment and infrastructure projects. The central government could even set up a specific wing in India's Ministry of Commerce and Industry that works closely with state governments — especially border states — so that trade and infrastructure cooperation with neighbouring countries is not hampered by excessive bureaucracy.

'Power diplomacy' is no longer enough for Indian states to manage their own affairs. It is time for India's border states to be given more power and autonomy to improve economic ties with its neighbours.

7

Rising Defence Manufacturing in India

"We have the reputation of the largest importer of defence equipment.... We too need to increase our defence preparedness. We need to modernize our defence forces," Modi said.

He said that a strong Indian defence industry will make India more secure. It will have room for the public sector, private sector and foreign firms.

Make in India—the theme of Aero India 2015, derived from the government's larger campaign of the same name—aims to transform the country into a manufacturing powerhouse and advocates boosting of exports, and incentivize import substitution. The 10th international edition of the aerospace and aviation exhibition, which opened on Wednesday, runs till 22 February.

Inaugurating the air show on Wednesday, Modi said India will need about 200,000 skilled people in the defence and aerospace industry in 10 years. "There are studies showing even a 20-25% reduction in imports could directly add up to 120,000 highly skilled jobs," he said.

Modi said foreign companies can use India as an export hub and as part of a supply chain. The prime minister said India must bridge the gap between prototype and production. He said India needs to improve the acquisition and approval process and India will ensure that its technology does not fall into the wrong hands. The government, he said, is introducing a technology development fund and export policy has been made simple, clear and predictable.

He also said the government will ensure the tax system does not discriminate against domestic manufacturing in comparison to imports. India's goal is to provide a level-playing field for Indian and foreign firms. The government is introducing significant reforms to defence offset policies to enable high value exports, he added.

India's defence offset policy mandates that foreign contractors source components and systems from local vendors for at least 30% of the value of government orders above Rs.300 crore.

"Offset is a crucial instrument. I want India's offsets policy not as a means to export low-end products but to acquire state-of-art technology and skills," the prime minister said.

Modi said that India needs to increase defence preparedness as it has huge requirements to manage internal security. He said the air show is not a trade fair of defence equipment but a platform to showcase India's defence manufacturing sector. "More than 250 Indian firms and foreign firms are here. This is the largest ever air show."

The air show will also include sectors such as defence manufacturing and airport infrastructure besides aerospace, defence and civil aviation. There are around 72 military and civil aircraft on display at the show.

Among the foreign military aircraft on display are the F-15C Eagle, Lockheed F-16C, Boeing KC-135 Stratotanker, Boeing C-17 A Globemaster III, Boeing P-8A Poseidon, Rafale Dassault and EMB-145 I.

Foreign civil aircraft include Pilatus PC-12 NG, Dassault Falcon 2000, Phenom 100E, Boeing B75, A75, Viking, Catwalk, WASP, RRJ 95, EMB 505, Bell 407 GX Helicopter, King Air 350 ER, 19-seater Turbo Prop AI Industry, Zlin Z-50 LX, Oma Sud Sky Car, Dassault Falcon 7X and Dornier 228-New Gen. "If we could raise the percentage of domestic procurement from

40% to 70% in the next five years, we would double the output in our defence industry. Imagine the impact in terms of jobs created directly and in the related manufacturing and services sector," Modi said.

He said that the government is reforming defence procurement policies and procedures. "There would be a clear preference for equipment manufactured in India. Our procurement procedures will ensure simplicity, accountability and speedy decision-making," he said.

The government has raised the permitted level of foreign direct investment in the defence sector to 49%.

"This can go higher, if the project brings state-of-the-art technology. We have permitted investments up to 24% by foreign institutional investments. And there is no longer a need to have a single Indian investor with at least a 51% stake," Modi said.

Industrial licensing requirements have been eliminated for a number of items. Where it is needed, the process has been simplified, he said.

India is expecting a total defence budget allocation to be $620 billion between financial year 2014 and 2022 of which 50% would be on capital expenditure.

The annual opportunity for Indian companies—both public sector undertakings and private companies—is expected to reach $41 billion in size by financial year 2022 and $168 billion of cumulative opportunity between fiscal 2014 and 2022, driven by domestic and external demand.

This is according to a report released by the lobby group Federation of Indian Chambers of Commerce and Industry (Ficci) and financial services company Centrum Capital Ltd early February 2015. The report noted that the domestic defence sector spends have seen continuous underspending vis-à-vis budgets, due to procedural delays.

Majority of the spending were for maintenance and salaries of the forces rather than for buying new equipment.

In the aerospace value chain, there is significant movement and capability creation being seen at sub-system levels in aerostructures, avionics, and actuation and control, said Rahul Gangal, partner, aerospace and defence, Roland Berger Strategy Consultants, when asked about new capabilities added by the government in defence manufacturing.

"In the areas of engines and related components, India as a supply base is still nascent and development will take time. In the areas identified, there is capability that is evolving at multiple levels and across multiple technical and process competencies," Gangal said.

India is forecast to spend $250 billion over the next decade to upgrade its military, which still largely relies on Russian equipment it bought from the 1960s to the 1980s, and catch up with strategic rivals like China.

DEFENCE MANUFACTURING IN INDIA

The Indian tycoon and the founder of conglomerate Reliance Group, Anil Ambani, wants to make missiles, helicopters and submarines. His plan is to turn Reliance into a major defence company and he has already bid for INR 840 billion (EUR 11 billion) in government contracts, as per a recent report by the news agency-Reuters. Though Reliance Group is latest in the race, many defence firms are keen to 'Make in India'. A domestic telecom equipment maker Himachal Futuristic Communications (HFC) is one of the private firms eyeing defence projects. The company has already been granted industrial licences for a range of products which include electronic fuses, electro optical devices and communication equipment along with the permit for assembling electronic warfare systems, radars and design, development and manufacturing of aircraft, including helicopters, says Bela Banerjee, director, HFC.

With more than USD 200 billion (EUR 176 billion) capital expenditure expected in the next 8 to 10 years, and with one of the fastest growing defence budgets in the world at 10 to 11 pc growth rate, India focuses on strengthening defence facilities and building manufacturing capacity. Of late, the government has been on the mission. According to the department of industrial policy and promotion (DIPP), responsible for formulation and implementation of promotional and developmental measures for growth of the industrial sector, the commerce ministry has granted 333 industrial licences to private firms for defence manufacturing, which includes names like Mumbai based Micronel Global Engineers, Kolkata based Naistoco India and OIS Advanced Technology based in New Delhi. There are more familiar names too like, Punj Llyod Aviation, Bharati Shipyard, Ashok Leyland Defence Systems, AMW Motors and then there are big, established ones such as Bharat Forge, Tata Group, Larsen & Toubro (L&T), Mahindra Group, to name a few.

So, the reason for this rush to be part of the defence sector is mostly the result of Prime Minister Narendra Modi's emphasis on defence manufacturing as part of his 'Make in India' campaign. Last year, Modi said that with 60 pc of India's defence requirements met through imports, local defence production is at the heart of the 'Make in India' programme. Launched on September 25, 2014, the idea of 'Make in India' is now more than 20 months old.

Private players - the real beneficiaries

According to AK Gupta, secretary, department of defence production, ministry of defence, the private sector now has the opportunity to pick up a 25 pc share of defence production. "Around 25 pc of the defence PSUs (public sector undertakings) turnover can be off-loaded to the private sector, and the ministry has already de-licensed 60-70 pc of the production. PSUs in defence sector have a cumulative turnover of about INR 500 billion," he said during a conference at DefExpo which took place in Goa in March 2016.

"Under the 'Make in India' programme, the government has awarded 56 defence manufacturing permits to private sector entities in the past one year compared with 47 granted in the preceding three years," says Anurag Garg, director- strategy and defence leader at professional services network headquartered in London, PwC (PricewaterhouseCoopers), adding, "Make in India has become the new mantra in the

Indian defence industry and within the industry, private sector is the centre of attraction.

This is quite evident from some of the big measures taken so far like hike in the foreign direct investment (FDI) from the earlier 26 pc to 49 pc, streamlining of defence industrial licencing, rationalisation of taxes, etc. Ultimately, private sector is the biggest beneficiary."

"In the case of the INR 500 billion (EUR 6.6 billion) P-75I project for procurement of six conventional submarines for the Indian Navy, the Modi government has changed the previous government's decision to import two submarines, followed by four to be licence-manufactured by public sector shipyards, and decided to construct all the submarines in domestic shipyards, with the further provision that the private sector would be given a fair chance to compete to get the contract," says Col K V Kuber, independent consultant, aerospace and defence.

In an interview with a defence news portal, Jan Widerström, country head and chairman of Saab (Swedenbased defence firm), said, "Make in India is definitely on our agenda. Our footprint in India is expanding fast. We now have eight Indian partner companies working with us." Its new fighter jet-Gripen E, which is said to have improved avionics system, is also considered under 'Make in India'. Not only Saab, but other players like America's Boeing and Lockheed Martin have also shown interest in making their aircrafts (F/A-18 and F-16) in the country. The opportunity is not only confined to foreign firms but domestic private firms have a significant opportunity, mentions Garg from PwC, adding, "The major players in the space have been investing for the past decade or more like Bharat Forge, Tata Group or L&T and have built a portfolio in electronics, land systems, missiles and aerospace products. Most of these are either in talks or have already signed the deals with the foreign Original Equipment Manufacturers (OEMs)." There were some similar announcements made during the DefExpo in Goa last March. Bharat Forge has tied up with Israel defence tech firm Rafael Advanced Defence Systems, Elbit Systems and UK-based Rolls Royce. Similarly, Tata Group has tied up with US-based firms Sikorsky Aircraft, Lockheed Martin and Boeing. For more than 15 years, India has tried to engage the private sector in defence production. But domestic defence manufacturing is still dominated by the defence public sector undertakings (PSUs) and the Ordnance Factories Board (OFB), which together command 80-90 pc share. Of late, however, Indian private companies have shown interest in the defence equipment business and have applied for industrial licences from the ministry of commerce to locally manufacture military equipment, including airplanes and warships.

A report by domestic brokerage ICICI Securities, published in January 2016, stated that imports contribute almost 75 pc of the defence equipment needs, while public sector and domestic private sector players contribute only 20 pc and 5 pc respectively. "While the growth of the defence sector will follow along its strategic and technological requirements, the domestic defence industry is still in its infancy—which translates into a huge opportunity for investors and Indian enterprises," the report by the brokerage firm said.

DPP - to boost 'Make in India'

In April this year, Defence Procurement Policy (DPP) 2016 was unveiled, in which 'Make in India' was the key highlight. A new procurement category — Indigenously Designed, Developed and Manufactured (IDDM) — has been introduced and accorded top priority, which means the government is leaving no stone unturned to give a boost to Make in India. The Make in India category has been divided into two categories — 'Buy (Indian)', with 40 pc indigenous content, and 'Buy and Make (Indian)' having an overall indigenous content of 50 pc, whereas DPP 2013 laid down minimum percentage of indigenous content for each acquisition route, which was 30 pc. "The IDDM and Buy and Make Indian categories will help global OEMs and Indian companies forge partnership for co-development and co-production. The integration of Indian companies in the global supply chain will help the establishment of defence manufacturing," says Garg from PwC. The 'Make' procedure is divided into two categories – projects under Make I category will involve government funding of 90 pc, released in a phased manner, and based on the progress of the scheme, as per terms agreed between ministry of defence and the vendor.

While, projects under Make II category will involve prototype development of equipment or system or platform or their upgrades, or their sub-systems or sub-assembly or assemblies or components with a focus on import substitution, for which no government funding will be provided for prototype development purposes.

And it has considered the interests of Micro, Small and Medium Enterprises (MSMEs) too. To bring the MSMEs into the loop, projects with an estimated cost of development of up to INR 100 million (EUR 1.3 million) under the first category and INR 30 million (EUR 395,000) under the second category will be earmarked for them. These projects will be opened to others only if MSMEs do not evince any interest.

"The prioritisation of Buy (IDDM) in procurement category and 'Make' project is aimed to provide handholding to 'Make in India' initiative and has the potential to increase the contribution of manufacturing output to 25 pc of country's GDP," says Col Kuber, adding, "With the DPP 2016 in place, it has become increasingly apparent to all concerned that the defence manufacturing capability cannot be built in isolation and requires the active involvement of the private sector." Boston Consulting Group (BCG) estimates that the defence sector has a potential of increasing the defence-manufacturing workforce by one million people within five years. Every million directed job created in defence manufacturing will create additional 0.5 million in indirect jobs through sub-contracts and vendors.

Looking forward

The government is doing its bit with programmes like Make in India to enhance the industrial capacity and manufacturing facilities of the companies – both Indian and foreign – need to respond to the changes. Garg from PwC says,

"To be able to qualify and continue to play in most defence programmes in India, it would be important for foreign companies to have some local presence via transfer of technology, co-development, manufacturing, and for Indian companies to enhance their capabilities to locally design and manufacture.

And global OEMs (Original Equipment Manufacturers) need to respond to these changes, by forging relations with large players in Make in India. Though it is happening but still it is not sufficient." It is envisaged that under the Make In India programme, at least half of total India's weapon and equipment needs in the next 10 to 12 years worth more than USD 100 billion (EUR 88 billion) is likely to be produced domestically; so the opportunity is galore.

"The government is taking initiative to encourage greater private participation in the defence sector and emphasis on other local manufacturing requirements, opening up the sector for the foreign investors," adding, "With the global price pressure, India is likely to become a large sourcing base for components and sub-systems thus energising the MSME (micro, small and medium enterprises) sector due to large and relatively low cost engineering talent pool." With initiatives such as Make in India, India's dream to be self-reliant in defence production seems more achievable than before! The Indian aerospace, defence and homeland security sector has emerged as an gorgeous investment occasion for global and domestic players, SMEs and defence public sector undertakings (DPSUs). Increased FDI will enable the domestic industry to advantage in areas of design, modernism and state-of-the-art manufacturing, all critical for India's national safety. A vibrant defence developed base, through increased indigenisation, will provide additional impetus to Make in India, creating service, self-reliance and geo-political stability.

INDIA INDIGENISATION IN DEFENCE MANUFACTURING

India is at the cusp of metamorphosing from a top regional player to one with global clout. As India's geo-political and economic ambitions grow, it needs to develop robust indigenous manufacturing capabilities and ecosystem to secure its ambition for self-reliance in the Aerospace and Defence industry.

Currently, the country allocates about 1.8 percent of its GDP to defence spending and imports about 70 percent of defence equipment. Owing to the dynamic security environment, India's defence requirements are likely to increase in the foreseeable future making indigenous development of modern defence hardware and technology a top priority for the government.

Glass half full: A Sea of Opportunity

The fact that India ranks amongst the top 10 countries in the world in terms of its military expenditure, makes it one of the most attractive markets for defence. With the government's agenda to reduce import dependence in defence by 35-40 percent it is actively promoting indigenous defence manufacturing with initiatives like Make in India and policy reforms including allowing 100 percent Foreign Direct Investment (FDI). Even the recently launched Defence Procurement Policy (DPP) is seen as a game changer to ensure faster pace in procurement, especially through newly introduced categories under indigenously designed, developed and manufactured (IDDM) provisions. Following the Central government's footsteps and recognising the huge potential from the defence sector, several states are also offering incentives and concessions in the form of aerospace clusters or Special Economic Zones (SEZs) for developing an ecosystem where all core and ancillary activities related to defence manufacturing can co-exist.

With the Defence Minister's intention of procuring about US$10 billion worth of defence products per year in the next 5 to 10 years, and the government undertaking several initiatives and reforms, there is a sea of opportunity available for all stakeholders in the sector. For example OEMs as well as SMEs in the defence manufacturing sector are focussing on moving from a buyer-seller to a co-developer and co-manufacturer relationship. They have not only come together and formed strategic partnerships to support the development of a sustainable supplier base for the defence sector, but have also moulded themselves quickly to foster a culture of innovation and R&D. So far, they have demonstrated a huge amount of potential and capability to deliver on this promise.

Glass half empty: necessary steps to hasten indigenisation

India offers tremendous opportunities in engineering services, supply chain sourcing and associated maintenance, repair and overhaul-related activities, however to achieve self-reliance we need to create a robust ecosystem that can address the capacity and capability requirements for the industry. While the government is taking numerous measures to bolster defence manufacturing, the pace of modernisation must be balanced with both short and long term initiatives. Here are some necessary steps that must be adopted to enable long term indigenisation:

a) Partnering for success: We believe that co-development and co-manufacturing is the way forward to achieve the vision of turning India into a global high value manufacturing destination not just for the home market but also for export. India harbours an immense amount of potential that can be tapped into by way of key strategic partnerships that add value across the entire length and breadth of R&D, manufacturing and supply chain. Foreign OEM's have already started leveraging these benefits, and are encouraging Indian industry to adopt best practices for global quality standards in their manufacturing processes to lead to the creation of a gold standard supply chain and defence manufacturing ecosystem in India.

b) A skilled talent pool: As per government estimates, a reduction in 20-25 percent in defence related imports could directly create an additional 100,000 to 120,000 highly skilled jobs in India. To be ready for the opportunities of the future, the industry needs to build and train talent to address the growing needs of the market. In addition, the academia and industry needs to forge partnerships to encourage research and technological advancements and create a talent pool that is industry ready.

c) Robust supply chain: A strong supply chain is critical for a defence manufacturer looking to optimize costs. Gradually, a handful of Indian SMEs are playing a key role in the global supply chain of OEMs. With the government's offset policies, procurement policies and regulatory incentives spurring the growth of a domestic defence industry, the SMEs need to play a more active role in developing a robust supply chain.

d) Infrastructure development: Lack of adequate infrastructure drives India's logistics costs upwards thus reducing the country's cost competitiveness and efficiency. While the government is investing in this area the pace of development needs to pick up considerably and public-private participation can go a long way in hastening this process.

TENDENCIES IN THE GLOBAL DEFENCE INDUSTRY

The global defence industry has undergone profound changes in recent years. Changes in demand for military weapons and equipment, the allocation of resources for national security, national and international security priorities especially by major states, among others, have affected the defence industry in many ways. While the Cold War era witnessed a massive military build-up by many countries, thus fuelling demand for this lucrative sector, the immediate post-Cold War period witnessed just an opposite scenario. Demand for military equipment went down during the late 1980s and early 1990s. Budgetary allocations for security sectors fell. Military downsizing occurred. In just a period of half-a-decade, roughly from 1987 to the early 1990s, the defence industry witnessed a different scenario and shrank considerably. It had to shift priorities to adjust to the new environment. In brief, since the end of the Cold War, the defence industry has faced numerous challenges from all quarters. Most of the decline in the volume of arms production took place during the early and mid-1990s. During this time, significant down-sizing, rationalisation and diversification (primarily into dual-use and civilian production) were witnessed in the defence-industrial sector.

Mergers and acquisitions during the 1990s resulted in the creation of a few giant companies like Boeing, Lockheed Martin, British Aerospace, Northrop Grumman, EADS, and others. This also resulted in many smaller companies either having to merge with big ones or having to shift their priorities toward civilian production, thus leaving the defence sector. Defence industries of major countries like the United States and of Western Europe were affected most during this period although countries like Russia, Israel, South Africa, Brazil, India, and others were also affected. Arms reductions during the 1990s were extensive and fetched a sizeable 'peace dividend'.

It was desirable that such a decade of disarmament should have been extended. However, as evidence suggests, indicators of disarmament and conversion now show stagnation; in many cases even a reverse trend toward a strengthening of military postures are witnessed. A decade of cuts in military expenditure ended in 1998/99 when it went up again. The upward trend in military expenditure is likely to continue in future. The 11 September 2001 terrorist attacks in the United States are likely to result in a major shift in defence-industrial developments because of their impact on security requirements at national and international levels. But this is not to suggest that the upward trend in military expenditure was a product of such an unfortunate event.

This trend had already started in the late 1990s, primarily because of increased military spending by countries like the United States and regions like the Middle East and South and East Asia. In this changed scenario, the defence industry seems to gear up to meet new challenges. As procurement budgets have started to swell again and are likely to stay that way, new opportunities are expected for the defence industry. In fighting terrorism, additional defence programmes initiated by countries like the United States will most likely change the structure of the defence industry. While it is expected that giant weapons producers, especially in the United States, are likely to benefit most from the on-going 'War on Terror', national defence industries elsewhere are also likely to reorient themselves to meet future challenges. In brief, the global defence industry, after a period of significant downsizing and rationalisation, is likely to enter into a phase of renewed attention. Demand for smart weapons, increased emphasis on military technology including investment in R&D, growing demand for aerospace and cutting-edge technology products, are all likely to boost defence-industrial activities in many parts of the world.

Trends of India's Defence Industry

Trends in global defence industry have impinged India in many ways. India's defence industry has witnessed significant changes since the end of the Cold War. In the 1990s, changes in both institutional and policy spheres became more prominent. The most far reaching change that has occurred in recent years in India's defence-industrial sector is related to its opening up to the market. Long protected as a closed sector, India's defence industry has now opened up for private participation. As if this was not enough, it is also showing enough willingness to become an exporter and dares to venture into the competitive global arms market. How far it will succeed in its objectives is examined elsewhere, but changes are certainly a product of and response to the contemporary changes in the global industrial defence scenario. At the same time, it is also showing willingness to diversify its range of products, which not only include modern weapons systems but also technologies for wide and popular civilian uses. The Indian defence-industrial sector targets the national, and even global, civilian market to sell its products, especially in the fields of civilian space, medical, and electronics. Thus conversion through diversification has been witnessed in many areas of defence production in India.

India's defence industry has come a long way from being at the lowest end of the production spectrum, catering to the maintenance and repair and overhaul of imported weapons, to a stage where it can boast of designing and developing a range of state-of-the-art weapons systems. Half a decade of defence-industrial experience in India shows that while it started from scratch, it has been able not only to learn and absorb various stages of production intricacies but also produce complex systems that are primarily an indigenous activities. Another important factor is that the Indian defence industry has produced various weapons systems under licenses acquired from various foreign sources.

Although the first Prime Minister of India, Jawaharlal Nehru, believed in 'self sufficiency' in arms production, which became a policy mantra for subsequent years, it had to be supplemented by what is roughly called 'self-reliance in defence'. Self-reliance does not preclude accessing external sources for technology and systems, or external help in any stage of the production cycle. It is the degree of dependency on external sources that is tested in the case of India's quest for self-reliance. India opted to choose an incremental path, in which it was necessary to continue to meet urgent requirements through imports while striving hard on achieving indigenous capabilities in defence production. Both policies continued till the late 1980s and many of the components of both still continue till today. The 1990s witnessed a series of far-reaching initiatives in the field of national security, of which defence industry was a critical component.

The creation of six Special Task Forces to reform major aspects of national defence coordination and management, under the Chairmanship of the then Defence Minister in 1994 may effectively be considered as the first major step after a long time to initiate and implement much-desired reforms in the defence-industrial sector. This was followed by a series of intensive interactions between various organs of the armed forces, government departments and institutions like the Confederation of Indian Industries (CII). The 'Army-Industry

Partnership', a partnership between CII and the Indian Army to get acquainted with each other's needs and to facilitate channels of communication between the armed forces and the private industry, was a result of this process and, in turn, led to other cooperative initiatives. Events like India's nuclear tests in mid-1998 and the Kargil conflict in mid-1999 provided grounds for an intense debate on various aspects of India's national security. Also, as a by-product of the current disinvestment programme, which is primarily aimed toward lessening or wiping out government control and responsibilities in state-owned public enterprises in India, the debate on a reform of the defence industry got a major boost as demands for a privatisation of and private participation in this hitherto closed sector grew more in tune with the changing times.

In January 2001, the Government of India initiated a series of major initiatives that, among others, included Foreign Direct Investment (FDI) up to about 26 percent and full private participation in certain sectors in the defence industry. This policy indeed marks a critical departure from the past. Followed by this, the Group of Ministers (GoM) Report on 'Reforming the National Security System' was made public in early 2001. This laid stress on reforms in all-encompassing aspects of national security, of which changes sought in higher defence management emphasised the need to create specific institutions like the Defence Acquisitions Board to adapt and facilitate changing needs of the defence industry.

While these far-reaching institutional and policy-oriented changes have been underway for quite some time especially since the early 1990s, the demand for private participation has assumed significance in recent years. In such a scenario, analyses of India's defence-industrial sector and policies have become critically important to understand the complex web of linkages that determine national policies in the defence-industrial sector. This, in turn, needs a closer look into the past performance of the defence industry, lessons learnt and a peep into the likely future course.

Research Objectives

The objectives are primarily four-fold. First, we will examine critical aspects of defence-industrial policies adopted by India in the past and link those to performance. It will examine the factors that have influenced India's defence production and their co-relationship with policies and decision-making in this sector. Second, we will examine the main trends during the 1990s, during which major policy changes occurred. It will critically examine the impact of such policy changes. Third, we will examine the contemporary scenario. Fourth and last, it will look into future problems and prospects. The last two are essential in understanding the intricacies involved in India's defence-industrial strategies and are expected to give some clues related to the future course of action in this sector.

Some of the major queries that will be examined here are: Why a quest for self-reliance in the past? Has the policy of self-reliance paid off? If not, what are the options for the future? Why the changes in defence-industrial policies during the 1990s? Are the objectives achievable? What are likely options for the future? Does it have scope for more diversion, thus leading to conversion through the increase in civilian production, in future? We will invariably try to find answers to these queries, although not necessarily in the same order.

Methods and Sources

We will follow a general descriptive-analytical approach. The scope is limited somewhat to policy analyses due to constraints in the availability of information. This is because India's defence industry has long been a 'closed' sector and thus been under exclusive government control. It is only in recent times that it has opened up, thus leading to an availability of information in a low to medium scale. We will also follow a historical method whereby it will emphasise linkages at policy- and decision-making levels to performance, and this is important in understanding the nature of development that this sector has undergone for the past half-a-century. Available data on specifics will be evaluated. Emphasis will be on an evaluation and interpretation of data from primary (especially government) sources. In brief, the overall approach will be descriptive and analytical.

Literature on the subject is scarce. At international level, the study of India's defence industry has attracted very little attention. The same is true at national level. Barring a few books, written by scholars like K. Subrahmanyam, Air Marshal Samir Sen, Major General Pratap Narain, Chris Smith, WPS Sidhu, and others, substantial work is not evident on this subject. Occasional research papers by G. Balachandran, Rahul Roy-Choudhury, Ajay Singh and others have also focused on limited themes. Secondary and tertiary sources are scarce. Primary sources, however, constitute the most important component of this study. Annual Reports (published by the Ministry of Defence, Government of India), Annual Reports of major Defence Public Sector Units (published by respective organisations), periodic reports published by the Comptroller and Auditor General of India, Parliament Secretariat and similar other reports constitute primary sources for this endeavour. Select interviews with senior government officers, analysts and industry-watchers have been taken into account.

MADE IN INDIA : DEFENCE MANUFACTURING IN INDIA

It is in strategic interest of a nation aspiring to be the regional power to develop indigenous and internationally competitive defence industry base. Presently, India is one of the largest importers of conventional defence equipment. According to government statistics, roughly 60% of India's defence requirements are met through imports.

India has the potential to emerge as a global platform for defence research, manufacturing, supply chain sourcing, software development, and offsets, which will strengthen our defence capabilities and spur industrial development as well as exports in this sector.

Government is also carrying out reforms in defence procurement to increase efficiency, invite foreign players with excellent capabilities and encourage domestic industry. It has introduced policies to strengthen technology transfer, including liberalized FDI in defence production. The report of Committee of Experts for Amendments to Defence Procurement Policy (DPP) 2013 is a progressive step in this direction. Also, Make in India the new flagship program of Government of India has put a renewed emphasis on creating a conducive policy environment for improving domestic defence manufacturing.

These radicle initiatives present opportunities for the foreign companies to enter India and local companies to collaborate and design, develop and showcase their engineering strength. This will also further India's objective to create jobs, catalyze technology development, and transform India into a self-reliant nation with export capabilities in defence sector. India's existing wealth of talent, technology and cost advantages together can help make defence products globally competitive.

It is a proud moment for us to share with you the report on "Make In India-An overview of Defence Manufacturing in India" at the momentous occasion of 11th Indo- US Economic Summit: Taking the Bilateral Trade to USD 500 Billion. Indian government is supporting the creation of a vibrant domestic defence manufacturing base in the country. Policy environment in India has never offered so many tangible opportunities to pursue co-development and co-production projects. We welcome you to come and Make in India!

India has the third largest Army, the fourth largest Air force and the seventh largest Navy in the world. India is among the top 10 countries in the world in terms of military expenditure and world's largest arms importer. India allocates about 1.8% of its GDP towards defence spending, of which 40% is allocated to capital acquisitions and only about 30% of India's equipment is manufactured in India, mainly by public sector undertakings. Even when defence products are manufactured domestically, there is a large import component. All these factors make the Indian defence market one of the most attractive globally and provides an immense opportunity for both domestic and foreign players in the defence sector.

India's Defence Industry

The post-independence industrial policy placed the production of defence items in the reserve List making it mandatory for production to be taken up only by the public sector. The sector for the first time was opened up to 100 percent Indian private sector participation in 2001. Reforms in the defence industrial sector and the acquisition policy have been one continuous process since then, beginning with the formulation of DPP 2002 and its successive revisions, formulation of the Defence Production Policy and the issuance of Joint Venture guidelines.

Indian defence industry is dominated by defence public sector undertakings (DPSUs) and ordnance factories (OFs) which contribute about 90% of the total domestic defence manufacturing output. The 41 ordnance factories are spread across 26 different locations and employ close to 1,25,000 people. The DPSUs and OFs manufacture a wide spectrum of equipment including small arms and field guns, ammunitions, explosives, armoured vehicles, transport vehicles, clothing, parachutes and general stores. DPSUs account for approximately 65 percent of the total industrial output of the defence public sector enterprises.

Combined, the DPSUs and OFs have played a critical role in building a domestic industrial base in this sector as they typically outsource 20 to 25% of their production requirements to private companies. In addition to the public undertakings, there is a small but growing number of medium large private companies that have already entered, or, are seriously evaluating entry into the market. These are in addition to about 6000 MSMEs that have largely depended upon the DPSUs for survival. The Indian defence industry's import export ratio is inferior to countries with a much smaller defence industrial base. India's arms imports are now almost three times as high as those of the second and third largest arms importers—China and Pakistan. India is among the top five arms importer, besides China, Pakistan, the UAE and Saudi Arabia.

Since opening up of the defence industry for private sector participation, the Department of Industrial Policy and Promotion (DIPP) has so far issued 222 Letters of Intents (LOIs) and issued Industrial Licences (ILs) to more than 150 companies for manufacture of a wide range of defence items. 46 companies have so far reported commencement of production.

The licenses have been issued to the Indian private sector for manufacture of Military Aircraft, Unmanned Aerial Vehicles, Radars, Electronic Warfare Systems, Ship borne platforms, Armoured Vehicles etc. In the recent years, many Indian private industries have been involved in a small way with several defence 'Make' projects. These are Integrated Materiel Management Online System (IMMOLS), Integrated Air Defence Command and control system (IACCS) Tactical Communication System (TCS), Battlefield Management Systems (BMS) and Futuristic Infantry Combat Vehicles (FICV). While (IMMOLS) and (IACCS) have been deployed, TCS, BMS and FICV are in the early stages of development. Award of major projects under 'Make' category to Indian private industries is a new beginning in Indian defence industrialization.

Larsen & Toubro, Tata group, Pipapav Defence and Offshore Engineering Ltd., Reliance Industries Ltd., Mahindra and Mahindra, Ashok Leyland Defence Systems, Piramal System and Technologies are some of the key Indian players in the defence industry.

Make In India

The Indian defence industry's import-export ratio is inferior to countries with a much smaller defence industrial base. The 'Make in India' policy for the defence sector aims to reverse the current imbalance between the import of defence equipment and indigenous manufacture of defence equipments without adversely affecting the requirements, capability and preparedness of the user. Therefore, achieving self reliance and reducing dependence on foreign countries in defence is a necessity today rather than a choice, both for strategic and economic reasons. The requirement for domestic production of defence equipment is more than for any other sector because it will not only save precious foreign exchange but will address the national security concerns. 'Make in India' policy aims at facilitating investments and fostering innovations for the manufacturing sector in India. Government being the only consumer, 'Make in India' in defence sector will be governed by the defence procurement policy of India. The Government policy of promoting domestic defence industry is adequately reflected in the Defence Procurement Policy, wherein preferential treatment is given to "Buy (Indian)" and "Buy and Make (Indian)" categories of acquisition over "Buy (Global)". As the Indian Companies may not have adequate capabilities in terms of technology, they are encouraged to partner with foreign companies for joint ventures, technology transfer arrangements and tie-ups.

RISING WEAPONS MANUFACTURING IN INDIA

Considering the national wealth it commands India's hard power shouldn't be dismissed. As a matter of fact, as early as 1947 India possessed the best trained military in Asia. A strong British core was the rock upon which a professional institution was molded and outfitted with a proper navy and air arm.

In the decades that followed a growing domestic arms industry improved this state of affairs. There was no realm Indian scientists and engineers ventured that didn't impact its military advancement. India also cultivated its allies from opposite sides of the Iron Curtain, an approach that remains profitable to this day as Delhi cuts deals with both Russia and the US.

So as the 20th century surrendered to the 21st India emerged as a leading arms importer while its military-industrial complex struggled with the development of cutting-edge weapons.

Glaring shortages in materials and capabilities persist in India's massive armed forces. But new hardware, from tanks to stealth warships, are rolling out of state-owned factories with alarming frequency. This is a sure sign India is preparing for an active role in global affairs.

Just like China India is arming itself to fortify its economic advancement and dominate the Asian continent. Its current path might be frustrating but the intent is clear: India is the would-be arsenal of the free world.

Akash

The medium-range Akash surface-to-air missile (SAM) is another successful offspring of the IGMDP.The Akash is so far the most potent air-defense system ever developed by India's military-industrial complex. Its performance is comparable to the Russian Buk and the US Hawk but Indian sources claim it's superior to Western SAMs.

After 20 years in development the Akash entered production by 2006 with orders being fulfilled until the present. The Akash deploys in batteries of 12 missiles and is designed to guard sensitive facilities, mechanized formations, and national airspace. Although India lags behind China when it comes to its air-defense network it compensates by having a large selection of foreign suppliers who can either sell or jointly develop new systems. The Akash, however, is touted for being completely Indian–96% of it, at the most.

The success of the Akash laid the groundwork for future programs that improve on the original. Rather than agree to a license-built variant of a Russian or French system, the Akash is tailor-made for its ultimate customer: the Indian military. A total of 3,000 Akash missiles are deployed with the army and air force.

Kalvari-class SSK

For a country that commands an entire ocean the Indian Navy's submarine fleet is a modest one, numbering less than 15 boats. This shortcoming in the face of China's rapid naval expansion is now being addressed with a commensurate blue water build up. At the forefront of this effort are, naturally, submarines. In the mid-2000s India partnered with France for the acquisition of half a dozen Scorpene-class diesel-electric submarines. These were to be constructed at the facilities of

Mazagon Dock Shipbuilders Ltd. over a 10 year period. The boats are locally made but the weapons and equipment inside are Franco-German systems.

The Scorpene is a small submarine that packs a serious punch and can launch torpedoes and anti-ship missiles. Since it entered service in 2005 Chile, Malaysia, and Brazil have acquired their own Scorpenes. But India is its largest international customer so far.

The first of its class the INS Kalvari, which took its name from the original Kalvari submarine from the previous century, was commissioned in April, 2015, and begins operations in September, 2016. If there are no delays its sisters will join the fleet each year at Kadamba naval base until 2019 or 2020.

Arihant-class SSBN

India and China are the only Asian countries actively building nuclear submarine forces. With the latter's efforts shrouded in secrecy and speculation, the Indian Navy's first Arihant-class SSBN comes with a refreshing amount of hype and genuine transparency.

India's need for a nuclear submarine arose in 1971 but like other ambitious defense programs it wasn't until the cusp of the 21st century before work on the Arihant began. (In 1998, to be specific.) When finally launched in 2009, it took several years and considerable assistance from Russia before its nuclear reactor was prepared. This breakthrough was followed by grueling sea trials.

India's experience operating Russian submarines had a great influence on the Arihant, which displaces at 6,000 tons and is powered by an 83 megawatt reactor. The navy's only nuclear-powered submarine, INS Chakra, is a massive Soviet-era Typhoon SSBN on lease until the advent of the Arihants, which externally resemble their Western European counterparts. Once commissioned in 2015, the first of six Arihant-class SSBN's serve as 1/3rd of India's nuclear triad. This ensures a second strike capability should an apocalyptic war erupt in the near future.

Shivalik-class frigate

As early as the 1970s India was far ahead of most Asian countries–except Japan–when it came to warship construction. With its experience operating British and Russian vessels, making the leap to local shipbuilding was inevitable.

A trio of Godavari-class guided missile frigates were commissioned during the 1980s and their success later inspired a requirement for newer advanced warships. These begat another trio of Brahmaputra-class frigates commissioned from 2000-2005.

But with the advent of stealth features and complex supply chains the navy still needed cutting edge assets that were just as capable as their Western European peers. Capabilities like deploying land attack cruise missiles, i.e. BrahMos, were essential too. During the 1990s plans were readied for the navy's next-generation frigates armed with a combination of Russian and Israeli systems.

Only three 4,900 ton Shivalik-class frigates were built and commissioned from 2010 to 2012. The Indian Navy is now preparing to commission a quartet of its upcoming stealth corvettes, the Kamortas.

Dhruv

A peculiar feature of India's sprawling military-industrial complex is despite abundant time and resources, it struggles to accomplish its own self-appointed goals. A stark contrast is nimble Israel, which achieved tenuous independence a year after India. Within six decades Israel leapfrogged from the Uzi to cyberwarfare and is recognized today as a world-class arms exporter. India's lazy approach to militarization does eventually succeed and proof of this is the Dhruv. Although designated as an Advanced Light Helicopter (ALH), the Dhruv performs the same role as the German Bo-105 or the US UH-1. It's a twin-engine utility helicopter designed to ferry troops and supplies. The Dhruv also qualifies as one of the oldest programs initiated by state-owned aerospace giant Hindustan Aeronautics Limited (HAL).

Originally conceived in 1984, production of the Dhruv only began in 2001 and by 2007 several dozen had been delivered to the army. The Dhruv is now flown by each branch–including the Coast Guard–and HAL has so far developed four variants, the last is ALH Mark IV Rudra attack helicopter. In a remarkable first, the Dhruv enjoyed limited export success from 2009 to 2010.

The Indian military expects to operate 200 Dhruvs and 76 Rudras before 2020.

LCH

Although India will spend an estimated $4 billion on Boeing Apaches and Chinooks for its air force, HAL is busy with the finishing touches for its vaunted Light Combat Helicopter.

The LCH's origins date to 2006, when a requirement was determined for a high altitude gunship that surpassed the performance of the dependable Mi-35 Hind.

By 2007 a prototype was unveiled during an air show in Bengaluru. The LCH's Technology Demonstrator 1 or TD-1 variant underwent its first flight test in 2010. The improved TD-2 flew again in 2011.

Weighing 5.5 tons and powered by twin turboshaft engines, the LCH's appearance is typical among current generation attack helicopters. Its armaments consist of a nose-mounted cannon and four hardpoints for rockets and missiles.

From 2012 until 2015 the LCH underwent further testing and its TD-3 variant can fly at subzero temperatures in the Himalayas–a feat most helicopters aren't designed for. The first batch of LCH's are expected to enter service by 2017. Its current production orders are large, with 65 helicopters for the air force and 114 for the army.

Su-30MKI

The Indian Air Force bridged the air-superiority divide in the late 1990s when HAL acquired licensed manufacturing rights to the Russian twin-seater Su-27UBK.

The investment has paid off in strategic dividends and since production commenced in 2002, the IAF have received 205 of the 270 Su-30MKI's it ordered. As a twin-engine aircraft with canards and Western European avionics, an Su-30MKI's performance characteristics are superior to most third and even fourth-generation fighters.

The Su-30MKI's capabilities are so impressive, from superb range, maneuverability, and armaments, that it altered the IAF's total war strategy in case of a future conflict with either Pakistan or China.

Even the Russians were awed by it and the Sukhoi Company is now building its own Su-30MK based on the Indian variant.

Nag

Even if it possesses large quantities of French, Israeli, Russian, Swedish, and US anti-tank weapons the Indian Army has yet to deploy a locally made ATGM. Beginning in the 1980s, however, the DRDO and its sister agency the DRDL launched various missile programs.

Its unclear what year the Nag was first prototyped but in 2010 it was successfully tested against inert tanks at a Rajasthan firing range. The 190mm Nag missile is comparable to the US-made TOW and the Hellfire. It's armed with a tandem HEAT warhead and has a maximum range of 4,000 meters (4 km).

Its operation, however, is similar to the Russian Khrizantema or the Chinese ATF-10. A battery of Nag missiles are mounted on a tracked carrier vehicle–a modified BMP-2–and these serve as tank hunters during combined operations.

On the other hand, the Nag's performance is reminiscent of the US FGM Javelin, albeit with impressive differences. It's a fire-and-forget missile that uses a high angle of attack to defeat its target. The Nag's optical seeker is allegedly jam resistant and it uses a smokeless propellant to conceal its flight path.

The Indian Army has already placed orders for hundreds of Nag missiles. An airborne variant of the Nag called the Helina is being tested.

BMP-2

The Indian Army is the second largest user of the BMP-2, which it renamed the "Sarath," outside Russia. Since licensed production commenced in 1987, a reported 1,200 or 1,500 BMP-2's have been made in the subcontinent. A further 363 will enter service in the coming years.

Despite its questionable armor protection–a flaw that can be rectified with upgrades–and cramped interior, the BMP-2 is a robust fighting vehicle. Designed to be fully amphibious and armed with a powerful 30mm gun, the BMP-2 still qualifies as a formidable opponent in any battlefield.

But the OFB and the Indian Army appear to have taken liberties with their BMP-2, using its hull and chassis for a SAM system, a self-propelled gun, a mortar carrier, a bulldozer, an engineer vehicle, a reconnaissance vehicle, and as a platform for the Nag missile,. i.e. the Namica.

Although Indian manufacturers can build an APC to replace the BMP-2, the Indian Army isn't budging. The Indian BMP-2 is destined for extensive modernization, with a better engine and armaments, to keep it viable until and perhaps beyond 2025.

Arjun

The production of tanks is a powerful indicator that a country has a strong industrial base. India reached this stage by the 1960s and after it fought three wars with Pakistan and another with China a new requirement arose for a true world-class battle tank.

India already manufactured a capable modern tank, the Vijayanta, and would later build licensed T-72 and T-90S tanks. So a new MBT superior to any rival in South Asia wasn't beyond its reach.

To this day literature about the Arjun's origin is scarce. But the Arjun does strongly resemble the original Leopard 2 and according to a profile published by the US Army's Armor magazine in 1998, its R&D was undertaken by the Combat

Vehicles Research and Development Establishment (CVRDE). In the period between 1983 and 1985 the Arjun was successfully prototyped and it strongly resembled the German Leopard 1 with its squarish turret, 120mm main gun, and 1,400 horsepower MTU diesel engine.

But the Arjun was a flop. Where other countries–Israel and Japan, for example–successfully launched MBT programs from scratch it took the Arjun three decades before it finally reached the Indian Army in 2011. With its performance characteristics lagging behind the DRDO enlisted Israeli defense contractors to upgrade it thereby creating the Arjun Mark II.

Having thousands of Russian tanks means the Indian Army needs just 242 Arjuns. Since there are no plans for exporting it the Arjun remains a promising MBT that never got to prove itself.

K9 Vajra

For the first time ever India has turned to an East Asian country for help with developing an advanced weapon system. Renamed the Vajra, the 155mm self-propelled gun is a license-built K9 Thunder with Indian production run by the conglomerate Larsen & Toubro with the help of South Korea's Samsung Techwin.

Larsen & Toubro are also collaborating with France's Nexter on a towed artillery piece.

When the expected 100 K9 Vajra's are delivered they replace the army's aging batteries of British 105mm Abbots and Russian 122mm Gvozdikas. Previous attempts to develop and mass-produce an indigenous self-propelled gun begat systems that fell short of modern standards, including a repurposed Arju tank chassis mounted with a crew-served artillery piece.

With the Vajra, however, the Indian Army receives a world-class product that surpasses its peers in NATO and even Russia. But the Vajra won't satisfy the Indian Army's enormous appetite for maximum firepower. According to its Field Artillery Rationalisation Plan, a total of 2,820 pieces need to be acquired before decade's end.

Light Field Gun

The 105mm L118 field gun is one of the most remarkable modern artillery pieces ever produced in the UK. Barely weighing two tons and designed to be transportable by land, sea, or air, it's used by at least 20 different countries.

The L118 first entered service with the British Army in 1975 and was soon snapped up by allied countries, including a modified variant for the US Army. The L118's biggest draw is it can be flown into any theater with difficult terrain and operated without fuss.

The Indian Army is fond of it too and several hundred Light Field Guns are counted among more than 2,000 towed and self-propelled artillery pieces in its arsenal.

Delhi-class destroyer

Each of these destroyers are a complete package armed with torpedoes, anti-ship and cruise missiles, and able to repel any airborne threat. Crewed by 390 sailors and officers the Delhi-class are fitting actors in any show of force. But their origins are quite colorful.

A recurring theme in modern India's rise as a military power is the unpredictable course that bedevils its weapons manufacturing.

Whether it's assault rifles or aircraft carriers, what the Indian government and its partner agencies begin have a startling tendency to meander, bog down, diverge, and complexify before the outcome arrives.

This is the experience of the Delhi-class guided missile destroyers. Conceived as a hybrid design combining the best aspects of Soviet surface combatants the Delhis were supposed to be furnished in Ukraine before their launch in India.

What happened was years of delays and changing requirements altered its function and appearance.

But the Delhis came out alright and in 1993, 1996, and 2001 each of the vessels received their commissions. With 70%

of their parts supplied by local contractors to Mazagon Dock Shipbuilders Ltd., the Delhi-class are truly made in India.

Kolkata-class destroyer

With its long experience building surface combatants, it should come as no surprise the Indian Navy wants them faster, larger, and deadlier. Hence the 7,500 ton Kolkata-class that have supplanted the older Delhis in every possible metric.

But the Kolkatas were also a success for Israel, i.e. Israeli Aerospace Industries (IAI), who not only supplied its MF-STAR radar but the Barak 8 SAMs, which is the navy's favorite anti-aircraft system after its trusted 30mm AK-630 CIWS'.

The Kolkatas were also designed to deploy the naval version Brahmos and like the Delhis, their hangars fit two Dhruv helicopters.

The Indian Navy intends to commission the last of its three Kolkata destroyers by 2016. These will then serve alongside a quartet of newer destroyers that share the same hulls–the Visakhapatnam-class.

INS Vikrant

Since India and China are poised to become rival powers state-owned shipyards from both countries are actively building next-generation warships. With two PLAN Liaoning-class carriers reportedly under construction in Dalian the Indian Navy isn't letting itself fall behind.

In 2013 it received its long-delayed Vikramaditya, which underwent a decade of expensive rebuilding in Russia. A second aircraft carrier's hull was completed at Cochin Shipyard Ltd. that same year. This was the INS Vikrant named after India's first British-made carrier.

Today the Vikrant is mostly complete with its runway and island installed. By the time it's commissioned it deploys 30 MiG-29K's and anti-submarine helicopters along with 1,600 crew members.

Once at sea the Vikrant's appearance and operation resembles its sibling Vikramaditya. It's worth noting the PLAN's upcoming carriers share the same short takeoff design of their Indian counterparts.

The irony here is not very subtle since both navies will deploy ships based on Soviet-era Kiev-class STOBAR carriers.

Vidhwansak

The extent of India and South Africa's commerce in weapons is difficult to ascertain. But at the turn of the last century an urgent requirement for large caliber anti-material rifles brought the Denel NTW-20 to the Indian Army's attention.

The OFB soon began manufacturing the NTW under license, renaming it the *Vidhwansak*. Recognizable for its large barrel, prominent muzzle brake, and squarish carrying handle that frames its scope, the bolt action NTW is known for its powerful 20x110mm round that can reach targets 1.8 km away.

The only comparable rifle to the Vidhwansak is the Croatian RT-20. But the OFB does offer a degree of customization to its largest rifle–operators can choose if they want it chambered in 20mm, 14.5mm, or 12.7mm.

Weighing 100 lbs and ideally carried by two soldiers, the Vidhwansak does sacrifice ease-of-use for accuracy and range. This explains why the Indian Army is looking for an alternate large caliber sniper rifle.

40mm MGL

It isn't clear how long the OFB has been manufacturing licensed copies of the Milkor multi-grenade launcher. When fully loaded, the MGL can fire a half dozen 40x46mm grenades in two seconds at targets up to 400 m away. India's *jawans* certainly have a reliable grenade launcher at their disposal for years to come.

The MGL's existence dates to the early 1980s, when a South African inventor built a revolver-type grenade launcher in his workshop. Andries C. Piek's creation was accepted by the South African Defense Force (SADF) in 1983 and its popularity soon spread all over the world, including the US where it has become a favorite of Marines and special forces operators.

A terrifying force multiplier in any type of combat, the MGL is proof that simple weapons always last longest.

Carl Gustaf

Could it be the ultimate recoilless rifle? The 84mm Carl Gustaf was first used by the Swedish Army in 1948. Its simple design and powerful warhead established its sterling reputation in at least 20 militaries, including the Indian Army. In 1964 (M2) and 1991 (M3) improved variants were developed by the Swedish defense contractor Saab.

Today. the Carl Gustaf qualifies as a short-range anti-tank weapon although it's just as frequently used to suppress enemy defenses and blow things up. It enjoyed a resurgence among NATO forces in Afghanistan where it helped level the battlefield against the ubiquitous RPG-7. Both weapons are evenly matched and have sufficient oomph to knock out modern armored vehicles.

The OFB manufactures both the Carl Gustaf M2 and M3, which suggests it first acquired licensing rights as far back as the 1960s. The Carl Gustaf serves as the army's entry level tank killer when soldiers don't have to use missiles. Saab is now developing smart munitions and a fire control system for the Carl Gustaf and these may soon reach India.

MO-120 mortar

This French heavy mortar from the 1950s might be an anachronism in this age of smart munitions, but it's dependable enough to enjoy continued use.

The original MO-120-RT was designed and manufactured by Thomson-Brandt. Its impressive range (up to 5 km) and ease-of-use endeared it to many foreign armies, including the US Marine Corps.

In what appears to be a genuine case of historic irony, the MO-120 is used by the successor states that replaced the fabled Gunpowder Empires: Turkey, Iran, Pakistan, and India. It deserves mention how each of these countries have enormous requirements for artillery and other crew-served weapons. It's unknown how many MO-120's are used by the Indian Army, but the OFB still considers it part of its product line.

AKM

Due to circumstances whose logic is difficult to comprehend, 30 years ago India became one of the largest customers for the AK-47 and its derivatives. The twist is it ignored directly purchasing the rifles from the Soviet Union, its main military supplier, and sourced the guns from Eastern Europe instead.

Unspecified numbers of AK's have since reached India via Bulgaria, Poland, the Czech Republic, and even China. Commandos, paratroopers, entire army regiments, paramilitaries, and local police are equipped with AK's and prefer it over the standard issue INSAS, which is patterned after the AK-47. For the sake of convenience, the Ordnance Factory Board (OFB) builds unlicensed AKM's to meet overwhelming demand from the security forces.

The Indian military's reluctance to formally adopt the AK-47 almost triggered a lawsuit by Russia's Izhmash in 2004 and left its state-owned small arms plants in a bizarre conundrum. The AK-47 is an excellent rifle but, as in the case of the disappointing INSAS, it's better to just borrow its parts.

Even today, after exhaustive trials to find a new assault rifle, the best local alternative for Indian soldiers uses an AK-pattern receiver and firing mechanism.

Dhanush

During the 1980s India became the largest international customer for the Bofors FH-77B, a 155mm towed howitzer made in Sweden. A total of 410 of these guns were delivered from 1986 until 1991. In 1987, however, a convoluted scandal involving shady arms dealers and bribery erupted and forever tarnished the Bofors name in the national consciousness. Sadly, what was called the Bofors scandal slowed down India's arms imports for decades.

But the FH-77B was a very capable artillery piece and proved its mettle during the Kargil War in 1998. The problem was these Swedish guns didn't have an indefinite service life and the Indian Army knew it badly needed more of the same rather than the familiar 105mm's. Although Russian artillery pieces were always an option, these had neither the range nor the sophistication of their Western European counterparts.

In early 2015 the OFB marked another breakthrough–one that could soothe the army's gripes over their big guns. After successful testing from 2011 to 2014, the locally made copy of the FH-77B called the Dhanush possessed the same features but with greater range and pre-installed targeting software. (The OFB acquired the FH-77B's schematics from a transfer-of-technology agreement.)

The Indian Army expects the Gun Carriage Factory to deliver 144 guns in the next few years. A total of 414 pieces along with continuous mass-production are required by 2020. A truck mounted system utilizing the Dhanush may or may not enter service.

Milan

France has been a faithful supplier of the Indian military since the 1960s and this profitable relationship endures to this day. Besides AMX-13 light tanks and Mirage jets, France's popular ATGM is also prized by the Indian military.

India's longstanding rivalry with Pakistan meant anti-tank weapons would have an enormous role in any conflict over the Line of Control (LoC). This was true in 1965 and 1971 and would remain so for any future showdown. The Milan was an excellent choice of missile when it was introduced by France in 1972. Its ease-of-use and ability to penetrate three feet of armor at medium-range established its reputation as a bestseller.

Since then, 300,000 of its wire-guided tandem HEAT missiles have been sold around the world. The Milan is license-built in Germany, Spain, Turkey, and India by state-owned Bharat Dynamics Ltd. As recently as 2009 the Indian Army replenished its stocks of Milans by ordering 4,100 missiles from France.

The Milan wasn't the only ATGM India settled on since the military also stocks large quantities of license-built Konkurs and the lethal Kornet. In 2014 India even purchased half a billion dollars worth of Israeli Spike missiles. But the Milan isn't disappearing any time soon.

Tejas Light Combat Aircraft

The IAF always wanted its own indigenous fighter jet. Take it from the decorated Air Marshall M.S.D. Wollen, who oversaw the development of what became the Tejas LCA during his time as HAL's chairman.

As early as 1969 the Indian government began planning for an advanced fighter jet that used a proven jet engine. It took 20 years before consultants from Dassault Aviation helped establish the design features of the LCA from 1987 to 1988–hence its delta wing configuration–but a viable prototype wasn't ready until 1995.

In the meantime, the IAF made do with an estimated 260 Soviet MiG-21 and MiG-27's, which served as the branch's ordained dog fighters since the days of Indira Gandhi. Since the IAF already flies a vast fleet of fourth-generation Su-30MKI's, the LCA was meant to replace the aging MiGs.

Like many Indian defense projects, the LCA had a protracted development across 40 years. Its first flight was in 2001 and testing continued until 2011. The IAF have an initial order for 40 Tejas LCA Mark I's and 250 additional Mark II's are expected by 2020. The Indian Navy also needs at least 56 carrier-based Tejas LCA's within the same time frame.

After decades of development hell, the Tejas LCA could be the next Mirage III and prove itself the ultimate cheap fighter jet.

Pinaka

Like many countries that acquired rocket artillery from the former Soviet Union, India moved away from its Grads and began developing its own system in 1986. Unfortunately where countries like Israel, China, South Korea, Turkey, Iran and even North Korea succeeded, the Armament Research and Development Establishment (ARDE) tasked by the DRDO with developing an indigenous MLRS struggled for years.

The Pinaka was already tested and viable in the period from 1994-1995 but it wasn't operational until 2000. The Pinaka marked a departure from the crude BM-21 it was meant to replace. Its launcher was armed with two cells holding a dozen 214mm rockets. The entire system was mounted on an 8×8 truck and could bombard targets 40 km away.

Its laborious development and low-rate production forced the Indian Army to acquire large numbers of the BM-30 Smerch in 2006. Today less than a hundred Pinaka Mark I's are in service. A new variant with a longer range, the Pinaka Mark II, is undergoing tests. Even with its sluggish progress the Pinaka deserves a place next to current multi-launch rockets systems.

Agni

India is a latecomer in the ballistic missile game. Despite access to both Western and Eastern Bloc technology during the Cold War, acquiring a long-range missile arsenal wasn't a pressing concern for its military. Even when the DRDO initiated its Integrated Guided Missile Development Program (IGMDP) during the 1980s, the fruits of this ambitious effort didn't arrive until almost a quarter century later. So it is with the Agni. Rather than a name for a single missile, the Agni represents a lineage of launch systems produced after India's successful nuclear tests in 1998. The Agni I is a conventional short-range road mobile ballistic missile that can deliver a large payload 1,200 km away. The Agni II is an improved variant of its predecessor with an even greater range.

The Agni III, IV, and V are intermediate-range systems capable of delivering nuclear warheads to anywhere in South and Central Asia. The Agni V in particular is currently being developed to launch multiple nukes over a rival country's major cities. But a lot of work remains to be done and India's full second strike capability won't be in place until the 2020s.

BrahMos

It's the deadliest conventional missile in the world. Or is it?

Untested in combat, the supersonic BrahMos represents a rare success in multinational defense cooperation outside Europe. In 1998, the governments of Russia and India launched a $250 million joint venture to manufacture a next-generation cruise missile based on proven technology, i.e. the P-800 Yakhont.

The BrahMos, a combination of the names *Brahmaputra* and *Moskva*, proved a sound investment that wasn't cursed by the Indian defense industry's endemic delays. Several years of testing led to actual production by 2004. The Indian Navy inducted it the following year and the ground-launched version was accepted by the army in 2007.

The BrahMos is a single warhead ramjet-driven system meant to operate from ground-based launchers, aircraft, warships, and submarines. Its range is between 300 and 500 km depending on the variant. Its payload, which can be armed with an 800 lb high explosive warhead, supports submunitions as well.

To further emphasize the BrahMos potential lethality–it's considered superior to anything used by NATO or the US.

Prithvi

Given its sterling bilateral ties with Russia, India never acquired ballistic missile technology from the Eastern Bloc. As its nuclear weapons program advanced, however, a requirement arose for a modern delivery system, i.e. a missile.

Beginning in 1983, the IGMDP sought to produce a road mobile surface to surface weapon for delivering conventional payloads. Its envisioned role was to degrade and destroy vital enemy infrastructure during a ground offensive.This doctrine made the forthcoming missile analogous to the Soviet Scud-series or the US-made ATACMS.

By 1988 testing commenced for what became the Prithvi I, a nine-meter tall conventional rocket with a 2,200 pound payload and a modest range of 150 kilometers. Production commenced in 1994 and the Indian Army maintains a small arsenal of Prithvi's today. An improved variant, the Prithvi II, is still undergoing tests in the Bay of Bengal.

The Prithvi II has more than twice the range of its predecessor and can be armed with a nuclear warhead. Once operational, it will be capable of ground, air, and sea launches. A naval variant of the Prithvi called the Dhanush is believed to already be in service since 2010.

FN FAL

From old school revolvers to nimble Sterlings, the OFB manufactures a bewildering variety of small arms and ammunition. But India's state-owned gun maker is unique for being the last, if not one of the last, bastions of the 7.62x51mm SLR.

The SLR, which is the British designation for the Belgian FAL, became a NATO standard rifle in 1953. Photographs can be found showing Indian soldiers armed with it during the Second India-Pakistan War in 1965. Given the size of India's military and police forces, the OFB could be the largest producer of the SLR outside Europe.

Over the decades the OFB eventually built significant numbers of the Soviet AKM, its own family of indigenous rifles, and R&Ded new small arms. But the SLR hasn't completely gone away and might never will. Why should it? It's a perfect semi-automatic rifle.

FN MAG

Frabique Nationale, known today as FN Herstal, created an immortal weapon when it combined the gas operated firing mechanism of the Browning Automatic Rifle with the feed of a German MG. 34. The result was a belt-fed machine gun that's now used in every continent and license-built by at least a dozen countries.

When introduced in 1958 it was quickly adopted by the UK as the L7 GPMG and the rest of NATO soon followed. Recognizable for its extended barrel, box shaped receiver, and distinctive carrying handle, it saw widespread use in the Middle East and Asia.

As a former British colony and a member of the Commonwealth, the Indian military stuck to their L7 (and the original BREN, to some extent) with its high rate of fire and impressive range, which reaches 1.5 kilometers. The OFB manufactures three variants for infantry, vehicles, and aircraft.

More thank half a century since its arrival the same L7 beloved by India is still rated excellent by soldiers everywhere.

NSV

In 1969 Soviet weapon designers began working on a new multipurpose 12.7mm machine gun to replace the cumbersome DShK, which dated to World War Two and was used throughout the Eastern Bloc.

By 1974 the NSV (an acronym for the inventors Nikitin, Sokolov, Volkov) commenced production and was soon indispensable for the Red Army and its allies. Weighing just 50 pounds and accurate up to 1,500 meters (1.5 km), the NSV was a formidable heavy machine gun that had no equivalent in the West. Its design also reflected its possible use against low-flying aircraft.

It's unclear when India began mass-producing the NSV. But after testing the Soviet T-72 during the early 1980s the schematics for the NSV were no doubt passed on to the OFB. Since then the Indian Army no longer bothered with another machine gun and like the Russians, the NSV is a permanent fixture on the army's tanks and vehicles.

8

Rising Indian Nuclear Power

India has a flourishing and largely indigenous nuclear power program and expects to have 14,600 MWe nuclear capacity on line by 2020. It aims to supply 25% of electricity from nuclear power by 2050.

Because India is outside the Nuclear Non-Proliferation Treaty due to its weapons program, it was for 34 years largely excluded from trade in nuclear plant or materials, which has hampered its development of civil nuclear energy until 2009.

Due to these trade bans and lack of indigenous uranium, India has uniquely been developing a nuclear fuel cycle to exploit its reserves of thorium.

Now, foreign technology and fuel are expected to boost India's nuclear power plans considerably. All plants will have high indigenous engineering content.

India has a vision of becoming a world leader in nuclear technology due to its expertise in fast reactors and thorium fuel cycle.

India's primary energy consumption more than doubled between 1990 and 2011 to nearly 25,000 PJ. India's dependence on imported energy resources and the inconsistent reform of the energy sector are challenges to satisfying rising demand.

Electricity demand in India is increasing rapidly, and the 1052 billion kilowatt hours gross produced in 2011 was more than triple the 1990 output, though still represented only some 750 kWh per capita for the year. With huge transmission losses

– 222 TWh in 2011, this resulted in only about 774 billion kWh consumption. Gross generation comprised 836 TWh from fossil fuels, 33 TWh from nuclear, 131 TWh from hydro and 53 TWh from other renewables. Coal provides 68% of the electricity at present, but reserves are limited. Gas provides 15%, hydro 12%. The per capita electricity consumption figure is expected to double by 2020, with 6.3% annual growth, and reach 5000-6000 kWh by 2050, requiring about 8000 TWh/yr then. There is an acute demand for more and more reliable power supplies. One-third of the population is not connected to any grid.

At mid-2012, 203 GWe was on line with 20.5 GWe having been added in 12 months. In September 2012 it had 211 GWe. The government's 12th five-year plan for 2012-17 is targeting the addition of 94 GWe over the period, costing $247 billion. Three quarters of this would be coal- or lignite-fired, and only 3.4 GWe nuclear, including two imported 1000 MWe units planned at one site and two indigenous 700 MWe units at another. By 2032 total installed capacity of 700 GWe is planned to meet 7-9% GDP growth, and this was to include 63 GWe nuclear. The OECD's International Energy Agency predicts that India will need some $1600 billion investment in power generation, transmission and distribution to 2035. India has five electricity grids – Northern, Eastern, North-Eastern, Southern and Western. All of them are interconnected to some extent, except the Southern grid. All are run by the state-owned Power Grid Corporation of India Ltd (PGCI), which operates more than 95,000 circuit km of transmission lines. In July 2012 the Northern grid failed with 35,669 MWe load in the early morning, and the following day it plus parts of two other grids failed again so that over 600 million people in 22 states were without power for up to a day.

A KPMG report in 2007 said that India needed to spend US$ 120-150 billion on power infrastructure over the next five years, including transmission and distribution (T&D). It said that T&D losses were some 30-40%, worth more than $6 billion per year. A 2012 report costs the losses as $12.6 billion per year. A 2012 report costs the losses as $12.6 billion per year. A 2010 estimate shows big differences among states, with some very high, and a national average of 27% T&D loss, well above the target 15% set in 2001 when the average figure was 34%. Installed transmission capacity is only about 13% of generation capacity.

Nuclear power supplied 20 billion kWh (3.7%) of India's electricity in 2011 from 4.4 GWe (of 180 GWe total) capacity and after a dip in 2008-09 this is increasing as imported uranium becomes available and new plants come on line. Some 350 reactor-years of operation had been achieved by the end of 2011. India's fuel situation, with shortage of fossil fuels, is driving the nuclear investment for electricity, and 25% nuclear contribution is the ambition for 2050, when 1094 GWe of base-load capacity is expected to be required. Almost as much investment in the grid system as in power plants is necessary.

The target since about 2004 has been for nuclear power to provide 20 GWe by 2020, but in 2007 the Prime Minister referred to this as "modest" and capable of being "doubled with the opening up of international cooperation." However, it is evident that even the 20 GWe target would require substantial uranium imports. In June 2009 NPCIL said it aimed for 60 GWe nuclear by 2032, including 40 GWe of PWR capacity and 7 GWe of new PHWR capacity, all fuelled by imported uranium. This 2032 target was reiterated late in 2010 and increased to 63 GWe in 2011. But in December 2011 parliament was told that more realistic targets were 14,600 MWe by 2020-21 and 27,500 MWe by 2032, relative to present 4780 MWe and 10,080 MWe when reactors under construction were on line in 2017.*

* "the XII Plan proposals are being finalized which envisage start of work on eight indigenous 700 MW Pressurised Heavy Water Reactors (PHWRs), two 500 MW Fast Breeder Reactors (FBRs), one 300 MW Advanced Heavy Water Reactor (AHWR) and eight Light Water Reactors of 1000 MW or higher capacity with foreign technical cooperation. These nuclear power reactors are expected to be completed progressively in the XIII and XIV Plans."

The 16 PHWRS and LWRs are expected to cost $40 billion. The eight 700 MWe PHWRs would be built at Kaiga in Karnataka, Gorakhpur in Haryana's Fatehabad District, Banswada in Rajasthan, and Chutka(in Madhya Pradesh.

After liability legislation started to deter foreign reactor vendors, early in 2102 the government said it wanted to see coal production increase by 150 Mt/yr (from 440 Mt/yr) to support 60 GWe new coal-fired capacity to be built by 2015. This would involve Rs 56 billion new investment in rail infrastructure.

Longer term, the Atomic Energy Commission however envisages some 500 GWe nuclear on line by 2060, and has since speculated that the amount might be higher still: 600-700 GWe by 2050, providing half of all electricity. Another projection is for nuclear share to rise to 9% by 2037.

INDIAN NUCLEAR POWER INDUSTRY DEVELOPMENT

Nuclear power for civil use is well established in India. Its civil nuclear strategy has been directed towards complete independence in the nuclear fuel cycle, necessary because it is excluded from the 1970 Nuclear Non-Proliferation Treaty (NPT) due to it acquiring nuclear weapons capability after 1970. (Those five countries doing so before 1970 were accorded the status of Nuclear Weapons States under the NPT.)

As a result, India's nuclear power program has proceeded largely without fuel or technological assistance from other countries. Its power reactors to the mid-1990s had some of the world's lowest capacity factors, reflecting the technical difficulties of the country's isolation, but rose impressively from 60% in 1995 to 85% in 2001-02. Then in 2008-10 the load factors dropped due to shortage of uranium fuel.

India's nuclear energy self-sufficiency extended from uranium exploration and mining through fuel fabrication, heavy water production, reactor design and construction, to reprocessing and waste management. It has a small fast breeder reactor and is building a much larger one. It is also developing technology to utilise its abundant resources of thorium as a nuclear fuel.

The Atomic Energy Establishment was set up at Trombay, near Mumbai, in 1957 and renamed as Bhabha Atomic Research Centre (BARC) ten years later. Plans for building the first Pressurised Heavy Water Reactor (PHWR) were finalised in 1964, and this prototype – Rajasthan 1, which had Canada's Douglas Point reactor as a reference unit, was built as a collaborative venture between Atomic Energy of Canada Ltd (AECL) and NPCIL.

It started up in 1972 and was duplicated Subsequent indigenous PHWR development has been based on these units, though several stages of evolution can be identified: PHWRs with dousing and single containment at Rajasthan 1-2, PHWRs with suppression pool and partial double containment at Madras, and later standardized PHWRs from Narora onwards having double containment, suppression pool, and calandria filled with heavy water, housed in a water-filled calandria vault.

The Indian Atomic Energy Commission (AEC) is the main policy body. The Nuclear Power Corporation of India Ltd (NPCIL) is responsible for design, construction, commissioning and operation of thermal nuclear power plants.

At the start of 2010 it said it had enough cash on hand for 10,000 MWe of new plant. Its funding model is 70% equity and 30% debt financing.

However, it is aiming to involve other public sector and private corporations in future nuclear power expansion, notably National Thermal Power Corporation (NTPC) – see subsection below. NTPC is very much larger than NPCIL and sees itself as the main power producer. NTPC is largely government-owned. The 1962 Atomic Energy Act prohibits private control of nuclear power generation, though it allows minority investment. As of late 2010 the government had no intention of changing this to allow greater private equity in nuclear plants.

DEFENCE MANPOWER OF NUCLEAR WEAPON

A nuclear weapon is an explosive device that derives its destructive force from nuclear reactions, either fission or a combination of fission and fusion. Both reactions release vast quantities of energy from relatively small amounts of matter. The first fission ("atomic") bomb test released the same amount of energy as approximately 20,000 tons of TNT. The first thermonuclear ("hydrogen") bomb test released the same amount of energy as approximately 10,000,000 tons of TNT.

A modern thermonuclear weapon weighing little more than 2,400 pounds (1,100 kg) can produce an explosive force comparable to the detonation of more than 1.2 million tons (1.1 million metric tons) of TNT. Thus, even a small nuclear device no larger than traditional bombs can devastate an entire city by blast, fire and radiation. Nuclear weapons are considered weapons of mass destruction, and their use and control has been a major focus of international relations policy since their debut.

Only two nuclear weapons have been used in the course of warfare, both by the United States near the end of World War II. On 6 August 1945, a uranium gun-type device code-named "Little Boy" was detonated over the Japanese city of Hiroshima. Three days later, on 9 August, a plutonium implosion-type device code-named "Fat Man" was exploded over Nagasaki, Japan. These two bombings resulted in the deaths of approximately 200,000 Japanese people—mostly civilians—from acute injuries sustained from the explosions. The role of the bombings in Japan's surrender, and their ethical status, remain the subject of scholarly and popular debate.

Since the bombings of Hiroshima and Nagasaki, nuclear weapons have been detonated on over two thousand occasions for testing purposes and demonstrations. Only a few nations possess such weapons or are suspected of seeking them. The only countries known to have detonated nuclear weapons—and that acknowledge possessing such weapons—are (chronologically by date of first test) the United States, the Soviet Union (succeeded as a nuclear power by Russia), the United Kingdom, France, the People's Republic of China, India, Pakistan, and North Korea. In addition, Israel is also widely believed to possess nuclear weapons, though it does not acknowledge having them. One state, South Africa, has admitted to having previous fabricated nuclear weapons in the past, but has since disassembled their arsenal and submitted to international safeguards.

Types

There are two basic types of nuclear weapons: those which derive the majority of their energy from nuclear fission reactions alone, and those which use fission reactions to begin nuclear fusion reactions that produce a large amount of the total energy output.

Fission Weapons

All existing nuclear weapons derive some of their explosive energy from nuclear fission reactions. Weapons whose explosive output is exclusively from fission reactions are commonly referred to as atomic bombs or atom bombs (abbreviated as A-bombs). This has long been noted as something of a misnomer, however, as their energy comes specifically from the nucleus of the atom. In fission weapons, a mass of fissile material (enriched uranium or plutonium) is assembled into a supercritical mass—the amount of material needed to start an exponentially growing nuclear chain reaction—either by shooting one piece of sub-critical material into another (the "gun" method) or by compressing a sub-critical sphere of material using chemical explosives to many times its original density (the "implosion" method). The latter approach is considered more sophisticated than the former and only the latter approach can be used if the fissile material is plutonium.

A major challenge in all nuclear weapon designs is to ensure that a significant fraction of the fuel is consumed before the weapon destroys itself. The amount of energy released by fission bombs can range from the equivalent of less than a ton of TNT upwards of 500,000 tons (500 kilotons) of TNT.

Fusion Weapons

The other basic type of nuclear weapon produces a large amount of its energy through nuclear fusion reactions. Such fusion weapons are generally referred to as thermonuclear weapons or more colloquially as hydrogen bombs (abbreviated as H-bombs), as they rely on fusion reactions between isotopes of hydrogen (deuterium and tritium). However, all such weapons derive a significant portion, and sometimes a majority, of their energy from fission. This is because a fission weapon is required as a "trigger" for the fusion reactions, and the fusion reactions can themselves trigger additional fission reactions. Unlike fission weapons, there are no inherent limits on the energy released by thermonuclear weapons. Only six countries—United States, Russia, United Kingdom, People's Republic of China, France and India—have conducted thermonuclear weapon tests. (Whether India has detonated a "true", multi-staged thermonuclear weapon is controversial.) All thermonuclear weapons are considered to be much more difficult to successfully design and execute than primitive fission weapons.

Thermonuclear bombs work by using the energy of a fission bomb to compress and heat fusion fuel. In the Teller-Ulam design, which accounts for all multi-megaton yield hydrogen bombs, this is accomplished by placing a fission bomb and fusion fuel (tritium, deuterium, or lithium deuteride) in proximity within a special, radiation-reflecting container. When the fission bomb is detonated, gamma and X-rays emitted first compress the fusion fuel, then heat it to thermonuclear temperatures. The ensuing fusion reaction creates enormous numbers of high-speed neutrons, which can then induce fission in materials not normally prone to it, such as depleted uranium. Each of these components is known as a "stage", with the fission bomb as the "primary" and the fusion capsule as the "secondary". In large hydrogen bombs, about half of the yield, and much of the resulting nuclear fallout, comes from the final fissioning of depleted uranium.

By chaining together numerous stages with increasing amounts of fusion fuel, thermonuclear weapons can be made to an almost arbitrary yield; the largest ever detonated (the Tsar Bomba of the USSR) released an energy equivalent of over 50 million tons (50 megatons) of TNT. Most thermonuclear weapons are considerably smaller than this, due to practical constraints arising from the space and weight requirements of missile warheads.

Other Types

There are other types of nuclear weapons as well. For example, a boosted fission weapon is a fission bomb which increases its explosive yield through a small amount of fusion reactions, but it is not a fusion bomb. In the boosted bomb, the neutrons produced by the fusion reactions serve primarily to increase the efficiency of the fission bomb.

Some weapons are designed for special purposes; a neutron bomb is a thermonuclear weapon that yields a relatively small explosion but a relatively large amount of neutron radiation; such a device could theoretically be used to cause massive casualties while leaving infrastructure mostly intact and creating a minimal amount of fallout. The detonation of any nuclear weapon is accompanied by a blast of neutron radiation. Surrounding a nuclear weapon with suitable materials (such as cobalt or gold) creates a weapon known as a salted bomb. This device can produce exceptionally large quantities of radioactive contamination. Most variation in nuclear weapon design is for the purpose of achieving different yields for different situations, and in manipulating design elements to attempt to minimize weapon size.

Weapons Delivery

Nuclear weapons delivery—the technology and systems used to bring a nuclear weapon to its target—is an important aspect of nuclear weapons relating both to nuclear weapon design and nuclear strategy. Additionally, development and maintenance of delivery options is among the most resource-intensive aspects of a nuclear weapons program: according to one estimate, deployment costs accounted for 57% of the total financial resources spent by the United States in relation to nuclear weapons since 1940. Historically the first method of delivery, and the method used in the two nuclear weapons actually used in warfare, was as a gravity bomb, dropped from bomber aircraft. This method is usually the first developed by countries as it does not place many restrictions on the size of the weapon and *weapon miniaturization* is something which requires considerable weapons design knowledge. It does, however, limit the range of attack, the response time to an impending attack, and the number of weapons which can be fielded at any given time.

With the advent of miniaturization, nuclear bombs can be delivered by both strategic bombers and tactical fighter-bombers, allowing an air force to use its current fleet with little or no modification. This method may still be considered the primary means of nuclear weapons delivery; the majority of U.S. nuclear warheads, for example, are free-fall gravity bombs, namely the B61.

More preferable from a strategic point of view is a nuclear weapon mounted onto a missile, which can use a ballistic trajectory to deliver the warhead over the horizon. While even short range missiles allow for a faster and less vulnerable attack, the development of long-range intercontinental ballistic missiles (ICBMs) and submarine-launched ballistic missiles (SLBMs) has given some nations the ability to plausibly deliver missiles anywhere on the globe with a high likelihood of success. More advanced systems, such as multiple independently targetable reentry vehicles (MIRVs), allow multiple warheads to be launched at different targets from one missile, reducing the chance of a successful missile defence. Today, missiles are most common among systems designed for delivery of nuclear weapons. Making a warhead small enough to fit onto a missile, though, can be a difficult task.

Tactical weapons have involved the most variety of delivery types, including not only gravity bombs and missiles but also artillery shells, land mines, and nuclear depth charges and torpedoes for anti-submarine warfare. An atomic mortar was also tested at one time by the United States. Small, two-man portable tactical weapons (somewhat misleadingly referred to as suitcase bombs), such as the Special Atomic Demolition Munition, have been developed, although the difficulty of combining sufficient yield with portability limits their military utility.

NUCLEAR STRATEGY

Nuclear warfare strategy is a set of policies that deal with preventing or fighting a nuclear war. The policy of trying to prevent an attack by a nuclear weapon from another country by threatening nuclear retaliation is known as the strategy of nuclear deterrence.

The goal in deterrence is to always maintain a second strike capability (the ability of a country to respond to a nuclear attack with one of its own) and potentially to strive for first strike status (the ability to completely destroy an enemy's nuclear forces before they could retaliate). During the Cold War, policy and military theorists in nuclear-enabled countries worked out models of what sorts of policies could prevent one from ever being attacked by a nuclear weapon.

Different forms of nuclear weapons delivery allow for different types of nuclear strategies. The goals of any strategy are generally to make it difficult for an enemy to launch a pre-emptive strike against the weapon system and difficult to defend against the delivery of the weapon during a potential conflict. Sometimes this has meant keeping the weapon locations hidden, such as deploying them on submarines or rail cars whose locations are very hard for an enemy to track and other times this means protecting them by burying them in hardened bunkers.

Other components of nuclear strategies have included using missile defence (to destroy the missiles before they land) or implementation of civil defence measures (using early-warning systems to evacuate citizens to safe areas before an attack). Note that weapons which are designed to threaten large populations or to generally deter attacks are known as strategic weapons. Weapons which are designed to actually be used on a battlefield in military situations are known as tactical weapons.

There are critics of the very idea of nuclear strategy for waging nuclear war who have suggested that a nuclear war between two nuclear powers would result in mutual annihilation. From this point of view, the significance of nuclear weapons is purely to deter war because any nuclear war would immediately escalate out of mutual distrust and fear, resulting in mutually assured destruction. This threat of national, if not global, destruction has been a strong motivation for anti-nuclear weapons activism.

Critics from the peace movement and within the military establishment have questioned the usefulness of such weapons in the current military climate. The use of (or threat of use of) such weapons would generally be contrary to the rules of international law applicable in armed conflict, according to an advisory opinion issued by the International Court of Justice in 1996. Perhaps the most controversial idea in nuclear strategy is that nuclear proliferation would be desirable. This view argues that, unlike conventional weapons, nuclear weapons successfully deter all-out war between states, and they are said to have done this during the Cold War between the U.S. and the Soviet Union. Political scientist Kenneth Waltz is the most prominent advocate of this argument.

The threat of potentially suicidal terrorists possessing nuclear weapons (a form of nuclear terrorism) complicates the decision process. The prospect of mutually assured destruction may not deter an enemy who expects to die in the confrontation. Further, if the initial act is from a rogue group instead of a sovereign nation, there is no fixed nation or fixed military targets to retaliate against. It has been argued, especially after the September 11, 2001 attacks, that this complication is the sign of the next age of nuclear strategy, distinct from the relative stability of the Cold War. In 1996, the United States adopted a policy of allowing the targeting of its nuclear weapons at terrorists armed with weapons of mass destruction.

Governance, Control, and Law

Because of the immense military power they can confer, the political control of nuclear weapons has been a key issue for as long as they have existed; in most countries the use of nuclear force can only be authorized by the head of government or head of state.

In the late 1940s, lack of mutual trust was preventing the United States and the Soviet Union from making ground towards international arms control agreements, but by the 1960s steps were being taken to limit both the proliferation of nuclear weapons to other countries and the environmental effects of nuclear testing. The Partial Test Ban Treaty (1963) restricted all nuclear testing to underground nuclear testing, to prevent contamination from nuclear fallout, while the Nuclear Non-Proliferation Treaty (1968) attempted to place restrictions on the types of activities which signatories could participate in, with the goal of allowing the transference of non-military nuclear technology to member countries without fear of proliferation.

In 1957, the International Atomic Energy Agency (IAEA) was established under the mandate of the United Nations in order to encourage the development of the peaceful applications of nuclear technology, provide international safeguards against its misuse, and facilitate the application of safety measures in its use. In 1996, many nations signed the Comprehensive Test Ban Treaty which prohibits all testing of nuclear weapons, which would impose a significant hindrance to their development by any complying country. Due to the strict entry into force criterion of the convention however, it had as of 2011 not entered into force.

Additional treaties and agreements have governed nuclear weapons stockpiles between the countries with the two largest stockpiles, the United States and the Soviet Union, and later between the United States and Russia. These include treaties such as SALT II (never ratified), START I (expired), INF, START II (never ratified), SORT, and New START, as well as non-binding agreements such as SALT I and the Presidential

Nuclear Initiatives of 1991. Even when they did not enter into force, these agreements helped limit and later reduce the numbers and types of nuclear weapons between the United States and the Soviet Union/Russia.

Nuclear weapons have also been opposed by agreements between countries. Many nations have been declared Nuclear-Weapon-Free Zones, areas where nuclear weapons production and deployment are prohibited, through the use of treaties. The Treaty of Tlatelolco (1967) prohibited any production or deployment of nuclear weapons in Latin America and the Caribbean, and the Treaty of Pelindaba (1964) prohibits nuclear weapons in many African countries. As recently as 2006 a Central Asian Nuclear Weapon Free Zone was established amongst the former Soviet republics of Central Asia prohibiting nuclear weapons.

In the middle of 1996, the International Court of Justice, the highest court of the United Nations, issued an Advisory Opinion concerned with the "Legality of the Threat or Use of Nuclear Weapons". The court ruled that the use or threat of use of nuclear weapons would violate various articles of international law, including the Geneva Conventions, the Hague Conventions, the UN Charter, and the Universal Declaration of Human Rights. In view of the unique, destructive characteristics of nuclear weapons, the International Committee of the Red Cross calls on States to ensure that these weapons are never used, irrespective of whether they consider them to be lawful or not.

Additionally, there have been other, specific actions meant to discourage countries from developing nuclear arms. In the wake of the tests by India and Pakistan in 1998, economic sanctions were (temporarily) levied against both countries, though neither were signatories with the Nuclear Non-Proliferation Treaty. One of the stated *casus belli* for the initiation of the 2003 Iraq War was an accusation by the United States that Iraq was actively pursuing nuclear arms (though this was soon discovered not to be the case as the program had been discontinued). In 1981, Israel had bombed a nuclear reactor being constructed in Osirak, Iraq, in what it called an attempt to halt Iraq's previous nuclear arms ambitions.

Disarmament

Nuclear disarmament refers to both the act of reducing or eliminating nuclear weapons and to the end state of a nuclear-free world, in which nuclear weapons are completely eliminated. Beginning with the 1963 Partial Test Ban Treaty and continuing through the 1996 Comprehensive Test Ban Treaty, there have been many treaties to limit or reduce nuclear weapons testing and stockpiles. The 1968 Nuclear Non-Proliferation Treaty has as one of its explicit conditions that all signatories must "pursue negotiations in good faith" towards the long-term goal of "complete disarmament". However, no nuclear state has treated that aspect of the agreement as having binding force.

Only one country—South Africa—has ever fully renounced nuclear weapons they had independently developed. A number of former Soviet republics—Belarus, Kazakhstan, and Ukraine—returned Soviet nuclear arms stationed in their countries to Russia after the collapse of the USSR.

Proponents of nuclear disarmament say that it would lessen the probability of nuclear war occurring, especially accidentally. Critics of nuclear disarmament say that it would undermine deterrence and could lead to increased global instability. Various American government officials, who were in office during the Cold War period, have recently been advocating the elimination of nuclear weapons. These officials include Henry Kissinger, George Shultz, Sam Nunn, and William Perry. In January 2010, Lawrence M. Krauss stated that "no issue carries more importance to the long-term health and security of humanity than the effort to reduce, and perhaps one day, rid the world of nuclear weapons".

In the years after the end of the Cold War, there have been numerous campaigns to urge the abolition of nuclear weapons, such as that organized by the Global Zero movement, and the goal of a "world without nuclear weapons" was advocated by United States President Barack Obama in an April 2009 speech in Prague. A CNN poll from April 2010 indicated that the American public was nearly evenly split on the issue.

Controversy

Even before the first nuclear weapons had been developed, scientists involved with the Manhattan Project were divided over the use of the weapon. The role of the two atomic bombings of the country in Japan's surrender and the U.S.'s ethical justification for them has been the subject of scholarly and popular debate for decades. The question of whether nations should have nuclear weapons, or test them, has been continually and nearly universally controversial.

Radioactive fallout from nuclear weapons testing was first drawn to public attention in 1954 when the Castle Bravo hydrogen bomb test at the Pacific Proving Grounds contaminated the crew and catch of the Japanese fishing boat *Lucky Dragon*. One of the fishermen died in Japan seven months later, and the fear of contaminated tuna led to a temporary boycotting of the popular staple in Japan. The incident caused widespread concern around the world, especially regarding the effects of nuclear fallout and atmospheric nuclear testing, and "provided a decisive impetus for the emergence of the anti-nuclear weapons movement in many countries".

Peace movements emerged in Japan and in 1954 they converged to form a unified "Japanese Council Against Atomic and Hydrogen Bombs". Japanese opposition to nuclear weapons tests in the Pacific Ocean was widespread, and "an estimated 35 million signatures were collected on petitions calling for bans on nuclear weapons".

In the United Kingdom, the first Aldermaston March organised by the Campaign for Nuclear Disarmament took place at Easter 1958, when several thousand people marched for four days from Trafalgar Square, London, to the Atomic Weapons Research Establishment close to Aldermaston in Berkshire, England, to demonstrate their opposition to nuclear weapons. The Aldermaston marches continued into the late 1960s when tens of thousands of people took part in the four-day marches. In 1959, a letter in the *Bulletin of Atomic Scientists* was the start of a successful campaign to stop the Atomic Energy Commission dumping radioactive waste in the sea 19 kilometres from Boston. In 1962, Linus Pauling won the Nobel Peace Prize for his work to stop the atmospheric testing of nuclear weapons, and the "Ban the Bomb" movement spread.

In 1963, many countries ratified the Partial Test Ban Treaty prohibiting atmospheric nuclear testing. Radioactive fallout became less of an issue and the anti-nuclear weapons movement went into decline for some years. A resurgence of interest occurred amid European and American fears of nuclear war in the 1980s.

Non-weapons Uses

Apart from their use as weapons, nuclear explosives have been tested and used for various non-military uses, and proposed, but not used for large-scale earth moving. When long term health and clean-up costs were included, there was no economic advantage over conventional explosives. Synthetic elements, such as einsteinium and fermium, created by neutron bombardment of uranium and plutonium during thermonuclear explosions, were discovered in the aftermath of the first thermonuclear bomb test. In 2008 the worldwide presence of new isotopes from atmospheric testing beginning in the 1950s was developed into a reliable way of detecting art forgeries, as all paintings created after that period may contain traces of cesium-137 and strontium-90, isotopes that did not exist in nature before 1945. Nuclear explosives have also been seriously studied as potential propulsion mechanisms for space travel.

INDIA'S NUCLEAR WEAPONS PROGRAMME

The end of World War II marked a revolution in world affairs - the recasting of nations and relations between nations, and the emergence of a new technology which fundamentally changed the role of warfare. Within the span of two years and two months, from 1945 to 1947, three critical events occurred whose reverberations have brought the threat of nuclear war in South Asia seemingly daily to the front pages of newspapers everywhere. The three events were - in chronological order - the establishment of the United Nations on 26 June 1945; the dramatic demonstration of the destruction of which even crude nuclear weapons are capable in August 1945; and the calamitous partition of British India into the modern states of India and Pakistan at midnight on 14-15 August 1947.

It is clear to everyone that the legacy of partition is a key driving force behind the nuclear standoff that now exists between India and Pakistan. Partition split apart a region that had been united for millenia amid communal massacres on a scale never before seen, leaving in its wake the unresolved issue of contested Kashmir - a Muslim-majority region held by Hindu-majority India. The skirmishing that has continued now for over fifty years, punctuated by outbreaks of full-scale war (in 1947, 1965, and 1971), have given both nations ample motivation to develop potent weapons to gain advantage over — or restore balance with — the other. Another motivation for India's acquisition of nuclear weapons, less often considered in the West, is the potential threat and regional challenge presented by the nuclear-armed state of China, which faces India along much of its northern border. Disputes covering 80,000 square kilometres of this border region exist:

- China currently occupies the Aksai Chin plateau adjacent to Ladakh in Kashmir;
- India occupies the North-East Frontier Agency claimed by China.

These territorial disputes, a legacy of British rule, erupted into the Sino-Indian War on 20 October 1962, when China launched a massive attack on India to which India was powerless to respond. India had relied for years on a warm relationship with the Soviet Union as a counterweight to China, but with the USSR facing down the United States at the same moment in the Cuban Missile Crisis, India was shocked to find the Politburo suddenly switching to support China in an effort to bolster its own position. PM Nehru was forced to appeal to the U.S. for help. U.S. naval air forces arrived off the coast, but before the USAF could deploy to India, China halted its attack on 21 November and partially withdrew. China continues to hold the Aksai Chin region captured in the initial advance. The legacy of this incident was the discovery that the Soviet Union was an unreliable ally, and the deep resolve not to be at a similar disadvantage with respect to China in the future.

Finally, an even less well known factor is a deep-seated drive to achieve international influence commensurate with India's size, and its importance throughout history as one of the world's principle civilizations. At the founding of the United Nations in 1945 the composition of the UN Security Council, the world's most influential and powerful international body, was fixed and has never changed from that time. By an accident of history India was not an independent state at that moment, and its only hope for representation at the conference was the Churchill administration, then in its closing days, which vehemently opposed India's national aspirations. As a result China - with a similar geographic size, population, and state of economic development - was given a seat on Security Council, but India was not. Nuclear weapons did not exist at the time the Security Council composition was debated, but over time the five Council members all acquired nuclear, then thermonuclear, arms. With the signing of the Nuclear Non-Proliferation treaty in 1970, and the replacement on the Council of the non-nuclear Taipei Chinese government with the nuclear armed government in Beijing shortly thereafter, the de facto principle that Security Council permanent members and the "nuclear club" were one and the same was firmly established.

The crucial importance of the desire for recognition of India as a world power in driving forward the nuclear weapons program, even overshadowing considerations of military necessity and deterrence is underscored by remarks by former weapons program leader Raj Ramanna: "There was never a discussion among us over whether we shouldn't make the bomb. How to do it was more important. For us it was a matter of prestige that would justify our ancient past. The question of deterrence came much later. Also, as Indian scientists we were keen to show our Western counterparts, who thought little of us those days, that we too could do it."

Thus it should be no surprise that India, now tied for third place among the world's largest economies (with Germany), and soon to become the most populous nation on Earth, has concluded that to be given its due in world affairs, it must become a member of the nuclear club as well. What is notable however is how the world's largest democracy developed such capabilities. The decisions were made by a handful of people, with virtually no input or oversight by the public or the legislature. India's nuclear weapons program from its outset has answered only to the Prime Minister's office, and only the Prime Minister and a select few of his or her appointees have ever had any say in its development and acquisition.

Origin of India's Nuclear Weapon Program

India's indigenous efforts in nuclear science and technology were established remarkably early. The first step was taken by Dr. Homi Jehangir Bhabha in March 1944 when he submitted a proposal to the Sir Dorab Tata Trust (established in honor of Bhabha's own uncle, Sir Dorab Tata) to found a nuclear research institute, over three years before independence and a year before the first nuclear weapon test.

This led to the creation of the Tata Institute of Fundamental Research (TIFR) on 19 December 1945 with Bhabha as its first Director. The new government of India passed the Atomic Energy Act, on 15 April 1948, leading to the establishment of the Indian Atomic Energy Commission (IAEC) not quite one year after independence. At that time Prime Minister Pandit Jawaharlal Nehru declared: We must develop this atomic energy quite apart from war - indeed I think we must develop it for the purpose of using it for peaceful purposes.... Of course, if we are compelled as a nation to use it for other purposes, possibly no pious sentiments of any of us will stop the nation from using it that way."

This note of ambivalence in Nehru's speech foreshadowed his policies on nuclear research for the next decade. Nehru took a prominent role in international politics, founding the Non-Aligned Movement, and advocating nuclear disarmament. However, he refused to foreclose India's nuclear option while other nations maintained nuclear arsenals and supported programs designed to bolster India's weapons potential. In 1954 the Indian nuclear program began to move in a direction that would eventually lead to establishment of nuclear weapons capability. On 3 January 1954 the IAEC decided to set up a new facility - the Atomic Energy Establishment, Trombay (AEET), later to become the "Indian Los Alamos". On 3 August 1954 the Department of Atomic Energy (DAE) was created with Dr. Bhabha as Secretary. This department answered directly to the Prime Minister and has continued to do so down to the present day.

The program grew swiftly. The atomic energy budget increased 12-fold from 1954 to 1956. By 1958 the DAE consumed one third of India's research budget. By 1959 AEET employed over one thousand scientists and engineers. In 1955 construction began on India's first reactor, the 1 MW Apsara research reactor, with British assistance. And in September 1955, after more than a year of negotiation, Canada agreed to supply India with a powerful research reactor - the 40 MW Canada-India Reactor (CIR). Under the Eisenhower Administration's "Atoms for Peace" program the US agreed to supply 21 tons of heavy water for this reactor in Februrary 1956, and the reactor was dubbed the Canada-India Reactor, U.S. or CIRUS (now commonly written as Cirus).

The acquisition of Cirus was a watershed event in nuclear proliferation. Although the sale was made with the understanding that the reactor would only be used for peaceful purposes (the heavy water contract at least made this explicit), it occurred before any international policies were in place to regulate such technology transfers and no provision for inspections were made. And in fact India was careful to ensure that no effective regulation would accompany the reactor. India refusing to accept fuel from Canada for the reactor and set up a program to manufacture the natural uranium fuel for Cirus indigeneously so as to keep complete control of the plutonium produced there. This program, led by metallurgist Brahm Prakash, succeeded in developing the techniques for producing the precisely manufactured, high purity material demanded by the reactor.

The reactor was a design ideal for producing weapons-grade plutonium, and was also extraordinarily large for research purposes, being capable of manufacturing enough plutonium for one to two bombs a year. The acquisition of Cirus was specifically intended by India to provide herself with a weapons option and this reactor produced the plutonium used in India's first nuclear test in 1974; provided the design prototype for India's more powerful Dhruva plutonium production "research" reactor; and is directly responsible for producing nearly half of the weapons grade plutonium currently believed to be in India's stockpile. The sale further set a precedent for similar technology transfers which greatly assisted Israel in obtaining its own plutonium production reactor from France shortly thereafter. The Atomic Energy Establishment, Trombay was formally inaugurated by PM Nehru on 20 January 1957. It acquired its present name — Bhabha Atomic Research Centre (BARC) — on 12 January 1967 when PM Indira Gandhi renamed it in memory of Dr. Bhabha who died in an airplane crash on 24 January 1966.

Apsara, fueled by enriched uranium from the UK, went critical on 4 August 1957, becoming the first operating reactor in Asia outside of the Soviet Union (though only days ahead of Japan's first reactor). Cirus achieved criticality at BARC on 10 July 1960.

As a nation India has always placed a premium on self-sufficiency. It is, in fact, the most self-sufficient large economy in the world and does not import any nuclear fuel. [The traditionally closed nature of economy though accounts for the import/export based Chinese economy far outstripping its growth from the late seventies to the early nineties.] Due to its vast domestic resources of thorium (a potential fuel for breeder reactors) but limited supplies of uranium, from the start of its nuclear program India has always placed strong emphasis on the development of breeder reactor fuel cycles. Breeder reactors require highly concentrated fissionable material for reactor fuel: either highly enriched uranium or plutonium. This provided a peaceful rationale for developing a plutonium separation capability, but the principal impetus for the India's first fuel reprocessing plant was to obtain a nuclear option.

In July 1958 PM Nehru authorized project Phoenix to build a plant with a capacity of 20 tonnes of fuel a year - sized to match the production capacity of Cirus. The plant was based on the U.S. developed Purex process and an American firm, Vitro International prepared the plans for it. Construction of the plutonium plant began at Trombay on 27 March 1961 and was commissioned in mid-1964.

India's civilian nuclear program was also established during this period. Discussions with American firms to construct India's first nuclear power plants at Tarapur were held in 1960-61. An interesting incident sheds light on Nehru's amd Bhabha's thinking at that time. In 1960 Kenneth Nichols, a former U.S. Army engineer who played significant roles in the Manhattan Project, represented Westinghouse in discussions on power plant construction. In a meeting with Nehru and Bhabha, Nichols relates that Nehru turned to Bhabha and asked: "Can you develop an atomic bomb?" Bhabha assured him that he could and in reply to Nehru's next question about time, he estimated that he would need about a year to do it.... He concluded by saying to Bhabha "Well, don't do it until I tell you to."

INDIA'S PARTICIPATION IN NUCLEAR COMMERCE

A key development in recent years has been the U.S.-India nuclear cooperation agreement, which was first unveiled in July 2005. This agreement and the subsequent endorsement of India's case by the Nuclear Suppliers Group (NSG) will enable India to engage in international nuclear trade. In return, New Delhi has agreed to allow safeguards on a select number of nuclear facilities that will be classified as "civilian" in purpose.

The remaining "military" facilities will remain off-limits to international inspectors. The agreement process required a number of steps, including passage of the Hyde Act by the U.S. Congress to authorize the United States government to negotiate a bilateral nuclear agreement with India (December 2006); adoption of a bilateral 123 agreement between India and the United States under the U.S. Atomic Energy Act; approval of a safeguards agreement between India and the International Atomic Energy Agency (IAEA) (August 2008); and an NSG waiver to its rules allowing Indian participation in nuclear trade (September 2008).

In October 2008, the bilateral '123' nuclear cooperation agreement was approved by the U.S. Congress and signed into law by President George W. Bush. In March 2009, the IAEA formally approved the Additional Protocol (AP) to the Indian safeguards agreement, which differs in several ways from previous APs concluded between the Agency and other states. India signed the safeguards agreement with the IAEA in February 2009, and subsequently the agreement was certified by the U.S. government in February 2010. The first two nuclear power plants, units at the Rajasthan Atomic Power Station (RAPS), have been formally placed under the safeguards agreement. In October 2009, India announced a plan to put 14 out of its 22 nuclear reactors under IAEA safeguards by 2014. In late July 2010, India and the United States signed a bilateral agreement on reprocessing spent fuel, in accordance with the '123' agreement between the two countries. The adoption of appropriate legislation dealing with liability in case of a nuclear accident represented a significant challenge. In August 2010, after contentious debate, the Indian Parliament approved the Civil Liability for Nuclear Damage Bill. The bill imposes liability not only on nuclear facility operators, but also on the suppliers of nuclear equipment and materials in the event of an accident. This clause has greatly concerned U.S. firms, which might find it difficult to obtain insurance coverage for such scenarios, making them less competitive than government-supported suppliers from other countries.

Following the NSG waiver, India signed nuclear cooperation agreements involving the supply of nuclear reactors and uranium, with France (October 2008), Russia (December 2008), Namibia (August 2009), and Argentina (October 2009). India also plans to sign an agreement with Kazakhstan, under which the Central Asian state will provide uranium to India and in return India may build several medium-sized 200 to 300MW nuclear reactors for Kazakhstan. Discussions on nuclear cooperation have also taken place with South Korea and Turkey. The Indian Nuclear Fuel Complex (NFC) received the first batch of 60 tons of uranium from Areva in March 2009, under a December 2008 agreement between the French company and the NPCIL to supply India with 300 tons of uranium. Additionally, the Russian company TVEL supplied a first batch of 30 tons of natural uranium fuel pellets to the NFC in April 2009.

According to Indian officials, New Delhi could import up to 40 nuclear reactors in the next decade. The U.S.-India Business Council stated that India might spend up to $175 billion to expand its nuclear sector in the next 25 years. According to October 2008 reports, in the next five years, India will construct 21 nuclear power facilities, including six French reactors (1,600MW each), four Russian reactors (1,000MW each), and four American reactors (1,500MW each).

In pursuit of these goals, agreements have already been struck with nuclear suppliers. In February 2009, the Nuclear Power Corporation of India Limited (NPCIL) and Areva concluded an agreement for the supply of two European Pressurized Reactors (EPR) of 1650MW each. In March 2010, New Delhi and Moscow signed nuclear deals under which Russia will construct 12 nuclear plants in India. In October 2009, New Delhi identified two locations, in the states of Gujarat and Andhra Pradesh that would host reactors constructed by GE Hitachi and Westinghouse. However, given the constraints on any agreement imposed by the civil nuclear liability law, it is unclear whether U.S. companies will conclude any reactor supply deals in the near future.

New Delhi has approved NPCIL's identification of five locations across the country which will host about 30 nuclear plants. A total of six reactors are currently under construction—work dating prior to the NSG waiver. These include two Russian reactors at Kudankulam, a 500MW fast breeder reactors at Kalpakkam, two 220MW PHWRs, and a 220MW unit at Kaiga.

Reliability of India's Nuclear Devices

There is considerable controversy over the yield and reliability of India's nuclear devices. When India tested its first fission device in May 1974, Indian scientists claimed the device had a yield of about 12 kilotons(kt).

However, that figure has been disputed by independent analysts who estimate that the yield was far lower, probably between 2 and 6kt. Similar controversy surrounds India's May 1998 tests.

After the first of round of tests on May 11, India's Department of Atomic Energy (DAE) announced that it had tested three nuclear devices: a fission device with a yield of 12kt; a thermonuclear device with a yield of 43kt; and a sub-kiloton device with a yield of 0.2kt. The figures were later revised to 45kt for the thermonuclear device and 15kt for the fission device.

However, these figures have been disputed by independent analysts, who — citing evidence from seismic data — claim that the cumulative yield of the Indian tests was more likely between 20 and 30kt, the implications being that the thermonuclear test likely failed. Senior Indian scientists including P.K. Iyengar have also publicly suggested that it is likely that the fusion device only burned partially.

However, the former head of India's Atomic Energy Commission (AEC) Dr. R. Chidambaram has claimed that a "post-shot" analysis of the Pokhran II tests confirmed that the May 1998 tests yielded about 60kt. Chidambaram subsequently asserted that the tests provided India with "the capability to design and fabricate nuclear weapons [in the range] of low-yields up to 200 kilotons." Following the May 11 tests, India carried out two tests of sub-kiloton devices on May 13 "to generate additional data for improved computer simulation of designs and for attaining the capability to carry out sub-critical experiments, if considered necessary."

Controversy regarding the 1998 tests was provoked once again in 2009 following the assertion by K. Santhanam, field director during the 1998 tests, that the thermonuclear test had failed, leading to calls by some senior scientists that New Delhi should conduct another test and should not join the Comprehensive Nuclear Test Ban Treaty (CTBT). In its response, the Indian government refuted these allegations, and reaffirmed its voluntary moratorium on tests.

Fissile Material Stocks

The plutonium for India's nuclear stockpile is most likely obtained from two research reactors: the 40 megawatts (MW) CIRUS and the 100MW Dhruva, which went critical in 1960 and 1985, respectively. The CIRUS reactor is capable of producing 9 to 10 kilograms (kg) of weapons-grade plutonium annually; the corresponding figure for the Dhruva reactor is 20 to 25kg. The irradiated fuel from the reactors is probably reprocessed at either the Plutonium Reprocessing Plant in Trombay (50 tons per year) or the Kalpakkam Reprocessing Plant (100 to 125 tons per year). The Department of Atomic Energy (DAE) plans to construct additional enriched uranium-fueled Light Water Reactors (LWRs) for future nuclear submarines, while also increasing uranium enrichment capability through the construction of a new facility.

According to published sources, India produces 20 to 40kg of plutonium annually and has probably accumulated 280 to 600kg of weapons-grade plutonium, enough to build 40 to 120 weapons. India also has a small stock of highly enriched uranium, but it is unclear if the HEU has been used to build nuclear weapons.

Custody, Command, and Control

India does not maintain a constituted nuclear force on a heightened state of alert. The nuclear-capable missiles, bombers, non-nuclear warhead assemblies, and fissile cores are maintained in a de-alerted state by their respective custodians — the individual armed services, the DRDO, and the DAE — with plans to reconstitute them rapidly during an emergency or national crisis.

India maintains a Nuclear Command Authority (NCA) at the apex of the command and control framework, which is controlled by the civilian authorities and includes the tri-service Strategic Forces Command (SFC), which administers the nuclear-capable missiles and aircraft. However, despite the existence of the SFC, the actual control of the delivery systems remains with the individual services.

NUCLEAR REACTORS DEPLOYED IN INDIA

The two Tarapur150 MWe Boiling Water Reactors (BWRs) built by GE on a turnkey contract before the advent of the Nuclear Non-Proliferation Treaty were originally 200 MWe. They were down-rated due to recurrent problems but have run well since. They have been using imported enriched uranium and are under International Atomic Energy Agency (IAEA) safeguards. However, late in 2004 Russia deferred to the Nuclear Suppliers' Group and declined to supply further uranium for them. They underwent six months refurbishment over 2005-06, and in March 2006 Russia agreed to resume fuel supply. In December 2008 a $700 million contract with Rosatom was announced for continued uranium supply to them.

The two small Canadian (Candu) PHWRs at Rajasthan nuclear power plant started up in 1972 & 1980, and are also under safeguards. Rajasthan 1 was down-rated early in its life and has operated very little since 2002 due to ongoing problems and has been shut down since 2004 as the government considers its future. Rajasthan 2 was restarted in September 2009 after major refurbishment, and running on imported uranium at full rated power.

The 220 MWe PHWRs(202 MWe net) were indigenously designed and constructed by NPCIL, based on a Canadian design. The only accident to an Indian nuclear plant was due to a turbine hall fire in 1993 at Narora, which resulted in a 17-hour total station blackout. There was no core damage or radiological impact and it was rated 3 on the INES scale – a 'serious incident'.

The Madras(MAPS) reactors were refurbished in 2002-03 and 2004-05 and their capacity restored to 220 MWe gross (from 170). Much of the core of each reactor was replaced, and the lifespans extended to 2033/36. Kakrapar unit 1 was fully refurbished and upgraded in 2009-10, after 16 years operation, as was Narora 2, with cooling channel (calandria tube) replacement. Following the Fukushima accident in March 2011, four NPCIL taskforces evaluated the situation in India and in an interim report in July made recommendations for safety improvements of the Tarapur BWRs and each PHWR type. The report of a high-level committee appointed by the Atomic Energy Regulatory Board (AERB) was submitted at the end of August 2011, saying that the Tarapur and Madras plants needed some supplementary provisions to cope with major disasters. The two Tarapur BWRs have already been upgraded to ensure continuous cooling of the reactor during prolonged station blackouts and to provide nitrogen injection to containment structures, but further work is recommended. Madras needs enhanced flood defences in case of tsunamis higher than that in 2004. The prototype fast breeder reactor (PFR) under construction next door at Kalpakkam has defences which are already sufficiently high, following some flooding of the site in 2004.

The Tarapur 3&4 reactors of 540 MWe gross (490 MWe net) were developed indigenously from the 220 MWe (gross) model PHWR and were built by NPCIL. The first – Tarapur 4 – was connected to the grid in June 2005 and started commercial operation in September. Tarapur 4's criticality came five years after pouring first concrete and seven months ahead of schedule. Its twin – unit 3 – was about a year behind it and was connected to the grid in June 2006 with commercial operation in August, five months ahead of schedule. Tarapur 3 & 4 cost about $1200/kW, and are competitive with imported coal. Future indigenous

PHWR reactors will be 700 MWe gross (640 MWe net). The first four are being built at Kakrapar and Rajasthan. They are due on line by 2017 after 60 months construction from first concrete to criticality. Cost is quoted at about Rs 12,000 crore (120 billion rupees) each, or $1700/kW. Up to 40% of the fuel they use will be slightly enriched uranium (SEU) – about 1.1% U-235, to achieve higher fuel burn-up – about 21,000 MWd/t instead of one third of this. Initially this fuel will be imported as SEU.

Kudankulam 1&2: Russia's Atomstroyexport is supplying the country's first large nuclear power plant, comprising two VVER-1000 (V-412) reactors, under a Russian-financed US$ 3 billion contract. A long-term credit facility covers about half the cost of the plant. The AES-92 units at Kudankulam in Tamil Nadu state have been built by NPCIL and also commissioned and operated by NPCIL under IAEA safeguards. The turbines are made by Leningrad Metal Works. Unlike other Atomstroyexport projects such as in Iran, there have been only about 80 Russian supervisory staff on the job. Construction started in March 2002.

Russia is supplying all the enriched fuel through the life of the plant, though India will reprocess it and keep the plutonium*. The first unit was due to start supplying power in March 2008 and go into commercial operation late in 2008, but this schedule has slipped by five years. In the latter part of 2011 and into 2012 completion and fuel loading was delayed by public protests, but in March 2012 the state government approved the plant's commissioning and said it would deal with any obstruction. Fuel loading was in September, and unit 1 started up in mid-July 2013, with unit 2 expected to do so early in 2014. Unit 1 was connected to the grid in October 2013 and is expected in commercial operation at full power early in 2014, with unit 2 following in October 2014. Each is 917 MWe net.

While the first core load of fuel was delivered early in 2008 there have been delays in supply of some equipment and documentation. Control system documentation was delivered late, and when reviewed by NPCIL it showed up the need for significant refining and even reworking some aspects. The design basis flood level is 5.44m, and the turbine hall floor is 8.1m above mean sea level. The 2004 tsunami was under 3m.

A small desalination plant is associated with the Kudankulam plant to produce 426 m^3/hr for it using four-stage multi-vacuum compression (MVC) technology. Another reverse osmosis (RO) plant is in operation to supply local township needs.

Kaiga 3 started up in February, was connected to the grid in April and went into commercial operation in May 2007. Unit 4 started up in November 2010 and was grid-connected in January 2011, but is about 30 months behind original schedule due to shortage of uranium. The Kaiga units are not under UN safeguards, so cannot use imported uranium. Rajasthan 5 started up in November 2009, using imported Russian fuel, and in December it was connected to the northern grid. RAPP 6 started up in January 2010 and was grid connected at the end of March. Both are now in commercial operation.

Under plans for the India-specific safeguards to be administered by the IAEA in relation to the civil-military separation plan, eight further reactors were to be safeguarded (beyond Tarapur 1&2, Rajasthan 1&2, and Kudankulam 1&2): Rajasthan 3&4 from 2010, Rajasthan 5&6 from 2008, Kakrapar 1&2 by 2012 and Narora 1&2 by 2014.

In mid-2008 Indian nuclear power plants were running at about half of capacity due to a chronic shortage of fuel. Average load factor for India's power reactors dipped below 60% over 2006-2010, reaching only 40% in 2008. Some easing after 2008 was due to the new Turamdih mill in Jharkhand state coming on line (the mine there was already operating). Political opposition has delayed new mines in Jharkhand, Meghalaya and Andhra Pradesh.

A 500 MWe prototype fast breeder reactor (PFBR) is under construction at Kalpakkam near Madras by BHAVINI (Bharatiya Nabhikiya Vidyut Nigam Ltd), a government enterprise set up under DAE to focus on FBRs. It was expected to start up about the end of 2010 and produce power in 2011, but this schedule is delayed significantly. Construction was reported 94% complete in February 2013. Four further oxide-fuel fast reactors are envisaged but slightly redesigned by the Indira Gandhi Centre to reduce capital cost. One pair will be at Kalpakkam, two more elsewhere.

In contrast to the situation in the 1990s, most reactors under construction more recently have been on schedule (apart from fuel shortages 2007-09), and the first two – Tarapur 3&4 – were slightly increased in capacity. These and future planned ones were 450 (now 490) MWe versions of the 202 MWe domestic products. Beyond them and the last three 202 MWe units, future units will be nominal 700 MWe.

The government envisages setting up about ten PHWRs of 700 MWe capacity to about 2023, fuelled by indigenous uranium, as stage 1 of its nuclear program. Stage 2 – four 500 MWe FBRs – will be concurrent. Construction costs of reactors as reported by AEC are about $1200 per kilowatt for Tarapur 3&4 (540 MWe), $1300/kW for Kaiga 3 & 4 (220 MWe) and expected $1700/kW for the 700 MWe PHWRs with 60-year life expectancy.

INDIA – NUCLEAR NEIGHBOURHOOD: CHALLENGES FOR INDIA

The situation that India faces today is unique; firstly, it shares common and disputed borders with both hostile neighbours; China has, according to several knowledgeable commentators and intelligence sources (of the West) built-up Pakistan's nuclear arsenal almost from scratch—providing designs, material, including fissile material, technology, delivery vehicles (either directly or through North Korea) and even conducted a weapons test in 1990 on its Lop Nor Test site, for Pakistan.

Today it is supplying reactors, which it claims will be under IAEA safeguards; but given the short shrift it has given the Nuclear Suppliers' Group, not to mention its obligations under the NPT in arriving at the agreement to do so, it is unlikely that the material from these reactors will remain for civilian purposes only. Thirdly and most dangerously, Pakistan has been using its growing nuclear arsenal as an umbrella under which it appears to feel that it can use sub-conventional attacks against India with little or no danger of (conventional) retaliation.

None of the above has been seriously disputed by either party; nor has the vague but ominous 'red lines' that Pakistan seems to have evolved regarding its stated doctrine of first use of nuclear weapons. It appears to have in mind the escalation of any conventional response from India to even an armed attack on Indian soil by its nationals, to a nuclear counter-response. The theories of deterrence would seem to not be applicable in a situation if there is a 'failure of rationality' on one side. Of course, it could very well be that the intention is to indeed give an impression of irrationality, to act as a deterrent to any action on India's part for fear that Pakistan would react 'irrationally'. This stand, of what has been termed 'a nuclear-weapon enabled terrorist threat' is supported by strong and consistent denials of culpability for any such 'non-state' attack and a reliance on its 'protector' and mentor, China, to handle the inevitable diplomatic furore that is bound to rise if the taboo on nuclear weapons is broken with however limited an application. India's doctrine calls for 'massive retaliation' in the event of a nuclear first strike; that would entail attacking counter-value targets, which could include cities and other population centres.

There would inevitably be calls for restraint on India's part, despite the enormity of the action by Pakistan and there is also likely to be some domestic resistance to attacks on cities or towns. In this, perhaps, worst-case but not improbable, scenario, what are India's options?

Difference between a 'declaratory' doctrine and an operational one; the latter can only be deduced from the information available on acquisitions and capabilities, statements of policy by albeit retired senior military men from Pakistan and such Western sources, presumably from intelligence inputs.

On the basis of these, it would appear that Pakistan has adopted a policy of battlefield use of its nuclear weapons, a likely escalation of a conventional confrontation to a nuclear level, arrangements for rapid deployment which could entail predelegation to unit commanders in the event of a loss of communications, (which is what apparently happened at Salala recently when 24 Pakistani soldiers were killed in an ISAF air attack on two border posts).

Sino-Pak nexus

Firstly, we need to take China's support of Pakistan for granted, even the use by the latter of non-state groups as a part of their foreign and security policy. This has been demonstrated repeatedly and not only in the UN Security Council, where China has blocked any forward movement on the naming of specific Pakistani nationals and sponsored groups as terrorists. Secondly, while the state of the internal instability in Pakistan is probably exaggerated in the media, Indian, Pakistani and the Western, there is no doubt that there is a considerable rise in religiosity with strong sectarian and intolerant strains in Pakistani society in general; this would have an inevitable impact on all state institutions, including the military.

At the same time, the military has not yet abjured its support for specific non-state groups as 'assets' in the furtherance of its foreign policy objectives. Some of the groups may well be out of control of the military, though there is little apparent effort to control them in any effective way, though some other groups, targeting the Pakistani state, are being attacked or negotiated with, according to press reports. Thirdly, while like many other developing countries, Pakistan's economy is currently in a very fragile condition, the worsening of relations with the US may adversely affect the budgetary support that Pakistan has been used to receive—China usually restricts itself only to project and commodity aid and does not give budgetary support to any of its allies, however close.

Notwithstanding these developments, the ambitions of Pakistan's military remain vaulting. Given these facts, it is clear that the situation is such that in the event of any crisis, or with the intention of creating one, India could face nuclear threats at multiple levels from Pakistan—it is not unlikely that these would be supported by China, which, however, will ensure that it is not directly involved.

The Pakistani nuclear doctrine, at least our knowledge of it, is today based on an interview given by Lt. General Khalid Kidwai (retd.), Director General of Pakistan's Strategic Plans Division to Paolo Cotta-Rassmussen and Maurizio Martinelli published by Pugwash International in 2002. There is, however, as has been noted elsewhere, a difference between a 'declaratory' doctrine and an operational one; the latter can only be deduced from the information available on acquisitions and capabilities, statements of policy by albeit retired senior military men from Pakistan and such Western sources, presumably from intelligence inputs. On the basis of these, it would appear that Pakistan has adopted a policy of battlefield use of its nuclear weapons, a likely escalation of a conventional confrontation to a nuclear level, arrangements for rapid deployment which could entail pre-delegation to unit commanders in the event of a loss of communications (which is what apparently happened at Salala recently when 24 Pakistani soldiers were killed in an ISAF air attack on two border posts) and increasing risks of inadvertent or accidental launch.

Ashley Tellis in his 2000 book on India's Emerging Nuclear Posture has written of the 'uncertainties' which arise from "The severe motivational and cognitive biases that have historically afflicted Pakistan's higher decision making institutions on matters of war and peace (which) raise fears about the prospect of extreme responses that might be precipitated in a crisis .... These failures of rationality ... could be compounded by exigencies of domestic politics, civil-military discord and biased and unreliable intelligence...." This posture is one which appears to be based on the assumption that India will not permit the situation to escalate, by considering a limited and targeted use of, for example, air strikes.

Bibliography

Ajey Lele: *Strategic Technologies for the Military : Breaking New Frontiers*, Sage, Delhi, 2009.

Alexander, J : *Military Technology and Equipment Technology*, Omega Pub, Delhi, 2008.

Allen Carlson, *Unifying China, Integrating with the World: Securing Chinese Sovereignty in the Reform Era,* Stanford: Stanford University Press, 2005.

Anil, K.C.: *Military and Democracy in India: Challenges, Politics and Power*, Sumit Enterprises, Delhi, 2009.

Bellamy, C.: *Knights in White Armour: The New Art of War and Peace*, London, Random House, 1997.

Bhaskara Rao: *Military Conversion : Impact on Science and Technology*, Discovery, Delhi, 2003.

Bhat, T.P. : *India and China : Trade Complementarities and Competitiveness*, Bookwell, Delhi, 2008.

Cathy Solheim: *Military Economics: Issues, Policies, and Solutions*, Washington, D.C., Island Press, 1995.

Davies.A.: *Telecommunications and Politics. The Secentralised Alternative*, London, Pinter, 1994.

Digumarti Bhaskara Rao: *Military Conversion : Impact on Science and Technology*, Discovery, Delhi, 2003.

Evelyn Goh, *Meeting the China Challenge: The U.S. in Southeast Asian Regional Security Strategies*, DC: East-West Center, 2005.

Friedman, G.: *The Future of War: Power, Technology and American World Dominance in the 21st Century*, N.Y., Random House, 1996.

Gaur, Mahendra :*Defence Import of India*, Delhi, Kalpaz Pub., 2006.

Goel, Suresh : *Military, Security and Intelligence Agencies*, MD Publications, Delhi, 2009.

James R Blaker: *Transforming Military Force : The Legacy of Arthur Cebrowski and Network Centric Warfare*, Pentagon Press, Delhi, 2008.

Juvale, R.P. : *Military Strategy, Manufacturing and Diplomacy*, Cyber Tech Publications, Delhi, 2010.

Kumar, Raj : *Weapons Manufacture and Military Technology*, Sumit Enterprises, Delhi, 2009.

Lovering, J.: *Labour and the Defence Industry: An Alliance for Globalisation*. Capital and Class, Delhi, 1998.

Mary, W.: *Military Space Force: the Cultural Dimensions of Authority*, Cambridge, Belknap Press, 1985.

Posen, B.R.: *The Sources of Military Doctrine*, Ithaca, 1984, Cornell Univ. Press.

Prabla, Dixit: *Communalism: A Struggle for Power*, New Delhi, Orient Longman, 1981.

Radhakrishna: *Military Ethics: Guidelines for Peace and War*, Sumit Enterprises, Delhi, 2009.

Rhodes, Richard, *The Making of the Atomic Bomb*, New York: Simon and Schuster, 1988.

Rita Raj: *Global Encyclopaedia of Military Education and Training*, Global Vision, Delhi, 2010.

Robert M Cassidy: *Counterinsurgency and the Global War on Terror : Military Culture and Irregular War*, Pentagon Press, Delhi, 2008.

Samuel P. Huntington: *The Soldier and the State : The Theory and Politics of Civil-Military Relations*, Natraj Pub, Delhi, 2005.

Sharma, G.K. and M.S. Jaswal: *Study and Practice of Military Law*, Deep and Deep, Delhi, 2006.

Shaun Narine, *Explaining ASEAN: Regionalism in Southeast Asia*, Boulder, CO: Lynne Rienner Publishers, 2002.

Singh, R.S.N. : *Asian Strategic and Military Perspective*, Lancer, Delhi, 2005.

Strange, Susan: *The Retreat of the State: The Diffusion of Power in the World Economy*, Cambridge: Cambridge University, 1996.

Sutton, J., *Technology and Defence Market Structure*, MIT Press, Delhi, 1998.

Wakamiya Yoshibumi, *The Postwar Conservative View of Asia*, Tokyo: LTCB International Library Foundation, 1999.

Index

W

❑❑❑